Visions of Vanaheim

Nornoriel Lokason

RavensHall Press

Visions of Vanaheim

Printed in cooperation with CreateSpace.

Published by Ravens Hall Press, an independent Pagan publisher
ravenshallpress.weebly.com

To Frey for your sacrifice.
To Njord for your peace.

Acknowledgements

Thanks first and foremost to my fans who follow my blog (whether WordPress or Tumblr), and have looked forward to this book - you give me an audience to write for. Thank you to those of you who have been supportive of me and sent me friendly and encouraging messages about the process of writing this book, and the difficulties surrounding it.

Thank you to Nicanthiel Hrafnhild and Catriona McDonald for your continued friendship and for providing me with a sounding board for Vanic stuff, as well as contributing material to this book. This book would not be possible without you.

A special thank you to Gefnsdottir (aka Gef) for also being someone I can talk with about the Vanir, and for the work you've done on behalf of the Vanatru community with being a resource.

Thank you to Clarence and Jarod, my beautiful Vanic loves, for your support, your love, your knowledge, and walking in beauty with me, sharing deep magic together. This book would not be possible without you either. My life would not be possible without you.

Thank you to Sandar, for all you have given on behalf of Vanaheim, for your work, for helping the realm to shed its skin and find renewal and healing. I am grateful to you more than you know. *Thandarë, salun.*

Thank you to my family by choice. Thank you for giving me a safe foundation to bring this work into being, and encouraging me to live up to my potential as a spirit-worker and scribe.

Thank you to my personal friends, especially the local ones, for giving me time away from the manuscript to recharge my brain cells and reminding me there is a world out there.

Thank you to the host of spirits I work with, especially to Eligos for inspiration, Asmodai for kicking my ass when I need it, and eternal gratitude to D. for your support and encouragement through the writing of this book, and the gift of your love, the song of my soul. *Herensia malatu, merendi, rivanha seiyan.*

Disclaimer

First and foremost, due to the fact that this book is about a group of entities known for obvious sexuality, there is some mild adult content. This book is not for children, nor those over the age of majority not capable of handling mature discussion.

While this book contains a fair amount of scholarship with research into primary sources as well as history, archaeology, and anthropology, there is an equal amount of personal gnosis, whether visions, experiential, or "filling in the blanks" from missing lore. Most of the personal gnosis is informed personal gnosis, through research and putting it into practice. Most of the personal gnosis is shared personal gnosis, corroborated by several people over 2007 to the present.

For the sake of continuity, the Common Germanic names have been used for each deity: "Freya" and "Frey" rather than "Freyja" and "Freyr".

Visions of Vanaheim is, as far as the author knows, the only explicitly Vanic text to come out since Thorsson's *Witchdom of the True,* and is far longer and more comprehensive, as well as from the perspective of an actual Vanic practitioner. Be that as it may, *Visions of Vanaheim* is not meant to be the last word on Vanic practice. This book makes no claims of carrying on an unbroken ancient tradition. Moreover, there is no central authority of Vanatru, no "Vanapope". This book does not speak for all devotees of the Vanir - just as any one Asatru book or website does not speak for the whole of Asatru. It is not necessary to agree with all of the viewpoints presented on this site to approach the Vanir or identify oneself as Vanatru or a Vanic pagan/heathen. This book is but one set of experiences, perceptions, and opinions; you must walk your own path for yourself, and seek your own truth.

Table of Contents

An Introduction to Vanic Practice

Allfather works,
the Alfar discern,
the Vanir know,
the Nornir indicate,
the Ividia brings forth,
men endure,
the Thursar await,
The Valkyruir long.
-Hrafngaldr Odins 1.

This is a book about the Vanir, the pantheon of Northern European gods whose primary domains are fecundity and prosperity. This book will examine archaeology, primary historical sources and folklore, and personal gnosis in piecing together what a Vanic religion might have looked like long ago, and how we can practice Vanatru in a way relevant to the needs of life in the 21st century. This book is not trying to assert that a Vanic religion came to us through the ages unbroken. Indeed, part of the mystery involves fitting together pieces of a puzzle both from what already exists in historical record, and what we can discern from our experience of the entities who live in Vanaheim. Nonetheless, a Vanic practice is worthy in its own right, and needed.

It is my hope that the writings in this book will garner interest in Vanatru, showing the relevance of Vanic ways in the 21st century, which is quickly escalating towards political, ecological, social, and economic crisis at a global level. The ultimate purpose of the pantheon known to us as the Vanir is to know the appreciation of everyday holiness that is sorely needed in a world full of malcontents seeking to destroy the world and/or themselves.

The Vanir are not pleased with the way things have fallen apart in a secular Western society, with our poison spreading to the other parts of the world. Drastic change is not going to happen overnight, and surely it would be hubris to think this book could inspire such needed change, but hopefully the words here can inspire people to think about the importance of the Vanir, their relevance in these chaotic times, and to be more aware of how our actions impact other people and the Earth itself, to be more aware of what is needed for honorable actions, and in building bridges with the Otherworld, have a better sense of perspective and relationships in our own. Hopefully, the Vanir can help us to re-learn what it is to be productive and honorable people, trying to help ourselves, help each other, and help our planet. It will take strong communities to work with strong Powers, and the option is now here to learn more about the Vanir, a Vanic-focused practice, and perhaps start your own Vanic tradition with like-minded folk.

Who are the Vanir?

The Vanir are one of three groups of gods in the Germanic pantheon (the others being Aesir and Jotnar/Rokkr), originating from the world of Vanaheim, and commonly holding domain over nature, fertility, and magic.

The Vanir as a set of entities are only mentioned in Old Norse primary sources and not the broader corpus of continental Germanic or Anglo-Saxon lore (of the Vanir, only Frey is seen outside Scandinavia, and there are no mentions of "Wenan" in Anglo-Saxon lore). This has led some scholars to speculate the idea of an Aesir-Vanir division is a later literary invention. To modern Vanic pagans, it cannot be disputed that the Vanir do have different spheres of influence than the Aesir, and indeed "feel" very different with regards to energy, the way they present themselves, and their agenda and workings in the world. The Aesir-Vanir war as recounted in the Voluspa only says that three of the Vanir joined the Aesir (this referenced also in Ynglinga Saga) – it does not say they ceased to be what they are.

Regarding the origins of the Vanir, and the implications of the Aesir-Vanir war, there seems to be two schools of thought among modern Vanic pagans.

The first school of thought is that the three ruling Vanir joining the Aesir represented a synthesis of parts into a greater whole.

The second school of thought is "the Vanir theory". This theory is based on archaeological evidence denoting a pan-northern-European set of fertility gods, with specific customs that were later associated with gods counted among the "Vanir" (e.g. Frey, Nerthus). The theory concludes that the gods we know as the Vanir are pre-Indo-European fertility gods, and the Aesir originated with the migrating Indo-Europeans coming from the Caucasus, and thus not are not from "the same pantheon"; that the story of the Aesir-Vanir war and subsequent merging of "Aesic" and "Vanic" traditions was based in the nomadic warriors conquering and intermarrying with the indigenous agriculturalists. This is a theory, and is not proven fact.

Because praxis follows theology, those whose beliefs are more in line with the first theory tend to practice the more Aesic-Vanic blended religion of heathenry reconstructed on the practices of the conversion era, or may just focus on the named Vanir within a heathen religious context; those whose beliefs are more in line with the second theory tend to see the Vanir as having their own separate customs and traditions (however it is not necessary to hold to the second theory to see the Vanir as having their own separate customs and traditions, one may just see that from them originating from a separate world than the Aesir).

As far as the Vanir themselves, according to the primary sources, there are three explicitly named Vanir: Frey, Freya, and Njord. Snorri mentions Njord's sister-wife, who many scholars and heathens agree is Nerthus, a goddess mentioned by Tacitus. Kvasir is another deity often named as Vanir, formed from the spittle of the Aesir-Vanir truce. Of the three primary named Vanir, the names Frey and Freya mean "Lord" and "Lady" respectively, and the name "Njord" is of uncertain meaning. Frey has domain over sunshine, rainfall, and the changing seasons. He is associated with farming, and was called upon at weddings. Njord, his father, is associated with fishing, and is noted for wisdom. Freya is a goddess of both love and war, as well as magic. Both Frey and Freya were often depicted in antiquity in an explicitly sexual way. If we count Nerthus (named by Tacitus) as Njord's sister-wife, she is associated with the fertility of the land and peace and prosperity among the people, with a yearly wagon procession conducted by a priest.

However, it takes more than three or four people to comprise an entire world, especially when fighting against the host of Asgard and winning. There has been corroborated gnosis among people who have been contacting the Vanir and making astral journeys to Vanaheim from 2007 onward that Vanaheim has a population in the tens of thousands, is tribally organized, and that individual Vanir unnamed by lore – who could be classified as "elves" (though this is oversimplifying it) and call themselves "Eshnahai", or "evergreen/undying" in their world's language – have continued relations with humans past the conversion era (many of them having guises of spirits known in folklore such as wulvers, merfolk, and huldre), and will work with interested humans today.

In addition to this there are some who identify or have previously identified as Vanic pagans who through esoteric work and research have discovered there are deities mentioned in the primary sources who fit the Vanic type; Sif would be an example of this.

In this book we will look at the different gods and goddesses of the Vanic pantheon, explicitly named by lore as Vanir, those speculated by Vanic pagans to be part of the Vanir, and a few unnamed by lore who were discovered by shared personal gnosis and are ready to be introduced to the world, as well as the tribes of Vanaheim.

The Vanir Theory

By Nicanthiel Hrafnhild

There is a theory concerning the Vanir that runs in the face of much of modern reconstructionist thought – namely, that the race of gods known as the Vanir are pre-Indo-European, and evidence and/or traces of them may be found in mythologies all across northern and central Europe, from Spain to Russia and from the Sámi to the Etruscans.

The premise of this theory is two-fold: 1. That the Vanir are an earlier race of gods than the Æsir and equivalent IE deities, part of a temporal and archeological procession reaching back to the earliest human inhabitants to be found in Europe; and 2. That the Vanir embody a system of archetypes that can be found, in almost staggeringly similar detail, throughout early European mythology.

First, to examine the primary premise. It has been suggested by some scholars that the Vanir, and correspondingly the Jötnar/Ettins, are an earlier, indigenous race of gods supplanted by the Indo-Europeans and their native gods. There is a motif throughout the reaches of IE culture and myth of the major gods supplanting or warring against one (often two!) other races of divine beings. The first enemy race is usually viewed in a highly negative and hostile light, from the Titans to the Giants to the Fomorians. The second enemy race, if there is one, is usually a supplanted and/or subsumed class of divine beings – the Fir Bolg, the Protogenoi (who are actually older than the Titans), and the Vanir. (Interestingly enough, in the early Vedic texts, it is the Vanir-like deities (the Devas) who are worshiped more, and the Æsir-like deities (the Asuras) who are eventually demonised and rejected.) In Europe itself, there are several tales of a war between the "middle" race and the conquering IE gods – the first Battle of Moytura results in the Fir Bolg capitulating to the Tuatha Dé Danann and fading from the scene; the tale of the Æsir-Vanir war in the Völuspá; the Abduction of the Sabine Women; Beowulf and Grendel/Grendel's mother.

Furthermore, until the Migration Era, there was no clear cultural distinction between the Celtic and Germanic tribes; even the Romans often got them mixed up! And as the archeological record shows, the Neolithic cultures of Europe were very often similar in cultural and religious expression, even at great geographic and temporal distances (e.g., the similarities between the Ertebølle culture from 5500-4000 BCE and the Beaker culture between 2500-1800 BCE) Thus, it is no stretch to assume that such cultural similarity might be due to common religio-cultural heritage and experience.

The second premise relies a bit more on UPG, since there is little evidence and lore about the Vanir, and virtually no mythology left over from the height of their cultus. But those modern folk who have worked with the Powers of the Land, in whatever European form they prefer, have found that there are certain forms and faces that the Vanir relate to, from the Pale Lady to the Lord of the Green, the King of Sea and Air, the Lord of the Wild Woods, the Lady of Passion, the Dark Mother, the Wild Father, the Witch-Queen and the Snow Queen and the Maker.

Thus the theory states the following:

1. The Vanir are the indigenous gods of Late Mesolithic and Neolithic Europe, following the introduction of horticulture and agriculture to the tribes that inhabited the continent. Previous to this, the Paleolithic and early Mesolithic cultures likely worshiped the gods known as Giants/Titans/Fomorians, focused entirely on hunting and gathering and nature over man.

2. These Vanic gods are not Indo-European, though some of them were adopted by the incoming cultures, which then separated into the cultural groups we know of today – Celtic and Germanic and Italic and Slavic. Thus, every European IE culture has remnants of the earlier worship embedded in their mythologies. This can particularly be seen in the cultures that directly neighbor the Germanic ones, the Celts and (to a lesser extent) the Slavs, leading to the nomenclature "Vanacelt" among some Vanic people.

3. The most likely way to revive the lost cultus of the Vanir is through comparative mythology and syncretism, particularly with systems of witchcraft and other "low" religio-cultural expressions. This has led to many Vanatru folks working with Druidry, Wicca, Strega and other non-Heathen influences in addition to the Germanic practices.

A Northern Tradition Timeline

The purpose of this timeline is to present a theory that northern Europe had three successive cultures with different religious practices, deeply steeped in those cultures. The timeline is particularly focused on what appears to be "the Vanic era", to give some food for thought, and perhaps inspiration, as to the way the Vanir would like to be honored: even if we do not have enough information on exactly what was done, and what we do know of is not practical or probable for the modern day, we can be inspired by the information anyway.

500,000 BCE
Lower Acheulean -These were tool users who left Africa to successfully colonize Eurasia.

300,000 BCE
Clactonian - Artifacts were found in Essex; Swanscombe in Kent and Barnham in Suffolk, of early, crude chopping tools made of flint, and the tip of a worked wooden shaft.

80,000 BCE
Mousterian - Artifacts were found in the Dordogne region of France and all over Europe; handaxes, racloirs and points made of flint were found.

40,000 BCE
Châtelperronian (France) - At this time, Neanderthals and modern humans occupied Europe together. Denticulate (toothed) stone tools were found from this era, including a distinctive flint knife with single cutting edge and a blunt,

curved back. There was also jewelry which indicates the Neanderthals may have been more sophisticated than previously thought.

30,000 BCE

Aurignacian - Tools are found here with complex art, including figurines that depict faunal representations of the time period associated with extinct mammals, such as mammoths, rhinos, and the European horse, along with anthropomorphized depictions inferred as some of the earliest evidence of religious belief and practice. There was also the use of bone and antler for tools such as needles and harpoons.

The **Lion Man** was found in the Hohlenstein-Stadel cave of Germany's Swabian Alb and dated at 32,000 years old, is associated with the Aurignacian culture. It is the oldest known anthropomorphic animal figurine in the world.

Gravettian (France) - A common artifact from this era is a small pointed restruck blade with a blunt but straight back, used for big-game hunting (bison, horse, reindeer, and mammoth). There are also some early examples of cave art and the famous 'Venus' figurines.

The **Venus of Lespugue** is a Venus figurine, a statuette of a nude female figure from approximately 25,000 BC. This particular "Venus" figurine was discovered in 1922 in the Rideaux cave of Lespugue in the foothills of the Pyrenees. Approximately 6 inches tall, it was carved from tusk ivory. Unfortunately, it was damaged during excavation.

10,000 BCE

Solutrean (France) - The Solutrean era was named after the type-site of Solutre in the Macon district, Saone-et-Loire, eastern France, which appeared around 19,000 BCE. Solutrean finds have been also made in the caves of Laugerie Haute and Les Eyzies, as well as in the Lower Beds of Cresswell Crags in Derbyshire, England.

Solutrean tools have finely worked, bifacial points made with pressure flaking rather than cruder flint knapping. Using this method, delicate slivers of flint could be made into light projectiles as well as barbed and tanged arrowheads. Other characteristic tools of this industry include large thin spear-heads; long spear-points with the tang and shoulder on one side only; flint knives and saws that are chipped, not ground or polished; and scrapers with the edge not on the side, but on the end.

The finds of this era also include prehistoric art, as well as ornamental beads and bone pins. Bone and antler were used. Animals of this era include horse, reindeer, mammoth, cave lion, bear, rhinoceros, and aurochs.

Magdalenian (France) - The Magdalenian era was named after the type site of La Madeleine, a rock shelter located in the Vezere valley, commune of Tursac, in the Dordogne department of France.

The Magdalenian era is synonymous in many people's minds with reindeer hunters, although Magdalenian sites do also contain extensive evidence for the hunting of horse, red deer, and other large mammals present in Europe towards the end of the last ice age. The culture was geographically widespread, and later Magdalenian sites have been found from Poland in the east to Portugal in the west.

This culture spans the period between c. 18,000 and 10,000 BCE, towards the end of the last ice age. There are regular blade industries, as well as elaborate worked ivory, bone, and antler, which seemed to serve both functional as well as aesthetic purposes. Examples of Magdalenian mobile art include figurines and intricately engraved projectile points, as well as items of personal adornment including sea shells, perforated carnivore teeth for necklaces, and fossils.

The sea shells and fossils found in Magdalenian sites can be sourced to relatively precise areas of origin, and have been used to support hypothesis of Magdalenian hunter-gatherer seasonal ranges, as well as perhaps trade routes. Cave sites such as the famous Lascaux contain the best known examples of cave art from this era. The site of Altamira in Spain, with extensive and varied forms of art, has been suggested to be a site where multiple small groups of Magdalenian hunter-gatherers congregated. (Conkey 1980).

The oldest offering found in northern Europe is a pile of elkbones from Lundey in Denmark, dating from 10,000 BCE, thrown into the lake. There are four piles of bones each consisting of one elk.

Ahrensburg culture - This culture is named after village of Ahrensburg, which is in the German state of Schleswig-Holstein, 25 km northeast of Hamburg. Wooden arrow shafts and clubs were excavated here. At this time, the landscape of Northern Europe was tundra with bushy arctic white birch and rowan, and the most important prey was the wild reindeer.

The primary hunting tool was bow and arrow. At the Stellmoor site, well-preserved arrow shafts made from pine, as well as arrowheads of flintstone, were found, as well as a number of intact reindeer skeletons with arrowheads in the chest. These have been assumed to be sacrifices to higher powers. The settlements have findings of stone circles, most likely the foundations of hide teepees.

There is also evidence of extensive fishing during this time period, and carvings of animals made from amber, such as an amber elk found in Weitsche.

8,000 BCE
Sauveterrian - The name of the Sauveterrian era is derived from the type site of Sauveterre le Lemance in the French departement of Lot et Garonne.

The Sauveterrian culture extended through large parts of western and central Europe. Artefacts characteristic to this era include geometric microliths and micro-blades with backed points. Wood working tools are notably missing from sites. There is definite evidence of ritual burial.

The Sauveterrian culture is the source of the first Nordic culture, the Maglemosian.

The oldest boat in the world dates from this era, found near Pesse in the Dutch province of Drenthe. It is a wooden canoe made from a hollowed-out tree trunk, dating to about 8000 BCE.

7,500 BCE

Maglemosian (Scandinavia and surrounding areas) - The name of the Maglemosian culture came from a type site in Denmark, named Maglemose at Mullerup on western Zealand. The Maglemosian people lived in forest and wetland environments. At this time the sea level in northern Europe was much lower, and did not reach current levels until about 6000 BCE, at which time they inundated some of the territories of this culture. The Maglemosian peoples used fishing and hunting tools made from wood, bone, and flint. They appear to have domesticated the dog.

Star Carr is a very important site in the Maglemosian culture, located in North Yorkshire, England. The Star Carr site was discovered in 1947 during the clearing of a field drain. Its main feature is a birch brushwood platform standing on the edge of what was Lake Pickering. Star Carr was occupied from around 8770 BCE until about 8460 BCE, with a possible period of abandonment between 8680 to 8580 BCE. Hearths found further away from the water indicate temporary settlement, during the summer months, where hunters chased red and roe deer, elk, wild boar, and aurochs. The lake's mud preserved items dropped into it. Hunter's tools such as scrapers, as well as worked bone and antler, have been found. A notable find was perforated parts of skull and antlers of red deer. There was a fragment of a wooden oar which implies boats used to travel or fish. Beads made from stone and amber suggest there was personal adornment, and remains of a dog are indication of domestication of this animal. The most famous find from this site is the top part of a stag skull, complete with antlers. The skull had two holes perforated in it and scholars have speculated that it was used as a hunting disguise, or perhaps in ritual.

6,000 BCE

Kongemose (Scandinavia) - This was a hunter-gatherer culture in southern Scandinavia, and the origin of the Ertebolle culture. The characteristic find is long flakes of flintstone, used for making rhombic arrowheads, scrapers, drills, and awls. Bone daggers were often decorated with geometric patterns, stone axes were made, and other tools of horn and bone. Most of the economy was based on hunting red and roe deer, as well as wild boar, supplemented by fishing on the coasts.

Nøstvet and Lihult (Norway/Sweden) - The Nostvet people lived on open settlements, using honed axes made of various rocks such as quartz, quartzite and flint. They hunted seafowl and marine animals, besides fishing and gathering. The size of the settlements grows over time, and reflects an increase in the population as well as a more sedentary lifestyle. The Nostvet culture appeared around the Oslofjord and along the Norwegian coast up to Trondelag. The Lihult culture is found in Sweden. These cultures neighbored the Kongemose and later the Ertebolle peoples.

Ertebølle-Ellerbeck (Scandinavia and northern Germany) - During this period, the Northern European climate was warmer and moister than today. Deciduous forests covered Europe, and the Baltic was at higher levels than today, and was a salt sea, rather than a brackish one. The Baltic coastline was often flooded, Jutland was an archipelago, and marshes were extensive, with tracts of shallow water rich in fish.

The Ertebolle population settled on promontories, near or on beaches, on islands and along rivers and estuaries. Due to chance fluctuations in the sea level during Ertebolle occupation of the coast and subsequently, many of the culture sites are currently under 3m-4m of water. Some have been excavated; the artifacts are in an excellent state of preservation, protected by anaerobic mud.

The Ertebolle population derived its living from a variety of means, but chiefly from the sea, which they traversed in paddled dugouts, which were a few feet wide and propelled by paddles constructed of shafts to which leaf-shaped or heart-shaped blades were attached. They hunted whales and seals. To trap fish, the fishermen constructed fish fences of approximately 4m-long hazel sticks set upright in the mud at the bottom of shallow water. Wickiwork traps were also used. They angled with hooks made of red deer bone, of which at least one example has been found with line attached. They spear-fished with spears made of shafts to which hazel tines were attached.

Judging from the remains of animal bones at their sites, the Ertebolle people did hunt land animals: large forest browsers, fur animals and maritime birds. They gathered berries for consumption and also prepared a number of wild plants, judging from the seed remains of plants that could not be consumed without preparation. This includes raspberry (Rubus idaeus), wild strawberry, crab apple, and rose hips. There were seeds that could have been made into gruel, such as acorn and manna grass (Glyceria fluitans), and they also ate roots of the sea beet (Beta maritima) which is ancestral to modern domestic beets. Greens were boiled from nettle (Urtica dioeca), orache (Atriplex) and goosefoot (Chenopodium album). In fact, fragments of textiles from Tybrind Vig were woven in the needle-netting technique from spun plant fibers.

Huts were constructed of brush or light wood. Fire pits located outside the huts indicate that most village functions were performed outdoors, with the dwellings mainly used for storage and sleeping. Red ochre and deer antlers were placed in some graves, but not others. Female graves were found with the women wearing necklaces, and belts, made from animal teeth and shells. At Mollegabet, an individual was buried in a dugout, which some see as the beginning of Scandinavian boat burials. Skateholm also contained a dog cemetery, where dogs were also prepared with red ochre, and given antler and grave goods.

Pottery was manufactured from native clays tempered with sand, crushed stone and organic material. Two main types are found, a beaker and a lamp. The beaker is a pot-bellied pot narrowing at the neck, with a flanged, outward turning rim. The bottom was typically formed into a point or bulb (the "funnel") of some sort that supported the pot when it was placed in clay or sand. Later, technique and decoration became slightly more sophisticated: the walls were thinner and different motifs were used in the impressions: chevrons, cord marks, and punctures made with animal bones. Handles were sometimes added.

Paddles from Tybrind Vig show highly developed and artistic woodcarving. The Ertebolle people also polished and engraved not obviously functional pieces of bone or antler, with motifs that were predominantly geometric, occasionally with anthropomorphic forms. Jewelry was made of animal teeth and decorative shells. At Fano, polished amber representations of animals have been found, *including a boar*.

A young couple walking along Horsens Fjord, Denmark, in August of 2008 found a limestone, which archaeologists from the Horsens Museum believe to be from the Ertebolle Culture ca. 5400-3900 BCE. The scratched motif depicts a man with an erect phallus and two fish, wearing some sort of headdress with animal ears.

Swifterbant (Netherlands) - Like the Ertebolle culture, the settlements were concentrated near water. In this case, the settlements were along creeks, riverdunes and bogs. A transition from hunter-gathering to cattle farming, primarily cows and pigs, occurred around 4800-4500 BCE. The wetlands offered optimized conditions to explore both cattle and small scale cultivation of different crops. There was a discovery of an agricultural field in Swifterbant dated 4300-4000 BCE4. Animal sacrifices found in the bogs of Drente are attributed to the Swifterbant era, and suggest a religious role for cattle.

Pottery has been attested from this period.

4,000 BCE

Funnelbeaker culture (Scandinavia and surrounding areas) – Most people were still nomadic hunter-gatherers who followed the herds, but at some places they settled more permanently because they could find food there during the entire year (game, fish, berries, tubers, turnips, nuts, etc.). Around this time the wheel is also believed to have been introduced, the oldest wheel found in northern Europe dates from this era, and was found near Weerdinge in the Netherlands. It was made from a single piece of wood. The transition to farming as a predominant lifestyle was gradual but when it became more widely used it deeply influenced the traditional way of living. Agriculture and cattle-breeding demanded a more permanent settlement and bigger houses could be built because they were used much longer. The Funnelbeaker people ate fruit such as apples. In the fields, they grew barley, flax, peas, lentils, and beans, as well as grains such as emmer wheat (Triticum dicoccum) and einkorn (Triticum monococcum). From these ingredients, bread and porridge could be made. Livestock mainly consisted of cattle, swine, goats, and sheep. Oxen were used to pull plows and wagons. Riding on horseback was unknown as the Funnelbeaker peoples hunted horses for food. The ram seems to be seen as a fertility symbol during this time, and depictions have been found on pottery as well as clay figurines, particularly a ram figurine found near Jordansmuhl/Jordanow in Poland.

It has been argued that the introduction of farming was introduced by a wave of massive immigration, but scientists have performed DNA studies on the modern European population, comparing their DNA to the finds of bodies from this time, and have concluded most of the peoples of Europe are direct descendants of those who were the native population. The transfer to farming was most likely an adaptation of technology.

A typical Funnelbeaker village would only have a few families and less than 10 houses. Between the Dutch cities of Anloo and Eext in the province of Drenthe, there was a settlement found dating to the Funnelbeaker era, consisting of 4 houses, inhabited by about 20-30 people. Originally, short houses were used, eventually replaced by longhouses closely resembling the later Germanic longhouses. The average Funnelbeaker house was 33 to 49 feet long and 13 to 16 feet wide. As time progressed, the houses seem to have gotten larger, as people lived under one roof with their animals, and in many cases deceased ancestors - in Flogeln (Germany) a Funnelbeaker farm was found that had a back room with a grave in it while the middle room was used as a living room.

The Funnelbeaker culture was known for burying rather than cremating their dead. Individual graves and tombs were usually covered with a conical mound. In some cases the mound was joined with others to form a single big mound, rectangular in shape. The most spectacular graves from this era are tombs known as "hunebeds", primarily found in the province of Drenthe in the Netherlands, and the bundesland of Niedersachsen in Germany. Most people were buried with gravegifts, typically ornate funnelbeakers, buckets, bottles, cups, bowls, dishes, stone axes, bow and arrow, necklaces made of jet and amber, and oftentimes food.

The Funnelbeaker culture was also known for enclosures with palisades and ditches, built on hilltops or other areas that would be easy to defend. Most of these enclosures were found in the southern areas of the Funnelbeaker culture: central Germany and what is now the Czech Republic, occasionally in the northern parts like Sarup (on the island of Fyn in Denmark).

The oldest road in Europe dates from before the Funnelbeaker culture (approximately 4600 BCE) and was found in Germany north of Osnabruck. Findings include roads and bridges that led from a village into the nearby bog and stopped halfway, most likely used for religious purposes especially as what can only be inferred as offerings have been found around them. The main bog offerings seem to be pottery, food, tools, and weapons. Near Gingst on the island of Rugen, 50 to 60 pots (contents unknown) were offered by multiple generations of Funnelbeaker farmers. In a bog in the Dutch province of Drenthe, an offering pot was found that contained the remains of eggs, beaver meat, a duck, pikes (Latin name: Esox lucius), and a tench (Latin name: Tinca tinca), other offerings in the bog included cattle, sheep, birds, bones and antlers, and used axes. Near Weerdinge in Drenthe (Netherlands), a funnelbeaker was found with the remains of a pike and a red deer. There were amber beads in the bog as well.

Of course, we cannot leave this discussion without noting the bog bodies, most of whom date from the Funnelbeaker culture. The bodies were strangled, stabbed to death, decapitated, cut to pieces, and often several of these in one body, definite signs of ritual killing.

Chalcolithic (Central Europe) - Here we find the appearance of the first significant economic stratification and the probability of the earliest presence of Indo-European speakers.

Mining of metal and stone is developed in some areas, along with the processing of those materials into valuable goods. In particular, we find the beginning of the usage of copper in the Balkans, Eastern Europe, and Central Europe.

From c. 3500 onwards, Eastern Europe is infiltrated by people originating from beyond the Volga. This pushes the natives to migrate in a northwest direction to the Baltic and Denmark, where they mix with the natives of that region.

Both the metal industry and the migration seem to have its basis in the use of horses, which would increase mobility.

Ötzi the Iceman (Austria/Italy) - Otzi is the nickname given to a well-preserved natural mummy of a man from about 3300 BCE. He was found in 1991 in the Schnalstal glacier in the Otztal Alps, on the border between Austria and Italy.

Analysis of pollen and dust grains and the isotopic composition of his tooth enamel have shown he spent his childhood near the present village of Feldthurns (Velturno), north of Bolzano, but later went to live in valleys approximately 50 kilometers further north. Analysis of his intestinal contents show two meals, the last one about eight hours before his death: one of chamois meat, the other of red deer meat, both eaten with some grain (highly processed einkorn wheat bran) as well as roots and fruits.

Otzi was found to have carbon tattoos consisting of simple dots and lines on his lower spine, behind his left knee, and on his right ankle. It has been speculated that they may be related to energy meridians of acupuncture. Using X-rays, it was determined that he may probably have had arthritis in these joints.

Otzi wore a cloak made of woven grass and a coat, a belt, a pair of leggings, loincloth, and shoes, all made from different leather skins. He also had a bearskin cap with a leather chin strap. His shoes were waterproof and wide, probably designed for walking across the snow. They had bearskin soles, deer hide for the top panels, and netting of tree bark. Soft grass went around the foot and in the shoe, similar in function to modern socks. His belt had a pouch sewn to it that contained a scraper, drill, flint flake, bone awl, and a dried fungus to be used as tinder.

Other items found with Otzi include a copper axe with a yew handle, a flint knife with an ash handle, a quiver of 14 arrows with viburnum and shafts made of dogwood. There was also an unfinished yew longbow. In addition, he also had berries, two birch bark baskets, and two species of polypore mushrooms with leather strings through them. The birch fungus is known to have antibacterial properties, and was most likely used for medicine.

It is believed that Otzi was killed. He had an arrowhead lodged in one shoulder when he died, which would indicate death via blood loss.

3,000 BCE

Corded Ware/Battle Axe culture - This culture receives the name of Corded Ware from the cord-like ornamentation of pottery from this era, Single Grave from its burial custom of single graves, and Battleaxe from the characteristic grave offering to males - a stone battle axe.

The traditional view of the Corded Ware culture as a series of pan-European migrations from the steppe region of southern Russia has been abandoned. Corded Ware culture communities are now seen primarily as sedentary agriculturalists.

There are very few settlements, but the settlements that have been excavated show that agriculture was continued from the Funnelbeaker era, and domestic animals were kept. The majority, however, did follow a fully- or semi-nomadic pastoral way of life. There are wheeled vehicles (presumably driven by oxen), and the tarpan horse was commonly in use. Cows' milk was used systematically from 3400 BCE onwards, and changes in the slaughter age and animal size of sheep is evidence of sheep being kept for their wool.

The dead were mostly buried, under flat ground or below small tumuli. On the continent, the males lay on their right side, females on the left, with the faces of both genders oriented to the south. In Sweden, the graves were oriented north-south, men laying on the left side and women on the right, both facing east. Pottery in the shape of beakers is the most common burial gift.

The role of the Corded Ware culture in the history of the Indo-European peoples is actively debated. It is generally seen that the Corded Ware culture is the beginning of the Proto-Germanic language and Germanic culture.

The Swedish-Norwegian Battle Axe culture, or the Boat Axe culture, appeared circa 2800 BCE and is known from about 3000 graves from Skane to Uppland and Trondelag. This time has been referred to as "the age of crushed skulls" however, it appears that most of the "crushing" happened post-mortem in the ground, and the battle-axes were primarily a status object. Most of the settlements were on small, separate farmsteads that did not appear to have defensive protection, which would be another argument against this being a time of aggressors.

About 3000 battle axes have been found, in sites distributed over all of Scandinavia, but they are sparse in Norrland and northern Norway. Less than 100 settlements are known, and their remains are negligible as they are located on continually used farmland, and have consequently been plowed away.

This culture was based on the same agricultural practices as the previous Funnelbeaker culture, but the appearance of metal changed the social system. The Funnelbeaker culture had collective megalithic graves with sacrifices inside. The Battleaxe culture has individual graves with sacrifices for the individual.

A "death house" dating to this period was excavated in Turinge, in Sodermanland. The walls were once heavily timbered and held the remains of about twenty clay vessels, six work axes, and a battleaxe. There were also cremated remains of at least six people, which is the earliest find of cremation in Scandinavia.

The Atlantic and North Sea coastal regions of Scandinavia and the Baltic areas were united by a vigorous maritime economy, which permitted a wider geographical spread as well as a closer cultural unity than cultures on the continent. There have been found many rock carvings from this era, displaying "thousands" of ships, using the sea much like a highway.

Bell-Beaker culture - The Bell-Beaker culture lasted from approximately 2800-1900 BCE, and is the term for a widely scattered cultural phenomenon of prehistoric western Europe starting in the late Neolithic running into the early Bronze Age. The term, coined by John Abercromby, refers to common use of beaker pottery with a distinctive inverted bell-shape. It seems that the beakers were designed for the consumption of alcohol - beer and mead content were identified from certain examples. Studies of pollen analysis suggests increased growing of barley during that era, which can be used in brewing. However, other beakers have some organic residues associated with food, and still others were employed as funerary urns, and from this we can infer perhaps it being used ritually. Beaker-type vessels remained in use longest in the British Isles.

It is noted that Marija Gimbutas derived the Beakers from eastcentral European cultures that became "kurganized" through incursions of steppe tribes. Despite this, even supporters of the Kurgan hypothesis dispute that the Beaker culture peoples originate from the east. Recently, a Strontium isotope analysis of 86 people from Bell Beaker graves in Bavaria suggests that between 18-25% of all graves were occupied by people who came from a considerable distance outside the area. This was true of children as well as adults. This is indicative of some significant migration wave, and it seems that people migrated from the northeast to the southwest[1].

Bell Beaker settlements in Southern Germany show evidence of mixed farming and animal husbandry, and there are also finds of millstones and spindle whorls. There are some well-equipped child burials that seem to indicate sense of predestined social position and allude to a socially complex society.

Beakers arrived in Britain around 2500 BCE and fell out of use around 1700 BCE. During the Bell Beaker period, the Neolithic form of Stonehenge was elaborated extensively. Many barrows surround it, and an unusual number of "rich" or elite burials can be found nearby, including the famous Amesbury Archer. Yet another site of interest is Ferriby on the Humber estuary; this is where Western Europe's oldest plank built boat was recovered.

The Danish Beaker period was characterized by the manufacture of lanceolate flint daggers, related to the style of daggers circulating elsewhere in Beaker dominated

---

[1]Price, T. Douglas, Grupe, Gisela and Schroter, Peter.

Europe. Gold sheet ornaments and copper flat axes were the predominant metal objects. During this period, there was also the adoption of European-style woven wool clothes kept together by pins and buttons, in contrast to the earlier usage of clothing made of leather and plant fibers[2]. Two-aisled timber houses dating from this period in Denmark correspond to similar houses in southern Scandinavia, and at least parts of central Scandinavia and lowland northern Germany.

2,300 BCE

Unetice culture - This culture was named for a typesite located at Unětice, northwest of Prague. It is focused around the Czech Republic, southern and central Germany, and western Poland, dated from 2300-1600 BCE.

The culture is characterized by metal objects which include ingot torcs, flat axes, flat triangular daggers, and bracelets with spiral-ends, distributed over a wide area of Central Europe and beyond. Hoards of the ingot torcs and axes have been found, such as the hoard of Dieskau (Saxony) which contained 293 flanged axes. Burials are normally inhumations in flat graves with bent legs and arms, lying on the side, oriented north-south or northeast-southwest, with males buried on the left, women on the right side.

Some groups used hollowed out tree trunks for burial, and stone cairns are found in the Upper Rhine. Males were usually buried with copper triangular daggers, flint arrowheads, stone wrist-guards, and clay cups; women were buried with bone or copper pins, bone arm-rings, and bracelets with spiral ends. A burial in Leubingen was

---

[2] Bender Jorgensen 1992, 114; Ebbesen 1995; 2004

covered by a barrow that was still 8.5 m high. It contained a wooden tent-shaped chamber. The grave contained two burials and golden grave gifts. Unetice metalsmiths mainly worked only with pure copper. Alloys of copper with arsenic, antimony and tin to produce bronze became common only in the succeeding periods. Most of the settlements are "pile dwellings". Houses measured approximately 8 by 4 meters. In Southern Germany, two-aisled longhouses of up to 50m length and 5 m width were used.

2,000 BCE

Nordic Bronze Age/Proto-Germanic - The Nordic Bronze Age is generally considered to be the direct predecessor and origin of the Proto-Germanic culture of the Pre-Roman Iron Age. The Scandinavians joined the European Bronze Age cultures fairly late, however the Scandinavian sites present rich and well-preserved objects of wool, wood, bronze, and gold. Mycenaean Greece, Phoenicia, and Ancient Egypt have all been identified as sources of influence for Scandinavian artwork from this period, the foreign influence likely due to the amber trade. The amber found in Mycenaean graves from this period originates from the Baltic. Many petroglyphs depict ships, and several petroglyphs depict ships that have been identified as plausibly Mediterranean.

A pair of twin gods are believed to have been worshiped, and is reflected in a duality in all things sacred. Where sacrificial artifacts have been buried, they are found in pairs. In addition, a female or mother goddess is believed to have been widely worshiped: sacrifices (animals, weapons, jewelry and men) were found in small lakes and ponds. Bronze Age rock carvings may contain some of the earliest depictions of well known gods from later Norse mythology. A common figure in these rock carvings is that of a male figure carrying what appears to be an axe or hammer, which may probably have been an early representation of Thor. Other male figures are shown holding a spear; one example of a Bronze Age rock carving shows a spear-holding figure missing a hand, which may be a representation of Tyr. A figure holding a bow may be an early representation of Ullr. Ritual instruments such as bronze lurs have been found sacrificed, and are believed to have been used in religious ceremonies.

1,600 BCE

Nebra sky disk (Saxony-Anhalt) - The Nebra sky disk is a bronze disk of around 30 cm diameter, patinated blue-green and inlaid with gold symbols. The symbols appear to be a sun or full moon, a lunar crescent, and stars. There are two golden arcs along the sides, as well as another arc at the bottom surrounded by multiple strokes. The disk was recovered at a site near Nebra, Saxony-Anhalt in Germany, a prehistoric enclosure encircling the top of a 252 m elevation in the Ziegelroda Forest, known as Mittelberg ("central hill"). Ziegelroda Forest is said to contain around 1,000 barrows dating from the Neolithic era, oriented in such a way that the sun seems to set every solstice behind the Brocken (the highest peak of the Harz Mountains, and a place traditionally associated with witchcraft, i.e. Walpurgisnacht) some 80 km to the northwest. The sky disk itself has been dated to c. 1600 BCE.

The find confirms that the astronomical knowledge and abilities of the people of the European Bronze Age included close observation of the yearly course of the Sun, particularly the angle between its rising and setting points at summer and winter solstice. While Stonehenge was used to mark the solstices, this disk is the oldest known "portable" instrument which can be used for such measurements. There was initial suspicion that the Nebra sky disk was fake, the disk is now widely accepted as authentic. As the item was not excavated using archaeological methods, authenticating it has depended on microphotography of the corrosion crystals, producing images that could not be reproduced by a faker.

1,300 BCE

Unrfield culture - In the Urnfield period, inhumation and burial in single graves prevails, though some barrows exist. During the earliest phases of this culture, man-shaped graves were dug, often with a stonelined floor, in which the cremated remains of the deceased were spread. Later, burial in urns became prevalent. The size of the urnfields is variable; in Bavaria there were hundreds of urn burials, while the largest cemetery in Baden-Wurttemberg in Dautmergen had only 30 graves. The dead were placed on pyres, covered in their personal jewelery, which often shows traces of the fire and sometimes food offerings.

The cremated bone-remains are much larger than what was found from the Romans, which indicates that less wood was used. The urn containing the cremated bones was accompanied by other ceramic vessels, like bowls and cups. They may have contained food. Burnt animal bones were often found, which may have been placed on the pyre as food. Metal grave gifts included razors, weapons that were deliberately destroyed (bent or broken), bracelets, pendants and pins. Metal grave gifts became rarer towards the end of the Urnfield culture, while the number of hoards increase. Amber or glass beads were luxury items found in the graves of the elite.

Upper-class burials were placed in wooden chambers, or chambers with a stone-paved floor. They were covered with a barrow or cairn. These graves contain especially fine pottery, animal bones (usually pork), sometimes gold rings, and in exceptional cases, miniature wagons. Some of these burials contain the remains of more than one person.

Towards the end of the Urnfield culture, some bodies were burnt in situ and then covered by a barrow. In the early Iron Age, inhumation became the rule again.

About a dozen wagon-burials of four-wheeled wagons with bronze fittings are known from the early Urnfield period. In Milavče near Domažlice, Bohemia, a four-wheeled miniature bronze wagon bearing a large cauldron (diameter 30 cm) contained a cremation. This exceptionally rich burial was covered by a barrow.

Cattle, pigs, sheep and goats were kept by the Urnfield peoples, as well as horses and dogs. The cattle and horses were very small. Forest clearance was intensive in the Urnfield period. Probably open meadows were created for the first time, as shown by pollen analysis.

Wheat and barley were cultivated, as well as millet and oats. Rye had already been cultivated, although further west it was only a noxious weed. Pulses and the horse bean were also grown. Poppy seeds were used. Hazel nuts, acorns, apples, and pears were collected. In the settlement of Zug, remains of a broth made of spelt and millet have been found. In the lower-Rhine urnfields, leavened bread was placed on the pyre and burnt fragments have been preserved.

Flax seems to have been of reduced importance, maybe because wool came into predominant use for clothing. Wool was spun (finds of spindle whorls are common) and woven on the warp-weighted loom, bronze needles were found, used for sewing.

Typical bronze tools include winged and socketed axes. In the North, stone axes were still in use. The leaf-shaped Urnfield sword could be used for slashing, in contrast to the stabbing-swords of the preceding culture. Protective gear like shields and helmets was extremely rare and almost never found in burials. The best-known example of a bronze shield comes from Plzeň in Bohemia and has a riveted handhold.

There is well-made pottery dating from this era: biconical pots with cylindrical necks are especially characteristic, and fluted decoration is common. Pottery kilns were already known (Elchinger Kreuz, Bavaria), as is indicated by the homogeneous surface of the vessels as well. Other vessels include cups of beaten sheet-bronze with riveted handles, and large cauldrons with cross attachments. Wooden vessels have only been preserved in waterlogged contexts (one example being a find in Neuchatel), but may have been quite widespread. Hoards were very common in the Urnfield culture, deposited in rivers and swamps. As these spots were often quite inaccessible, they most probably represent gifts to the gods. In the river Trieux, Cotes du Nord, complete swords were found together with numerous antlers of red deer that probably had had a religious significance as well.

700 BCE

Strettweg Cart (southeast Austria) - From this period, an artifact was found of a four-wheeled cart with a goddess, riders with axes and shields, attendants and stags.[3]

500 BCE

Pre-Roman Iron Age - This is the earliest part of the Iron Age in Scandinavia, northern Germany, and the Netherlands north of the Rhine. All regions feature many extensive archaeological excavation sites, yielding a wealth of artifacts. The objects discovered suggest strong influences from the Celtic Iron-Age Hallstatt culture in Central Europe.

The Iron Age in northern Europe is distinct from the Celtic La Tene culture southwards, while still having been influenced by it. Around 600 BCE the northern people began to extract iron from the ore in peat bogs. The oldest iron objects found were needles, as well as edged tools, swords, and sickles. Bronze was now mostly used for decoration, especially in torcs.

---

[3] Landesmuseum Johanneum, Graz, Austria

Archaeologists have also found shield bosses, spearheads, scissors, sickles, knives, pincers, buckles, and kettles. The Gundestrup silver cauldron dates from this era as well as the Dejbjerg wagons of Jutland, two four-wheeled wagons of wood with bronze parts.

The Bronze Age tradition of burning corpses and placing the remains in urns continued. The Bronze Age ended due to the expansion of the Hallstatt culture from the south. The climate also deteriorated. The finds from Scandinavia are consistent with a loss of population, whilst the Jastorf culture expanded southwards.

It is widely accepted that these northern Iron Age people spoke Germanic languages. The late phase of this period sees the beginnings of Germanic migrations, starting with the invasions of the Teutons and the Cimbri.

Jastorf Culture (north Germany) - Named for a typesite in Jastorf, Lower Saxony, the Jastorf culture extended south to the fringes of the northern Hallstatt provinces.

The Jastorf culture is characterized by its use of cremation burials in extensive urnfields, using urns in the shape of houses. It is considered that religious beliefs changed in that time. There are few and modest grave goods, with weapon deposits completely absent.

Hallstatt culture (Central Europe) - Named for its type site, Hallstatt, a lakeside village in the Austrian Salzkammergut southeast of Salzburg. The Halstatt culture extended to Champagne-Ardenne in the west, through the Upper Rhine and the upper Danube, as far as the Vienna Basin and the Danubian Lowland in the east, from the Main, Bohemia and the Little Carpathians in the north, to the Swiss plateau, the Salzkammergut and to Lower Styria.

The Hallstatt culture exploited the salt mines. Inhumation and cremation co-occur. Members of the elite in the western zone were buried with sword or dagger, and in the eastern zone with an axe. The western zone has chariot burials. In the eastern zone, warriors were frequently buried in full armor. There was trade with Greece, attested by findings of Attic black-figure pottery in the graves of the elite. Other imported luxuries included ivory and wine, as well as red dye made from cochineal (seen at the Hochdorf burial).

The settlements were mostly fortified, situated on hilltops, and frequently included the workshops of bronze-, silver-, and goldsmiths. Towards the end of the period, very rich graves of high-status individuals under large tumuli are found near the remains of fortified hilltop settlements. They often contain chariots and horse bits or yokes.

Well known chariot burials include Býči Skala, Vix and Hochdorf. Elaborate jewelry made of bronze and gold, as well as stone stelae was found in this context.

While this culture is seen as Proto-Celtic rather than Germanic, we can see that it has similarities with Proto-Germanic cultures, and indeed we can see how they would be very close "cousins" both in custom and perhaps even religious belief.

0 CE

Roman Iron Age - The name "Roman Iron Age" comes from the influence that the Roman Empire had begun to exert on the Germanic tribes. In Scandinavia a great number of goods were imported, such as coins (more than 7000), bronze images, glass beakers, enameled buckles, and weapons. The style of metal objects and clay vessels was markedly influenced by the Romans. In the 3rd and 4th centuries, we see the first use of runes. There are also many bog bodies from this time in Denmark, Schleswig, and southern Sweden, found with weapons, household wares, and clothes of wool. Great rowing ships were found in Schleswig. The primary burial tradition was cremation, while there was still some inhumation. Through the 5th and 6th centuries, gold and silver became increasingly common.

400 CE

Germanic Iron Age - The Germanic Iron Age follows the Roman Iron Age, and the beginning is marked by the fall of the Roman Empire, with the rise of the Germanic kingdoms in Western Europe. During the Roman Empire's fall, much gold came into Scandinavia and there are excellent works in gold found dating from this period. Gold was particularly used to make scabbard mountings and bracteates. After the Roman Empire was gone, gold became scarce and the Scandinavians instead made objects of gilded bronze, mainly decorations of interlacing animals.

Witham shield (Britain, boar-emblem)[4] - This shield was discovered in the River Witham in the vicinity of Lincolnshire, in 1826. When the shield was first found, the archaeologists examining it could clearly see the shape of a wild boar on the front. The boar shape was cut from a piece of leather and fixed to the shield. The leather has since rotted away, but the shadow remains a different color in the bronze, and while it has mostly faded it can still be seen if looked at closely. There are small rivet holds across the center of the shield which show where the boar was originally fixed. The red color on the shield's boss was made of small pieces of red coral from the Mediterranean. The shield itself is a remnant, a decorative front which was fixed to a wooden back. Further excavation at the site has revealed posts that look like they are a foundation for a causeway, as well as artifacts that include a sword, spears, and part of a human skull with a sword fragment lodged in.

700-1100 CE

Viking Age - The Viking Age is the term for the period in European history, especially Northern European and Scandinavian history, spanning the 8th to 11th centuries, when Scandinavian Vikings explored Europe by its oceans and rivers, through both trade and warfare. The Vikings also reached Iceland, Greenland, Newfoundland, and Anatolia. Viking society was based on agriculture as well as trade with other peoples. They placed great emphasis on the concept of honor in combat as well as in criminal justice. This era coincided with the Medieval Warm Period (800-1300) and stopped with the start of the Little Ice Age

---

[4]http://www.britishmuseum.org/explore/highlights/highlight_objects/pe_prb/t/the_witham_shield.aspx

(1250-1850). The lack of pack-ice made for easier sea travel. Many scholars also believe a growing Scandinavian population was too large for the peninsula and there were not enough crops to feed everyone, which led to seeking more land to cultivate and feed the people.

The Viking age is considered to have ended with the establishment of royal authority in the Scandinavian countries, and Christianity becoming the dominant religion, put in the early 11th century for all of the Scandinavian countries.

From looking at archaeology, we can make the following suggestions:

-The first people in the Northlands were hunter-gatherers. Life was brutal and short. It is likely these people worshiped the elemental Jotnar as well as worked with the tribes of the Vanir, who had anthromorphic forms (e.g. Bear, Cat).

-The period when the gods of the Vanir might have been introduced to the Northern people looks probable to have started in the Maglemosian/Kongemose era, co-existing with the dominant Vanic Tribes cultus. The Vanir gods appear to have gained dominance during the Funnelbeaker/Ertebolle culture, to eventually be secondary with what looks to be co-existence with the Aesir gods coming into the Northlands from elsewhere beginning in the Bell Beaker culture into the Unetice and Urnfield cultures, with the Aesir dominant starting from the Bronze Age onwards.

-It is the thought of the authors that while gods have always existed and are not dependent on human worship to exist, they will reveal themselves to people as the people have need. We can see this as the Vanic tribes contacting humanity at a time when people needed to master the elements to survive, learning to hunt and later to grow food. These beings were revealed when the time was right and specific people were open. All of what we now know to be mythological primary sources - the Eddas as told to Snorri - were originally someone's personal gnosis, people who were in direct contact with the gods and related their stories to the people.

-The Vanir and the Jotnar can thus be thought of as deities that are not Indo-European, or pre-Indo-European. While names such as "Freya" and "Ran" are Germanic in origin, it is likely that the original names of these gods were lost as these societies were pre-literate. One of two things is likely to have happened: 1. the gods were called by a similar-sounding name by the original Pre-Germanic peoples, and the Germanic language thought "good enough" due to the characteristics of these gods, 2. the original names were lost completely and replaced by the Germanic names based on the gods' characteristics.

This is given some credence when you consider that most scholars cannot find a meaning for the name "Njord", as it seems to have no Indo-European root. The *Nj-*combination means that Njord is **not** etymologically similar to Jord ("Earth"), and Njord is perhaps a leftover of his name among the original Vanir cultus.

-The Hellenic Titans and the Celtic Fomorians hold the same place in their cosmology as the Nordic Jotnar, original gods who were later replaced by successive cultures and demonized.

-Rather than the Germanic peoples always having been separate and distinct as some would claim, there seems to be a lot of cross-pollination of customs and perhaps even belief and practice, particularly in relation to the early Celtic people, e.g. the influence of the Hallstatt/La Tene culture on the Proto-Germanic cultures. We also see frequent interaction with what has later become the Slavic culture, as well as the Mediterranean peoples to the south. While the gods themselves are individuals, there does seem to be certain commonalities across Europe even before the Indo-Europeans came forward and changed the culture.

We will never know for certain what was believed and practiced in those times, but it is fascinating to discover that what we know to be "the Germanic culture" had its origins with something more widespread over Europe, and things familiar to the Northern Tradition (boar motifs, deity depictions) were found long ago.

Works Consulted

Andersson, Magnus, Per Karsten, Bo Knarrstrom, and Mac Svensson. Stone Age Scania. Riksantikvarieambetets Forlag, 2004.

Bakker, Jan Albert. The Dutch Hunebedden: Megalithic Tombs of the Funnel Beaker Culture. International Monographs in Prehistory, 1992.

Blankholm, Hans Peter. On the Track of a Prehistoric Economy: Maglemosian Subsistence. Aarhus Univ Pr, 1996

Bradley, Richard. Ritual and Domestic Life in Prehistoric Europe. Routledge, 2005.

Davidson, H. R. Ellis and Gelling, Peter: The Chariot of the Sun and Other Rites and Symbols of the Northern European Bronze Age, 1969.

Fowler, Brenda. Iceman: Uncovering the Life and Times of a Prehistoric Man Found in an Alpine Glacier. University Of Chicago Press, 2001.

Harrison, Richard J. The Beaker Folk. Thames & Hudson, 1980.

Hodder, Ian. The Domestication of Europe. Wiley-Blackwell, 1991.

Jensen, Helle Juel. Flint Tools and Plant Working: Hidden Traces of Stone Age Technology: A Use Wear Study of

Some Danish Mesolithic and Trb Implements. Aarhus Univ Pr, 1994.

Jochim, Michael A. A Hunter-Gatherer Landscape: Southwest Germany in the Late Paleolithic and Mesolithic. Springer, 1998.

Kujit, Ian. Life in Neolithic Farming Communities - Social Organization, Identity, and Differentiation. Springer, 2000.

Larsson, Mats. The Early Neolithic Funnel-beaker Culture in South-west Scania. British Archaeological Reports, 1985.

http://politiken.dk/newsinenglish/article585168.ece

http://www.uni-leipzig.de/~ufg/reihe/files/lobufa13.pdf

Star Mother

"The cosmos is within us. We are made of
star-stuff. We are a way for the universe to
know itself."

-Carl Sagan

Star Mother is, in personal gnosis corroborated by
several spirit-workers (as well as directly from Vanic
elves), the progenitor of the Vanir and Creatrix of the
Multiverse, and (with the Serpent Twins) the closest thing
the Vanir have to a god that they will revere, in the sense
of ancestor worship.

Once upon a time, billions and billions of years ago,
there was a woman, lush and full and dark. And she dreamed.
And when she woke from her dreaming, she saw her reflection
in the Void, and fell in love with her, and they made love. And
with the orgasm of that union, the Multiverse exploded into
being.

When they made love again, she felt the need to be
filled, and when she shattered, she found another being there
with her, like her and not like her, parts that fit hers, dark where
she was bright, bright where she was dark, wild where she was
peaceful, peaceful where she was wild. They were two halves of
a whole, and in that, there was deep magic. They were Star
Mother and Horn Father, the first, the eldest.

Time passed, and in their love, they decided to create
more beings like themselves. Star Mother's belly grew, and when
it was time, out came a pair of twins, male and female, made of
Earth. "Be fruitful, and multiply," she told them, and they made
worlds, and gave them form, and paid attention to one most
particularly, which they called home.

Star Mother and Horn Father lay together again, and made the next pair of twins, made of Fire. They forged their own realm, and periodically would tear down what their elder siblings built, so their siblings could take joy in creating again.

Star Mother and Horn Father lay together yet again, and made the next pair of twins, made of Water. They too forged their own realm, balancing the creation and destruction of their siblings, done with the beauty and grace of lotuses floating on a pond.

Star Mother and Horn Father lay together once more, and the last set of twins was made of Air. They made a city high above the worlds, looking down on all, to sustain all that was made with breath and thought.

And there they are, and here we are.

Some time after Star Mother birthed the Serpent Twins, and the Serpent Twins made the world, the cycles of life and death, living and dying, began upon that world. And even though Star Mother knew it was necessary, and that life feeds on life, she still shed tears, feeling the pain of every living thing in its struggles, and in its dying process. Those tears were the only record kept of those lives and those pain, for eons. Eventually, she shed so many tears that she was almost drowning in them.

Star Mother decided she needed someone to talk to, as she did not want to overburden her husband with the pain. And so from a lock of her hair, she formed a being, serpent-shaped, and which she clad in black from the Void. She gave it life with her own breath.

The being one day looked at all of the tears, and told her that she might feel a little better if she had some breathing room. The being offered to move the tears, but moving around in the Void would take a long time in a slithery serpent body. So Star Mother breathed on the being again, and gave it wings and a tail. The bird, black as the Void, thanked Star Mother, and began to hang the tears in the Void. They all sparkled in the darkness, and as the bird hung the tears, the bird received the knowledge of what each tear was shed for, and spent a moment to honor that life, that memory. And from it, some of the tears, far far away from the world of the Serpent Twins, began to form life, while others just hung, shining in silent tribute to the memory of those who had gone before.

As many tears as were moved away from Star Mother, she cried more as the cycles of life and death continued, and more and more beings lived and struggled and died. And the being became overwhelmed with collecting the tears and moving them into the Void. One day, he plucked out his own feathers, wanting to peck himself to death. Where the feathers landed, they turned into birds of his own kind.

The birds talked amongst themselves, and decided to help Star Mother and the first of their kind by going into the world and assisting the best way they knew how. They eased the passage of the good souls dying, and brought vengeance to those who created more suffering in the world. And more than anything else, Star Mother was not the only one who remembered each life, anymore. The birds kept records of everyone.

As time went on, the number of Ravens grew. Just as their kind had helped Star Mother hang her tears, which became the stars in the sky, they are attracted to shiny things in the worlds, and brightness within people. They help bring out the shining in others. But just as the stars shine best in the darkness, and were forged in pain, the Ravens will often create darkness to test and forge the character of the shining ones.

As more time went on, and the Ravens spent so much time in the world that their time in the Void was a distant memory, one Raven decided to go back to the Void. He wanted to go beyond the farthest star, curious as Raven-kind is. He flew out into the stars, and as he passed the outer limits, the light from the stars began to turn his feathers white. A long time passed, and the other Ravens thought he was dead and would never return. But he did return, and could not speak of what he had seen. He was changed, though, and from that day onward, he led a small group of Ravens to tend to the souls that were leaving the world, ferrying them out to the stars, helped those who had left to come back again in their time, and collected light to heal the shining ones who were sick. These are known as the White Ravens, the priests of the Raven tribe, who are bound up in taboo and oaths, but whose work is necessary.

And so this is the Raven tribe, who bring ordeal, the darkness that brings out the brightest in the best and brightest, who bring ease of passage to the dying and pain to the wicked. Some heal, and help the dying move forward and the deceased return to us, as the first White Raven returned. And more than anything else, the Ravens remember. They preserve the memories of those who went before, and in addition, inspired others to keep certain thoughts and ideas alive, so they did not die with the person originally carrying them. While Star Mother still cries, she cries less, knowing that her tears are no longer the only thing that recognizes a person's pain, a person's life and death. The Ravens keep the memory, keep the stories of the land and all that has lived upon it.

-Eshnahai myth

She is Mother Night, Queen of Stars, Mother of All, Creator of All, Lady of Stars, Dark Mother, Void Mother. She is not the moon or a moon goddess, and is a separate entity from other goddesses associated with night.

She can be honored through mundane practices such as wishing on the first star at night, wishing on shooting stars, stargazing, and astronomy.

As her primary role in Eshnahai myth is self-impregnating woman-woman masturbation, followed by penetrative heterosexual sex with her son-consorts, it can be said that all genders and sexualities are rooted in her; she is the embodiment of sacred Vanic sexuality, the way the Vanir embrace life and passion.

I most admire her compassion for every form of life, her remembrance of lives and caring no matter how seemingly insignificant.

However, she is not a personal goddess, as she literally holds up the Universe and is thus not known for directly interacting with others. She is also outside of our concepts of morality and ethics, as she is the Void of Chaos that gave birth to Order.

If you would get to know her better, go out into the night and look at the stars. If you can, go to a remote area where there is no light pollution, where the stars are really clearly visible. See the world with fresh eyes, a sense of wonder in the everyday miracles around us. See the beauty in yourself and make love to it with your words and deeds, exploding your own Multiverse of possibility, opportunity, and beautiful wonders into being.

Horn Father

"You're the predator right up until you're
prey."
— *James S.A. Corey,* **Abbadon's Gate**

Horn Father is, in corroborated gnosis, the father of the Serpent Twins and one of the progenitors of the Vanir. He is also the creator of the animal tribes; he presides over a "sorting ceremony" into the tribes when groups of young adults come of age. He is Lord of the Hunt and leads the largest Wild Hunt procession from Vanaheim in its seasons.

When Star Mother was done laying with herself and the Multiverse exploded into being, she found she had created one like herself in every way, but male. They lay together and made four sets of elemental twins, who paired off together and brought different dimensions into form.

Horn Father came to the place that the twins of Earth made, and as his children terraformed worlds, and fauna, he made beasts to crawl and fly and swim upon the land and sky and sea. And then he hunted them, for life to feed on life, and the land to not be too full with living things.

When there were enough descendants of the twins of Earth, Horn Father separated them by group and gave them each an animal form and a task to do within the realm. And so it is to this day.

-Eshnahai myth

Horn Father is strong and wild and free, and can teach us strength and wildness and freedom.

Horn Father has a very utilitarian view of life; everything is food. You are special, but you are also not special. You someday will die. To work with Horn Father is to be hunted, to face your worst fears and darkness, to die to your old self to run free with him. He will make you honor the life that was given you in the short time you have to live it. He has a pragmatic view of death and suffering and may seem harsh, the opposite of his twin Star Mother who has compassion for all.

Horn Father is sexual with his mother-sister Star Mother, as well as with his twin/shard-self. He is the embodiment of male sexuality and both homosexual and heterosexual practices are sacred to him. Horn Father will also help those who wish to become men, regardless of what sex they were born into.

Horn Father can be connected with through mundane practices such as hunting, preparing meat, running, and cleaning a dead animal for bones, fur, etc.

To learn more about Horn Father, it is suggested that you observe the behavior of animals. Learn about the predatory animals of your bio-region. Own your shadow side, face your fears, go after the things you want in life. Get your hands dirty. Learn to see both sides of a story/issue, see things from others' point of view even if you ultimately disagree and don't stay in that mindset.

The Serpent Twins

Amor vincit omnia, et nos cedamus amori.
(Love conquers all things; so too shall we
yield to love.)
-Virgil

The Serpent Twins are the firstborn twins of Star Mother and Horn Father, the twins of Earth, who fucked the worlds into being and are the direct blood ancestors of all Eshnahai.

The twins of Earth gave this rock form, shaping the terrain, and creating flora and fauna in the ecstasy of their joining. They played together, eternally innocent in the garden of primordial Earth. They were passionately in love with each other, found each other beautiful, and everything they made together, was beautiful to them, touched by their love, and beautiful for it.

The twins of Earth counted all beings as their children, but in particular, they shaped sentient beings that myths would call giants, to play and be free as they were, while also protecting and continuing to shape their creation. And they had two sets of twins, each set being a polarity – Air and Earth, and Fire and Water.

The giants made other giants and other beings, and the twins of Air and Earth found them and began to live among their people. Meanwhile their father and mother, Ana and Ka'el - who were beginning to be referred to as the Serpent Twins, for their affinity for their favorite creation - kept to themselves, travelling the world, blessing it with their love and their passion and ecstasy.

After a long time, the Serpent Twins decided they had lived long enough, and there were many beings on the planet now, and they were no longer needed, and more importantly, that there was enough life that some of it needed to be culled, and they needed to set an example that entering the wheel of incarnation was not to be feared, but right and necessary. They came to their children, and their people, and gave themselves as a sacrifice, letting all of them consume them, and take a piece of them, so the spirits of the Serpent Twins continued to live on, inside all, and thus ensured that the process of creation, and the joy of it, would continue. The love of Ana and Ka'el for each other was great enough that they knew they would be someday reborn as twins again, making magic once more.

However, some time after this happened, there arose a conflict over how to deal with the rise of human. Some of the beings decided that humans were prey. The adopted children of the Serpent Twins decided that humanity was their kin and had potential to be like them someday, and so they broke away from the others - who would be known in later myths as giants - and led folk with them to found a new realm, wherein the changed their appearance and energy a bit to differentiate themselves from the ones they'd split from. The "elves" (or "Vanir") began to reach out to humanity as teachers, surrogate parents, and sometimes even as lovers and friends. Bridges were forged between worlds, and enough energy was exchanged that even when the people of the North left the old gods behind, they continued to remember the "elves", having relationships with the ones who had adopted spirits of place, or their ancestors.

   -Eshnahai myth

The Serpent Twins are a reminder of ultimate love: love so strong that it formed worlds in the chaos of desire, love that was willing to sacrifice itself to feed its beloved creation and set an example of the cycle of incarnation, love that knew it could transcend death and be reunited.

Ana and Ka'el were born opposite-sex twins, but over the course of their incarnation, "shed their skin" over and over again, changing gender and form at will. Thus all genders and all expressions of sex between consenting adults is literally sacred to them.

The Serpent Twins are not currently living - the current King and Queen are their avatars (and when they die the wheel of incarnation will begin again), but the King and Queen are also their own people (which will be explored later in this book) and are not worshiped by the Vanir, but seen as having a very important job. The Serpent Twins are still referred to in oaths ("by the Serpent Twins"), and their memory given reverence.

If one would honor them, the best way to do so is Love, open yourself to love (not necessarily romantic or sexual), and let it inspire you to create beautiful, wonderful things.

Njord

It is said by the Eldar that in water there lives
yet the echo of the Music of the Ainur more
than in any substance that is in this Earth;
and many of the Children of Ilúvatar hearken
still unsated to the voices of the Sea, and yet
know not for what they listen.
-J.R.R. Tolkien, The Silmarillion

Njord is a god of the sea, a patron of fishermen as
well as merchants whose commerce depends on items
brought in or out across sea. He is a god of peace and
prosperity, and known for his generosity and good nature,
which is not to be mistaken for being a pushover – he is
fierce in battle, he was the one who cut off Mimir's head
with an axe when he felt the terms of the Aesir-Vanir truce
insulted his people – but he is good at calming stormy
seas, both literally as well as metaphorically.

Gagnrad: Tell me tenthly, since thou all the origin of the
gods knowest, Vafthrudnir! Whence Niord came among the
Aesir's sons? O'er fanes and offer-steads he rules by hundreds,
yet was not among the Aesir born.
Vafthrudnir: In Vanaheim wise powers him created, and
to the gods a hostage gave. At the world's dissolution he will
return to the wise Vanir.
-VafÞrúðnismál (Poetic Edda)

The third among the Aesir is he that is called Njordr: he
dwells in heaven, in the abode called Noatun. He rules the
course of the wind, and stills sea and fire; on him shall men call
for voyages and for hunting. He is so prosperous and abounding

in wealth, that he may give them great plenty of lands or of gear; and him shall men invoke for such things. Njordr is not of the race of the Aesir: he was reared in the land of the Vanir, but the Vanir delivered him as hostage to the gods, and took for hostage in exchange him that men call Hoenir; he became an atonement between the gods and the Vanir.

Njordr has to wife the woman called Skadi, daughter of Thjazi the giant. Skadi would fain dwell in the abode which her father had had, which is on certain mountains, in the place called Thrymheimr; but Njordr would be near the sea. They made a compact on these terms: they should be nine nights in Thrymheimr, but the second nine at Noatun. But when Njordr came down from the mountain back to Noatun, he sang this lay:

> Loath were the hills to me, I was not long in them,
> Nights only nine;
> To me the wailing of wolves seemed ill,
> After the song of swans.

Then Skadi sang this:
> Sleep could I never on the sea-beds,
> For the wailing of waterfowl;
> He wakens me, who comes from the deep-
> The sea-mew every morn.

Then Skadi went up onto the mountain, and dwelt in Thrymheimr. And she goes for the more part on snowshoes and with a bow and arrow, and shoots beasts; she is called Snowshoe-Goddess or Lady of the Snowshoes. So it is said: Thrymheimr 't is called, where Thjazi dwelt, He the hideous giant; But now Skadi abides, pure bride of the gods, in her father's ancient freehold.

...Njordr in Noatun begot afterward two children: the son was called Frey, and the daughter Freya; they were fair of face and mighty.

-Gylfaginning (Prose Edda)

● ● ●

Odin placed Njord and Frey as priests of the sacrifices, and they became Diar of the Asaland people. Njord's daughter Freya was priestess of the sacrifices, and first taught the Asaland people the magic art, as it was in use and fashion among the Vanaland people. While Njord was with the Vanaland people he had taken his own sister in marriage, for that was allowed by their law; and their children were Frey and Freya. But among the Asaland people it was forbidden to intermarry with such near relations.

...Njord took a wife called Skade; but she would not live with him... Njord of Noatun was then the sole sovereign of the Swedes; and he continued the sacrifices, and was called the drot or sovereign by the Swedes, and he received scatt and gifts from them. In his days were peace and plenty, and such good years, in all respects, that the Swedes believed Njord ruled over the growth of seasons and the prosperity of the people. In his time all the diar or gods died, and blood-sacrifices were made for them. Njord died on a bed of sickness, and before he died made himself be marked for Odin with the spearpoint. The Swedes burned him, and all wept over his grave-mound.

-Ynglinga Saga

Njord is mentioned as a "priest of the sacrifice" along with his son, and I believe that the offerings we make to the Powers are part of an exchange -- we gift them, and they gift us.

I often see Njord walking along the beach, barefoot, watching the ebb and flow of the tides and smiling slightly, knowingly, seeing the patterns of the tides and wave formations as wyrd, and enjoying the beauty of the sea. I have seen Njord walking along the beach with his children, pointing out different varieties of seabirds, collecting shells, driftwood, sea glass and smooth rocks. Teaching his children to sing to the sea, and the cycles of precipitation that renew the sea and the water supply of the Worlds. That tears are a reminder that we are all alive, and a part of this cycle.

Njord has taught me to find the calm center within myself - to the place where the tides may ebb and flow, but never cease, and the water renews itself through evaporation and transpiration, precipitation, and runoff. I find taking long showers to be very relaxing when stressed out, and being at the beach and in direct contact with the sea recharges my batteries like nothing else. To flow with the water, to pour and drop down, billow into wave and roll out, is the nature of my calm center. To be liquid, to flow, and to know that I am part of the greater cycle of nature, and the Universe itself, and all things will work out in their time.

Njord is huggable, he is often smiling, with a twinkle in his blue eyes that hints of occasional mischief. He loves the Worlds because they are beautiful in their own way. He is much less intense than Odin, and much less into the idea of power and status. He's not too proud to sit down and build a sandcastle (or a sand turtle), or splash around with you in the sea. He loves laughter, and you can sense the vitality and life within his being without it becoming overwhelming or oppressive. His contentment and sense of rightness about things is infectious, and it's very hard for me to stay upset or grumpy for very long around Njord.

That being said, part of Njord's grandfatherly role towards me is teaching, or at least gentle guidance, which sometimes involves things I don't want to hear. However, this has helped me heal, and though I am not complete in my healing -- it's rather like peeling layers of an onion, from all the damage sustained -- I know that all things will work out in their time, and the journey is just as important as the destination. To sail on a ship from one land to another and be impatient with when you arrive is to not observe the waves, to not observe the patterns of the sea, the way the sky and sun reflects, particularly at sunrise and sunset, or the twinkling stars and bright moon at night.

Nerthus

If you have been in the vicinity of the sacred
– ever brushed against the holy – you retain
it more in your bones than in your head; and
if you haven't, no description of the
experience will ever be satisfactory.

-Daniel Taylor

Nerthus is the twin and consort of Njord. She lives alone on an island in Vanaheim that none are allowed to visit except Njord, sometimes her children, and her priest; she leaves the island once a year, to travel throughout Vanaheim and Midgard and bless the land with her presence, a time of merry-making and letting go of grudges and regrets, celebrating abundance and family.

After the Langobardi come the Reudigni, Auiones, Angli, Varni, Eudoses, Suarines and Nuithones, all well guarded by rivers and forests. There is nothing remarkable about any of these tribes unless it be the common worship of Nerthus, that is Earth Mother. They believe she is interested in men's affairs and drives among them. On an island in the ocean sea there is a sacred grove wherein waits a holy wagon covered by a drape. One priest only is allowed to touch it. He can feel the presence of the goddess when she is there in her sanctuary and accompanies her with great reverence as she is pulled along by kine. It is a time of festive holidaymaking in whatever place she decides to honor with her advent and stay. No one goes to war, no one takes up arms, in fact every weapon is put away, only at that time are peace and quiet known and prized until the goddess, having had enough of peoples' company, is at last restored by the same priest to her temple. After which the wagon and the drape, and if you like to believe me, the deity herself is bathed in a mysterious pool.

The rite is performed by slaves who, as soon as it is done, are drowned in the lake. In this way mystery begets dread and a pious ignorance concerning what that sight may be which only those who are about to die are allowed to see.

...Upon the right of the Suevian Sea the Aestyan nations reside, who use the same customs and attire with the Suevians; their language more resembles that of Britain. They worship the Mother of the Gods. As the characteristic of their national superstition, they wear the images of wild boars. This alone serves them for arms, this is the safeguard of all, and by this every worshiper of the Goddess is secured even amidst his foes. Rare amongst them is the use of weapons of iron, but frequent that of clubs.

-Tacitus, Germania

On the island of Rugen (a German island in the Baltic Sea) at Jasmund, near Stubbenkammer, remains can still be seen (notably the outer wall) of Hertha Castle, that have been standing there for many hundreds of years, since the Pagan period. In the castle the Pagans of Rugen would worship an idol of Hertha, who they saw as the Earth-Mother.

Near Hertha Castle is a dark, deep lake, with woodland and hillsides all around. Each year, on several occasions, the goddess bathed in the lake. She rode to the lake in a wagon concealed by a strange veil. The wagon was pulled by two cows. Only the goddess's sacred priest could travel with her. Slaves were the cows who pulled the wagon, but they were drowned in the lake once their task has been completed as any unsanctified human who saw the goddess was doomed to die. And for that reason we know nothing else about the cult of this goddess.

There are many strange tales about weird things that happen near the lake. Some people think these are due to the devil, who, they think, took the form of Hertha to lead the Pagans astray and as he (in the form of Hertha) was worshiped there, still lays claim to the lake. Other people believe the odd happenings are caused by an ancient queen or princess who was exiled to the lake.

A glamorous woman in frequently seen coming out of the woodland near the lake, especially when the moon is bright in the sky. This being goes to the lake where she bathes. She is accompanied by numerous female attendants. They all disappear but can still be heard splashing in the waters of the lake. Later they reappear and return to the woods wearing long white veils. But it is extremely perilous to watch all this, for any wanderer seeing these sights will feel drawn forcefully toward the lake where the white woman bathes. As soon as he has touched the water of the lake he will be powerless and the lake will engulf him.

It is said that the woman must lure one human into the lake each year. None are allowed to take boats or nets into the lake. Once some people risked bringing a boat onto the lake. It was left afloat overnight. When they came back next morning it was gone. A lengthy search was made and it was found at the top of a beech tree on the banks of the lake; Spirits of the lake had placed it there during the night and as the people were removing the boat from the tree they heard a mocking voice crying out from within the lake: "Nickel, my brother, and I did it!"

-J. D. H. Temme, "Die Volkssagen von Pommern und Rügen" (retold by Shaun D. L. Brassfield-Thorpe)

> *Erce, Erce, Erce, Mother of Earth,*
> *May the Almighty grant you, the Eternal Lord,*
> *Fields sprouting and springing up,*
> *Fertile and fruitful,*
> *Bright shafts of shining millet,*
> *And broad crops of barley*
> *And white wheaten crops*
> *And all the crops of earth.*
> *May God Almighty grant the owner,*
> *(And his hallows who are in heaven),*

That his land be fortified against all foes,
And embattled against all evil,
From sorceries sown throughout the land.
Now I pray the Wielder who made this world
That no cunning woman, nor crafty man,
May weaken the words that are uttered here.

Then drive forward the plough and cut the first furrow, then say:

Hail, Earth, mother of all;
Be abundant in God's embrace,
Filled with food for our folk's need.
-Acerbot (Anglo-Saxon Charm)

My first encounter with Nerthus came during the visionary experience when I oathed to Frey, in 2004. I had to be both in this world and Vanaheim, to "do it properly" before his family. Nerthus appeared as a very large woman, with a Venus-of-Willendorf type figure, and veiled. Anytime I would see Nerthus after that, in a visionary experience, she was veiled. When I moved out to Southern California, she allowed me to see her face. Of her face I cannot really speak because her eyes were so intense that it made the rest of her face almost un-noticeable. She had completely blue eyes, bright and blazing, not dissimilar to the Fremen in *Dune*. (It may be that her eyes were once a different color, perhaps brown, but they changed when she matured and took her role among the Vanir, according to my gnosis.)

Those who see Nerthus, who she reveals her true self to, are killed. One could argue the complex nature of the ceremony and the sacrifice of the slaves, but I believe these slaves gave themselves to Nerthus willingly, knowing she would kill them after they got to see her, but it was worth serving her, and worth seeing her, that they gave those final days in service to her and went to her upon death.

The concept of human sacrifice, including and especially *willing* human sacrifice, rubs moderns the wrong way, and in no way am I condoning suicide or homicide by this statement. However, in the 21st century we seem to all be terrified of death, seeking to prolong our lives as long as possible. In the Western world we also live in a secular society and it is thought that belief in anything Bigger than ones' self is a sign of mental illness. It should be patently obvious that a hoddess of Earth, intimately tied to health and fertility of soil and the life of the living things on the Earth, would also be connected with death. Life feeds on death, and Nature is the Great Recycler. The more society becomes detached from living closely to the Earth, the more that we depend on artificial means to keep us safe from that which we fear, the more we anger Nerthus.

In my own case, I still don't claim to understand why Nerthus chose to show me her true self, and work with me for a time. She may have taken interest in me due to my promoting Vanatru as a viable religious option. Nonetheless, the brief time I was working intensely with her, changed me inside and out, and gave me some new perceptions on the nature of sacredness, for which I am grateful to her, but processing the knowledge has been difficult to say the least.

There are two words to express the sacred in the Anglo-Saxon tongue -- a culture that likely worshiped Nerthus as Erce, the Earth Mother (as seen in the *Acerbot*)-- and those words are *halig*, from which we get our modern English "holy", and *wih*, which has cognates with the Norse *ve*, as in "temple", as well as the modern English "woe".

Halig is the kind of holiness the everyday person can aspire to -- a state of wholeness, finding wholeness within self, in healthy coexistence with the land, relationships with others, and communion with the Divine.

To be *halig* or to have *halig* is to have wholeness, to have health in body, mind, and spirit. It is a state of radiant well-being rather than blissful euphoria or serious solemnity. Njord, the consort of Nerthus, is very much a god of *halig*, as are his offspring. He is a god who inspires wholeness, who inspires a good quality of life that can be shared with others and given back to the Divine in gratitude.

Conversely, *wih* is not "everyday holiness", nor should it be. And while Njord is more *halig*, Nerthus is definitely more a goddess of *wih*. To be touched by Nerthus, to receive her blessings, is a gift precious enough it is only reserved for once a year. But the deeper connection with Nerthus was apparently worth dying for back in the old days, to experience her true nature, to commune with the reality of her being. To see her eyes -- the eyes are called the window of the soul by many cultures -- is to see Nerthus' Self, and is such a profound experience that life is never the same afterwards, and indeed to go back to the way things were is impossible.

Wih is the energy found in a temple, and within ritual tools (including deity statues). In modern paganism we seem to take a lot of this for granted, and I've seen too many pagan altars that attract random clutter and are not treated like the homes of the Divine that they are. There is a casual familiarity with objects used to cast spells and/or create sacred space, rather than seeing them as imbued with the power of the Divine – that which can heal, change, and even kill. Indeed, *wih* is cognate with the Latin *victim*, recalling the human sacrifices made to Nerthus.

One of the old words for "temple" was *ealh*, and in the Anglo-Saxon Rune Poem, the verse usually thought to be one about an elk is very particular about describing the energy within an *ealh*, or temple:

> The Eolh-sedge is mostly to be found in a marsh;
> it grows in the water and makes a ghastly wound,
> covering with blood every warrior who touches it.

If you see groves as being sacred sites, as well as temples being built on holy ground, this verse makes a lot more sense. If you consider that Nerthus's sacred places were lakes and bogs, this makes even more sense. The presence of the Divine – and especially Erce, herself - will "make a ghastly wound". Yes, it is important to cultivate relationships with the gods, to make them a part of our lives as they reach out to us. But we can never forget that they are gods, and sometimes to be in their presence is beautiful but also terrifying.

Nerthus is no exception, the fact that the one piece of lore we have explicitly discussing her by name refers directly to human sacrifice should be a lesson that dealing with the Vanir is not casual, and though she may well be invested in the peace, prosperity, and overall well-being of humanity, it comes at a terrible price.

Ergo, I feel that the occasion for celebration and peace with Nerthus' travels through the land was not just rejoicing in the fertility she brought to the soil, animals, and people, but the knowledge that she is holy and we all are hers in the end, given back to the Earth, whether buried in a mound or scattered ashes on the ground. We live, die, and are recycled out again. The mystery of

Nerthus is that we must enjoy the gifts of the Earth, because they can be taken away at any time. Life itself is too sacred to be consumed by petty jealousies and fighting; we must be mindful that she is all around, and she is holy.

While I do not believe the Venus of Willendorf figures found throughout Europe are Nerthus *per se*, I do use the Venus figures to represent Nerthus, being full-figured and unmistakably female, but faceless... too holy to look upon, for that kind of holiness means enslavement to her service... and death.

That I have seen Nerthus' eyes does not make me "special". Rather, it was her way of showing me a glimpse into her world and her ways, and what that would mean for me and those around me. To touch the Divine is also to pay a great price. Even if one survives the psychological intensity of the encounter, one does not walk away from the gods unchanged and indeed the "stain" of their holiness will be noticed by others, pushing the god-touched one into a liminal space. It also pushes those primary people in that one's life, into surrounding the liminal space, which can be difficult for most.

I am proud to serve the Vanir, that they would allow me the honor of serving them is amazing. But I am mindful that even in the ecstasy of their companionship, in sacred rites and carrying their blessings within me, it is also to die to myself. Most people, fortunately, are not meant to be in full time service to the gods. Indeed, the purpose of one who can communicate directly with the Powers, is ultimately to mediate between them and their people who may not have the same ability. However, what devotees would envy of the mediators, is not something to be envied, in the end. A gift demands a gift, power demands a price. To touch the Divine is to become less human, to visit their world is to straddle the hedge between this world and theirs. It is a beautiful place, but also a dangerous place. This is the lesson of Nerthus, to me: *If you would know us, and learn our ways, you will gradually lose your own.*

Frey

You'll remember me when the west wind
moves
Upon the fields of barley.
You'll forget the sun in his jealous sky
As we walk in fields of gold
-Sting, "Fields of Gold"

Frey is the son of Njord (and likely Nerthus), the twin brother of Freya, and one of three Vanir who were sent to Asgard as hostages following the Aesir-Vanir war. He is a god of fertility; he is typically portrayed with an erect phallus, and is connected with the cult of the elves, being called "Lord of Alfheim" (and as we will explore later in this book, Vanir are elves). As I once put it rather flippantly, "Frey is the god of elf cock". But there is more to him than just his cock, he is also a god of peace and prosperity, and abundance.

How should one periphrase Frey? Thus: by calling him Son of Njordr, Brother of Freya, and also God of Vanir, and Kinsman of the Vanir, and Wane, and God of the Fertile Season, and God of Wealth-Gifts.
-Skaldskaparsmal, VII.

Njordr in Noatun begot afterward two children: the son was called Frey, and the daughter Freya; they were fair of face and mighty. Frey is the most renowned of the Aesir; he rules over the rain and the shining of the sun, and therewithal the fruit of the earth; and it is good to call on him for fruitful seasons and peace. He governs also the prosperity of men.
-Gylfaginning XXIV.

Gymer hight a man whose wife was Orboda, of the race of mountain giants. Their daughter was Gerd, the fairest of all women. One day when Frey had gone into Hlidskjalf, and was looking out upon all the worlds, he saw toward the north a hamlet wherein was a large and beautiful house. To this house went a woman, and when she raised her hands to open the door, both the sky and the sea glistened therefrom, and she made all the world bright. As a punishment for his audacity in seating himself in that holy seat, Frey went away full of grief.

When he came home, he neither spake, slept, nor drank, and no one dared speak to him. Then Njord sent for Skirner, Frey's servant, bade him go to Frey and ask him with whom he was so angry, since he would speak to nobody. Skirner said that he would go, though he was loath to do so, as it was probable that he would get evil words in reply. When he came to Frey and asked him why he was so sad that he would not talk, Frey answered that he had seen a beautiful woman, and for her sake he had become so filled with grief, that he could not live any longer if he could not get her. And now you must go, he added, and ask her hand for me and bring her home to me, whether it be with or without the consent of her father. I will reward you well for your trouble.

Skirner answered saying that he would go on this errand, but Frey must give him his sword, that was so excellent that it wielded itself in fight. Frey made no objection to this and gave him the sword. Skirner went on his journey, courted Gerd for him, and got the promise of her that she nine nights thereafter should come to Bar-Isle and there have her wedding with Frey. When Skirner came back and gave an account of his journey, Frey said:

> Long is one night,
> Long are two nights,
> How can I hold out three?
> Oft to me one month
> Seemed less
> Than this half night of love.

This is the reason why Frey was unarmed when he fought with Bele, and slew him with a hart's horn. Then said Ganglere: It is a great wonder that such a lord as Frey would give away his sword, when he did not have another as good. A great loss it was to him when he fought with Bele; and this I know, forsooth, that he must have repented of that gift. Har answered: Of no great account was his meeting with Bele. Frey could have slain him with his hand. But the time will come when he will find himself in a worse plight for not having his sword, and that will be when the sons of Muspel sally forth to the fight.

-Prose Edda, Anderson translation

Indeed, before Thorkel left Thvera, he went to Frey's temple, and taking an old steer up thither, made this speech:-- "Thou, Frey," said he, "wert long my protector, and many offerings hast thou had at my hands, which have borne good fruit to me. Now do I present this steer to thee, in the hope that Glum hereafter may be driven by force off this land, as I am driven off it; and, I pray thee, give me some token whether thou acceptest this offering or not." Then the steer was stricken in such a way that he bellowed loud and fell down dead, and Thorkel took this as a favorable omen. Afterwards he was in better spirits, as if he thought his offering was accepted and his wish ratified by the god.

…before Glum left home he dreamt that many persons came to Thvera to visit the god Frey, and he thought he saw a great crowd on the sand-banks by the river, with Frey sitting on a chair. He dreamt that he asked who they were who had come thither, and they said, "We are thy departed kindred, and we are now begging Frey that thou may'st not be driven out of Thvera, but it is no use, for he answers shortly and angrily, and calls to mind now the gift of the ox by Thorkel the tall." At that point Glum woke up, and ever afterwards he professed that he was on worse terms with Frey.

-Viga-Glum's Saga

King Heithrek worshiped Frey, and he used to give Frey the biggest boar he could find. They regarded it as so sacred that in all important cased they used to take the oath on its bristles. It was the custom to sacrifice this boar at the 'sacrifice of the herd.' On Yule Eve the 'boar of the herd' was led into the hall before the King. Then men laid their hands on his bristles and made solemn vows. King Heithrek himself made a vow that however deeply a man should have wronged him, if he came into his power he should not be deprived of the chance of receiving a trial by the King's judges; but he should get off scot free if he could propound riddles which the King could not answer. But when people tried to ask the King riddles, not one was put to him which he could not solve.

-The Saga of Hervor and Heithrek, II, X.

There happened to be great sacrifices in the honor of Frey, and his idol had such a power that the devil spoke through it, and it had been given a young wife. People believed that they could have sexual intercourse. Frey's wife was pretty, and she had the dominion over the temple.

-Gunnar Helming's Saga, Flateyjarbok

The horse, it appears, was regarded as a favorite animal of Frey. At his temple in Throndheim it is said there were horses belonging to him.

...A highly-valued wooden statue of Frey was found in a temple in Throndheim, which King Olaf Tryggvason hewed in pieces in the presence of the people.

-*The Religion of the Northmen*, Rudolph Keyser

The worship of Frey, however, must also have been very popular in Norway, from which it passed to Iceland with the early settlers. As late as 998 the men of Thrandheim are represented as refusing to break their image of Frey at the command of King Olaf, 'because we have long served him and he has done well by us. He often talked with us, and told us things to come, and gave us peace and plenty.'

-The Religion of Ancient Scandinavia, **W.A. Craigie**

Finally, there is far less information in the Anglo-Saxon primary sources on Ing-Frea than there is in the Norse lore, however even from scant mentions we can assume Ingui was an important god to the Anglo-Saxon people, if not one of the most important.

For starters, it may be that the English people were named for Ing himself. In Tacitus' *Germania*, mythology is recounted of the Earth god Tuisto, his son Mannus, and his three sons, after whom many people are called – the Ingaevones are said to dwell next to the ocean. In the Nordic lore, Frey is the son of Njord the sea god, and so it would make sense for his people to live by the sea. Pliny notes the Ingaevones as consisting of the Cimbri, Teutons, and Chauci tribes. The Ingaevones form the majority of the Anglo-Saxon settlement in Britain, and the linguistic scholar Noah Webster speculated they gave England its name. John Grigsby (author of *Beowulf and Grendel*) remarks that on the continent, "they formed part of the confederacy known as the 'friends of Ing' and in the new lands they migrated to in the 5th and 6th centuries. In time they would name these lands Angle-land, and it is tempting to speculate that the word Angle was derived from, or thought of as a pun on, the name of Ing." At the very least, an Ingui is listed in the Anglo-Saxon royal house of Bernicia, and he was probably seen as the progenitor of all Anglian kings. Ing is most likely one and the same as Yngvi, the founder of the Yngling dynasty of Sweden. Since Frea or Frey means "lord", we can assume Ing or Ingui is the god's proper name, with Frea as his title.

In the Anglo-Saxon Rune Poem, a rune is named for him, with the corresponding verse

* * *
73

Ing was arest mid East-Denum
gesewen secgun, ot he siddan est
ofer wag gewat; wan after ran;
dus Heardingas done hale nemdun.
(Ing was first seen by men among the East-Danes,
till, followed by his chariot,
he departed eastwards over the waves.
So the Heardingas named the hero.)

The Danes are mentioned in the story of *Beowulf*, with Hrothgar referred to as "Lord of the Ingwine", or "friends of Ing".

Frey is a god of reliability and integrity, manifest in the seasonal cycles, which change, but you can always depend upon changing and being at the same time every year: the cycles within the season of birth, growth, and death of animals, and seed, root, bud, ripening, and harvest, to compost again, in the plant world. He is said to bring the sunshine as well as the gentle rain, and to bestow peace, pleasure, and prosperity on mortals. To my knowledge, peace, pleasure, and prosperity all involve being able to feel safe, and feel secure. This verse from the *Lokasenna*, spoken by Tyr (a god of justice, honesty, and integrity), exemplifies Frey's concept of integrity:

Frey is best
of all the exalted gods
in the Aesir's courts:
no maid he makes to weep,
no wife of man,
and from bonds looses all.

The women are not made to weep because Frey does not let them down. Frey looses us from our bonds, that is, what holds us back from enjoying life. Sometimes cutting these bonds can be painful, if one has become attached to their "post" for lack of anything better to compare it with. To be free -- to be truly free -- is very powerful, but also comes with responsibility. To be irresponsible is not freedom, it is illusion of thought and causing harm, thus bondage. To have an appropriate amount of responsibility, for one's words, deeds, and their impact, and to be empowered in those words and deeds, is to be free.

Frey is not like Santa Claus who will give you everything you want. Indeed Frey, as a deity tied both to horticulture/agriculture and the hunt (he had to get his antler from somewhere), he respects hard work and plenty of it. Frey is all about the long-term, not the quick fix. Instant gratification is not his *modus operandi*, and indeed, he has ways of teaching people hard lessons about getting what they pay for, and what they really value in life.

Nonetheless, to earn Frey's blessing is to hold onto something precious, something that time and changing with the times cannot depreciate. His blood is in the soil, and to gain Frey's favor is to plant seeds and take root. (When Frey does choose to communicate with people, he often uses metaphors of seeds, and growing seasons.)

I do see his primary domain, or sphere of influence, as being Life-Sustainer. This is quite a bit different than Odin who has a creation/destruction polarity, and Thor who is a protector first and foremost.

To modern devotees of Ing, he can be seen as the ultimate example of holding what you have. Frey is not as obvious of a warrior deity as Thor or Odin, but he is entrusted with the best sword in the Nine Worlds, later giving it to his etin-bride's family as a bride-price, and wielding an antler in its place, though it is noted he could kill with his bare hands. It would seem then that Ing is a defensive warrior, fighting for home and protecting the land, rather than the glory of war itself. The boar, his most sacred animal, is a very territorially aggressive beast. When Ing fights, it is to preserve what he holds most dear, as well as to return the land to a state of *frid* - peace among the tribe. His presence hallows and sanctifies. He is intimately bound with the health and fertility of the land, and his Swedish title of "Veraldar Gudh" - God of the World – can be seen as referring to the world in terms of daily life. He is the god of the sacred in the mundane, the little things that make life worth living, and what makes it worth preserving and fighting for.

The main mythos of Frey in Norse lore is that of his wooing of and marriage to the giantess Gerda, who may probably be one and the same as the troll-woman Thorgerda Holgabrudr mentioned in the Sagas and worshiped as a Goddess by Earl Haakon, and may also be one and the same as Hretha whose name means "glory" - recalling the light radiating from her when Frey saw her for the first time from Odin's high seat. Her name is related to our word for "garden" as well as our term "geard" or "garth", especially as denotes "innangeard" - the inner circle of trust, such as found in a tribe. Frey's marriage to Gerda the etin-bride is not only symbolic of the sacral king wedding and blessing the land, but also of another related term, "grith" – a state of truce with the outdwellers, especially if one is adopted into the tribe.

As such, Ing-Frey is a good deity to call upon for those who are frith-weavers, especially those who are building a kindred or organization, as well as those who are in a minority group and are working for the same rights as others and would be an example through non-violence and worthy deeds.

As a warrior, Frey is also helpful to fathers protecting their household, men who want to be more whole in their maleness, as well as those who may have been abused by men and need to relate to a masculine figure who is strong but balances strength with sensitivity, might with mercy. He is not overbearing. He is, indeed, a good deity for anyone who wants to appreciate life more, drawing upon his vitality to build and grow things of life, and be able to recognize their value and work to maintain them, even fighting to hold onto them if need be.

From Frey's perspective, the world is what it is, and it is best to connect with the world, to embrace its joys and pleasures as well as its sorrows and pain. Frey is, to me, what is good in this world. When I call Frey "God of the World", I don't just mean the sun and the rain and the growing things, but daily life itself.

Gerda

She walks in beauty, like the night
Of cloudless climes and starry skies;
And all that's best of dark and bright
Meet in her aspect and her eyes;
Thus mellowed to that tender light
Which heaven to gaudy day denies.

-Lord Byron

While the subject of Jotun-worship still remains a controversial and polarizing issue within modern heathenry, there is some evidence of it being part of elder heathen practice. The most famous mention of Gerda is of course the account of her marriage to Frey as given in *Skirnirsmal* as well as the *Prose Edda*. I personally believe Gerda is one and the same as Thorgerdr Holgabrudr, sister of Irpa, a goddess mentioned in three different Sagas.

Earl Hakon said: "It seems to me that the battle is beginning to go against us. I had thought it a bad thing to have to fight these men, and so indeed it turns out. Now this will not do. We must bethink ourselves of some wise course. I shall go up on land, and you are to look after the fleet meanwhile, in case they attack." Thereupon the earl went up on the island of Prim signed, and away into a forest, and fell on his knees and prayed looking northward. And in his prayer he called upon his patron goddess, Thorgerd Holgabrud. But she would not hear his prayers and was wroth. He offered to make her many a sacrifice, but she refused each one, and he thought his case desperate. In the end he offered her a human sacrifice, but she would not have it. At last he offered her his own seven-year-old-son; and that she accepted. Then the earl put the boy in the hands of his slave Skopti, and Skopti slew him.

Afterwards the earl returned to his ships and urged his men on to make renewed attack; "for I know now surely that victory will be ours. Press the attack all the more vigorously, because I have invoked for victory both the sisters, Thorgerd and Irpa."

Then the earl boarded his ship and prepared for the fight, and the fleet rowed to the attack, and again there was the most furious battle. And right soon the weather began to thicken in the north and the clouds covered the sky and the daylight waned. Next came the flashes of lightning and thunder, and with them a violent shower. The Jomsvikings had to fight facing into the storm, and the squall was so heavy that they could hardly stand up against it. Men had to cast off their clothes, earlier, because of the heat, and now it was cold. Nevertheless, no one needed to be urged on to do battle. But although the Jomsvikings hurled stones and other missiles and threw their spears, the wind turned all their weapons back upon them, to join the shower of missiles from their enemies.

Havard the Hewing was the first to see Thorgerd Holgabrud in the fleet of Earl Hakon, and then many a second-sighted man saw her. And when the squall abated a little they saw that an arrow flew from every finger of the ogress, and each arrow felled a man. They told Sigvaldi, and he said: "it seems we are not fighting men alone, but still it behooves us to do our best."

And when the storm lessened a bit Earl Hakon again invoked Thorgerd and said that he had done his utmost. And then it grew dark again with a squall, this time even stronger and worse than before. And right at the beginning of the squall Havard the Hewing saw that two women were standing on the earl's ship, and both were doing the same thing that Thorgerd had done before.

Then Sigvaldi said: "Now I am going to flee, and let all men do so. I did not vow to fight against trolls, and it is now worse than before, as there are two ogresses."

[All of Earl Hakon's enemies flee.]

Then they weighed the hailstones on scales to see what power Thorgerd and Irpa had, and one hailstone weighed an ounce.

-The Saga of the Jómsvíkings, Chapter 21

Earl Hakon was atttending a feast a Gudbrand's home. During the night, Hrapp the killer went to their temple. Inside it, he saw the statue of Thorgerd Holgi's-Bride enthroned, massive as a fully-grown man; there was a huge gold bracelet on her arm, and a linen hood over her head. Hrapp stripped off the hood and the bracelet. He then noticed Thor in his chariot, and took from him another gold bracelet. He took a third bracelet from Irpa. He dragged all three of the idols outside and stripped them of their vestments; then he set fire to the temple and burned it down. [...]

Early that morning, Earl Hakon and Gudbrand went out to the temple and found it burned down, with the three idols lying outside stripped of all their riches. Then Gudbrand said, 'Our gods are powerful indeed. They have walked unaided from the flames.'

'The gods have nothing to do with it,' said Earl Hakon. 'A man must have fired the temple and carried the gods out. But the gods are in no haste to take vengence; the man who did this will be driven out of Valhalla for ever.'

-Njal's Saga, Chapter 88

Of Sigmund it must be now told that he fell to talk with Earl Hacon, and told him that he was minded to leave warring and hie out to the Fareys [...]

And when he was fully bound, Earl Hacon said to him, "One should speed well one would fain welcome back." And he went out of doors with Sigmund. Then spake Hacon, "What sayest thou to this? In what dost thou put thy trust?" I put my trust in my own might and main," said Sigmund. "That must not be," the Earl answered," but thou shalt put thy trust where I have put all my trust, namely in Thorgerd Shinebride," said he. "And we will go and see her now and luck for thee at her hands." Sigmund bade him settle this matter as he would.

They set forth along a certain path into the wood, and thence by a little bypath into the wood, till they came where a ride lay before them, and a house standing in it with a stake fence round it. Right fair was that house, and gold and silver was run into the carvings thereof. They went into the house, Hacon and Sigmund together, and a few men with them. Therein were a great many gods. There were many glass roof-lights in the house, so that there was no shadow anywhere. There was a woman in the house over against the door, right fairly decked she was. The Earl cast him down at her feet, and there he lay long, and when he rose up he told Sigmund that they should bring her some offering and lay the silver thereof on the stool before her. "And we shall have it as a mark of what she thinks of this, if she will do as I wish and let the ring loose which she holds in her hand. For thou, Sigmund, shall get luck by that ring." Then the Earl took hold of the ring, and it seemed to Sigmund that she clasped her hand on it, and the earl got not the ring. The Earl cast him down a second time before her, and Sigmund saw that the earl was weeping. Then he stood up again and caught hold of the ring, and now, behold, it was loose; and he took it and gave it to Sigmund, and told him that with this ring he must never part, and Sigmund gave his word on it. With that they parted.

-Færeyinga Saga, Chapter 23

Furthermore, it says in **Skaldskaparsmal**:

They say that a king known as Holgi, after whom Halogaland is named, was Thorgerd Holgabrud's father. Sacrifices were offered to them both, and Holgi's mound was raised with alternately a layer of gold or silver-- this was the money offered in sacrifice-- and a layer of earth and stone.

It should be mentioned that Halogaland is in northern Norway, and Halogaland is one of the lands noted by the Liljenroths where the Hel-folk likely lived[5], and it seems likely that in a drowned coastline containing extensive mountainous fjords and islands, there would indeed be a cult of mountain Jotnar. "Thor" is closely related to the word "thurse" (and indeed, often an epithet for "giant") and in this instance would mean "Thurse-Gerda" or "Giant-Gerda" and would thus point to none other than the giantess Gerda, wed by Frey. As Gerda is said to be one of the mountain-dwelling Jotnar, origins in mountainous Halogaland would be in keeping with this gnosis. Her sister, Irpa, has a name equivalent to the Old Norse word *jarpr*, or "brown", and from here we can see her relationship with Gerda, whose name means "yard" and is related to "garden" – they are both Jotynjar directly connected with Earth, Irpa as the soil, Gerda with its cultivation. Irpa would most likely be "elder sister".

It is also said that Thorgerd was the "wife" of Earl Haakon, and indeed H.R. Ellis Davidson[6] mentions that Olaf I of Norway dragged out an image of Thorgerdr after Haakon's death and had it burned next to an image of Frey, which would suggest that Thorgerdr was beloved to Frey, and one and the same as Gerda. It is also telling that in heathen lore, Frey is the only god explicitly known to take a human spouse (the priestess-wife mentioned in the Saga of Gunnar Helming), and if Gerda took Haakon as mortal consort, this would indeed be an evenly matched pair.

---

[5] http://hem.passagen.se/helandia/index_en.htm
[6] Davidson, Hilda Ellis (1998). *Roles of the Northern Goddess.*

In any case, I believe Thorgerd is evidence of Gerda's cultus in heathen times, but short of building a time machine and going back into time there is no way to know for certain. Even if it were not true, there are people giving her honor now.

Too many refuse to honor Gerda at all – at least one heathen has said in my presence that Gerda is "hostile" and "tricked Frey with *seiðr*" – and those who do hail her often dismiss her as Frey's consort and nothing more. Yet she is much more of that.

If we see her as the same as Thorgerd, she is a powerful goddess in her own right, bringer of thunder and lightning, fierce in battle, bestower of power and authority. "Holgi" comes from the Proto-Norse *hailaga* meaning "holy"; Thorgerd is the holy-bride, and being called Shine-Bride relates to the mythos where Frey saw her light and fell in love with her. I think of this as being like light through the storm clouds, and tenebrescent clouds are in my opinion one of the most beautiful wonders of the natural world, and relate to Frey's role as Light-Bringer; Gerda is the strength that supports Frey in his work of bringing light and life to the land, the love that makes him feel whole, and inspires his love for all life.

In my personal gnosis, the light that Frey saw in his vision on Hlidskjalf, Odin's high seat, was of the light within Gerda's soul, her essence being almost blinding in its brightness, and Frey knowing that he had to have it, that she would complete him -- and their entire exchange of love is based on an exchange of light and darkness. Frey is a Light-Bringer, and filled with light of his own. But he needs a continual source, and Gerda is his light (rather like Sigyn is the innocent joy to Loki that inspires his humor and playfulness), her support of him in her quiet dignity, with meaningful words and even more meaningful touch, is what keeps Frey going. On those rare instances that her calm cool exterior is broken to flash a smile or break out in wild laughter, Frey feels most alive, and is able to take the love between them and give it to the committed lovers of Midgard.

Gerda also sees the moments that very few humans are ever able to see: Frey filled with pain, weeping, seeing the struggles of people in Midgard, and the senseless wars between the Jotnar and Aesir. Frey wants so very badly for everyone to have a good quality of life, and he takes it personally if there is suffering. Gerda's embrace gives him solace, and gives him the darkness he needs for his light to rest and regenerate.

And indeed, Frey would not have pledged himself to someone unworthy; to dismiss Gerda is to dismiss Frey's choice.

Those who have dealings with Gerda have remarked amongst themselves that Gerda is quiet. It is not something to take personally. Gerda's quiet is not so much based in shyness as it is in dignity: She feels that only fools talk to hear themselves talk, and that words should be reserved for something of meaning. Much more can be conveyed in body language, or a touch, or just noticing something, than actually speaking. Gerda's quiet also extends to attire - she is not glamorous like Freya, or stunning like Sif, but has her own understated class. Gerda's modesty in attire is also based in her attitude that there is more to her than her body, there is a mind full of wisdom that should be known and explored... and then only for those who she deems fit.

There is a corroborated gnosis that Gerda can teach about working with plant spirits, and the act of working the soil to be a grounding experience, and noticing the subtle growth of herbs and other garden plants as a mindfulness exercise. To notice the small details is to notice the health and well-being of a person or situation, when so many are focused on the bigger picture and their castles may fall apart due to the weakness of a few bricks. Gerda tends to the plants as lovingly as she would children – in fact, it could be rightly said that the greenwights are Gerda's children, the only children she will ever have.

I have had visions of Gerda being something akin to the archetypal hedgewitch, working in her enclosed garden, communing with the plant spirits, singing to them, and being rather solitary -- and fond of being solitary -- but open to those who could earn her trust with these secrets.

Gerda's solitary and wise connection to the Green World compliments Frey's role as God of the World, giver of prosperity and fertility to land and people – Frey directs it outwardly from land to people, and Gerda directs it in reverse, from her own self (or her laying with Frey) to the land. Frey is generous and gregarious, but needs a quiet space to recharge in order to keep giving of himself, and Gerda is his quiet space, his refuge – and moreover, the love that she gives to Frey, holds the power of her role to the Green World, allowing Frey to carry it with him when his wain goes forth.

I feel that it is impossible to honor Frey without understanding the goddess who owns his heart, who compelled him to "sell out" the fate of the Aesir by giving up the most powerful sword in the Nine Worlds. When Frey gave his sword to Gerda's family, both were aware of the costs involved: that if it should come to Ragnarok, the lines are already drawn and Frey will not survive.

However, they also understand Ragnarok to be just a prophecy, and the course can change. Frey giving up his sword was the manifestation of the desire to, on his part, end the fighting and hostilities between the Jotnar and Aesir, and try to weave frith between the two tribes, rather than continue the fighting. And so Frey tries to teach the people of Midgard about tolerance and acceptance, and Gerda does as well, in her own quiet, understanding way.

I have included Gerda here among the Vanir because even though she is Jotun-born, she was accepted among Frey's people – to marry a citizen of Vanaheim is to become a citizen yourself – and her sphere of influence with the Green World is very Vanic, as is the way she quietly works to promote peace and understanding alongside of her husband. She is worthy of honor and respect, and while she is not easy to approach or get to know, with time, effort, and patience, she may let you in to her secret garden, and prove herself to be a loyal friend, even one who will be a lethal foe to protect what she holds within the walls of her heart.

Freya

I can cast a spell
With secrets you can't tell
Mix a special brew
Put fire inside of you
But anytime you feel
Danger or fear
Instantly I will appear, 'cause

I'm every woman, it's all in me
Anything you want done, baby
I'll do it naturally
-Chaka Khan

Freya is the daughter of Njord (and likely Nerthus), the twin sister of Frey, and one of three Vanir who were sent to Asgard as hostages following the Aesir-Vanir war. Like her brother, she is connected with fertility, and portrayed in lore as being extremely sexual. However she is also a warrior and a mistress of magic, and a very complex figure.

How should one periphrase Freya? Thus: by calling her Daughter of Njordr, Sister of Frey, Wife of Odr, Mother of Hnoss, Possessor of the Slain, of Sessrumnir, of the Gib-Cats, and of Brisingamen; Goddess of the Vanir, Lady of the Vanir, Goddess Beautiful in Tears, Goddess of Love.
-Skaldskaparsmal 20

Freya is most gently born (together with Frigg): she is wedded to the man named Odr. Their daughter is Hnoss: she is so fair, that those things which are fair and precious are called hnossir. Odr went away on long journeys, and Freya weeps for him, and her tears are red gold. Freya has many names, and this is the cause thereof: that she gave herself sundry names, when she went out among unknown peoples seeking Odr: she is called Mardoll and Horn, Gefn, Syr. Freya had the necklace Brisingamen. She is also called Lady of the Vanir.

-Gylfaginning (Brodeur Translation)

Njord's daughter Freya was priestess of the sacrifices, and first taught the Aesir the magic art, as it was in use and fashion among the Vanir. While Njord was with the Vanir he had taken his own sister in marriage, for that was allowed by their law; and their children were Frey and Freya. But among the Aesir it was forbidden to intermarry with such near relations.

...Freya alone remained of the gods, and she became on this account so celebrated that all women of distinction were called by her name, whence they now have the title Fru (Frau in German); so that every woman is called fru (frau in German), or mistress over her property, and the wife is called the house-Fru (Ehefrau in German). Freya continued the blood-sacrifices. Freya had also many other names. Her husband was called Odr, and her daughters Hnoss and Gersemi. They were so very beautiful, that afterwards the most precious jewels were called by their names.

-Ynglinga Saga

East of Vanaquisl in Asia was the land called Asialand or Asiahome, but the folk that dwelt there was called Aesir, and their chief town was Asgard. Odin was the name of the king thereof, and therein was a right holy place of sacrifice. Niord and Frey Odin made Temple-priests thereover; but the daughter of Niord was Freya, and she was fellow to Odin and his concubine. Now there were certain men in Asia, whereof one was called Alfrigg, the second Dwalin, the third Berling, the fourth Grerr: these had their abode but a little space from the King's hall, and were men so wise in craftsmanship, that they laid skilful hand on all matters; and such-like men as they were did men call dwarfs. In a rock was their dwelling, and in that day they mingled more with menfolk than as now they do.

Odin loved Freya full sore, and withal she was the fairest woman of that day: she had a bower that was both fair and strong; insomuch, say men, that if the door were shut to, none might come into the bower aforesaid without the will of Freya.

Now on a day went Freya afoot by that rock of the dwarfs, and it lay open: therein were the dwarfs a-smithing a golden collar, and the work was at point to be done: fair seemed that collar to Freya, and fair seemed Freya to the dwarfs.

Now would Freya buy the collar of them, and bade them in return for it silver and gold, and other good things. They said they lacked not money, yet that each of them would sell his share of the collar for this thing, and nought else---that she should lie a night by each of them: wherefore, whether she liked it better or worse, on such wise did she strike the bargain with them; and so the four nights being outworn, and all conditions fulfilled, they delivered the collar to Freya; and she went home to her bower, and held her peace hereof, as if nought had befallen.

There was a man called Farbauti, which carl had to wife a carline called Laufey; she was both slim and slender, therefore was she called Needle. One child had these, a son called Loki; nought great of growth was he, but betimes shameless of tongue and nimble in gait; over all men had he that craft which is called cunning; guileful was he from his youth up, therefore was he called Loki the Sly. He betook himself to Odin at Asgard and became his man. Ever had Odin a good word for him, whatsoever he turned to; yet withal he oft laid heavy labours upon him, which forsooth he turned out of hand better than any man looked for: moreover, he knew wellnigh all things that befell, and told all he knew to Odin. So tells the tale that Loki knew how that Freya had gotten the collar, yea and what she had given for it; so he told Odin thereof, and when Odin heard of it he bade Loki get the collar and bring it to him. Loki said it was not a likely business, because no man might come into Freya's bower without the will of her; but Odin bade him go his ways and not come back before he had gotten the collar. Then Loki turned away howling, and most of men were glad thereof whenas Loki throve nought.

But Loki went to Freya's bower, and it was locked; he strove to come in, and might not; and cold it was without, so that he fast began to grow a-cold. So he turned himself into a fly, and fluttered about all the locks and the joints, and found no hole therein whereby he might come in, till up by the gable-top he found a hole, yet no bigger than one might thrust a needle through; none the less he wriggled in thereby. So when he was come in he peered all about to see if any waked, but soon he got to see that all were asleep in the bower. Then in he goeth unto Freya's bed, and sees that she hath the collar on her with the clasp turned downward. Thereon Loki changed himself into a flea, and sat on Freya's cheek, and stung her so that she woke and turned about, and then fell asleep again. Then Loki drew from off him his flea's shape, and undid the collar, and opened the bower, and gat him gone to Odin therewith.

Next morn awoke Freya and saw that the doors were open, yet unbroken, and that the goodly collar was gone. She deemed she knew what guile had wrought it, so she goeth into the hall when she is clad, and cometh before Odin the king, and speaketh to him of the evil he has let be wrought against her in the stealing of that dear thing, and biddeth him give her back her jewel. Odin says that in such wise hath she gotten it, that never again shall she have it.

"Unless forsooth thou bring to pass, that two kings, each served of twenty kings, fall to strife, and fight under such weird and spell, that they no sooner fall adown than they stand up again and fight on: always unless some christened man be so bold of heart, and the fate and fortune of his lord be so great, that he shall dare go into the battle, and smite with weapons these men: and so first shall their toil come to an end, to whatsoever lord it shall befall to loose them from the pine and

trouble of their fell deeds." Hereto said Freya yea, and gat her collar again.
-Sorla Thattur, chapters 1 and 2.13

Freya spake:
"Mad art thou, Loki, | that known thou makest
The wrong and shame thou hast wrought;
The fate of all | does Frigg know well,
Though herself she says it not."
Loki spake:
"Be silent, Freya! | for fully I know thee,
Sinless thou art not thyself;
Of the gods and elves | who are gathered here,
Each one as thy lover has lain."
Freya spake:
"False is thy tongue, | and soon shalt thou find
That it sings thee an evil song;
The gods are wroth, | and the goddesses all,
And in grief shalt thou homeward go."
Loki spake:
"Be silent, Freya! | thou foulest witch,
And steeped full sore in sin;
In the arms of thy brother | the bright gods caught thee
When Freya her wind set free."
-Lokasenna (Bellows), v. 29-32

Folkvangr is the ninth,
there Freya directs
the sittings in the hall.
She half the fallen chooses each day,
but Odin the other half.
-Grimnirsmal (Thorpe)

Freya rides with her favorite Ottar to Hyndla, a Vala, for the purpose of obtaining information respecting Ottar's geneology, such information being required by him in a legal dispute with Angantyr. Having obtained this, Freya further requests Hyndla to give Ottar a portion (minnisol) that will enable him to remember all that has been told him. This she refuses, but is forced to comply by Freya having encircled her cave with flames. She gives him the potion, but accompanied by a malediction, which is by Freya turned to a blessing: Fire I strike over thee, dweller of the wood! So that thou goest not ever away from hence.

Hyndla: Fire I see burning, and the earth blazing; many will have their lives to save. Bear thou the cup to Ottar's hand, the mead with venom mingled, in an evil hour!

Freya: Thy malediction shall be powerless; although thou, Jotun maid! dost evil threaten. He shall drink delicious draughts. All the gods I pray to favor Ottar.

-Hyndluliod, introduction, v. 46-48

Freya has four faces, which she chooses to reveal to people as she thinks appropriate (just as Odin has over 200 names, each of them reflective of a different part of himself, but all still Odin). There is Mardoll, Horn, Gefion, and Syr.

- Syr ("Sow") is the Battle Goddess. If you have never seen a mother boar protecting a sounder of piglets, you will not understand Freya riding her battle-boar, Hildisvin, coming to the defense of her people (especially when they want to protect those they love). To say that Freya has a temper is a vast understatement, and here she uses down-and-dirty fisticuffs as well as battle magic, most notably shrill keening to inspire fear in the heart of the opponent.

- Horn ("Flax") is the Fertility/Creatrix aspect of Freya, the Nature Goddess who for merely walking into a field, causes things to grow around her, responding to the vitality within her. Everything she touches does indeed change, for the healthier and more beautiful.

The name Horn suggests a connection with Holda the flax Goddess, and indeed it is a personal gnosis of mine that Freya was sent to her grandmother Holda for training and it is as Horn that she is most magical in a positive way. However, there is a strong undercurrent of being able to take away and recycle back out again, just as she creates.

- Mardoll (Sea-Bright) is the most benign face of Freya, when she appears as a young woman, and is very much Njord's daughter. I have seen Freya's Mardoll side when she is older but in a more playful mood. While Freya can often be very serious – such as when she becomes Syr, and works woe on evildoers – she has a great sense of humor, and enjoys fun and games. It is through Mardoll that she is also mother to Gersemi and Hnossa. However, it is also through Mardoll that Freya's prophetic abilities are made most apparent: surrounded by the mists of the sea, Freya can see the threads of wyrd reaching into the well of the Norns, and predict how things will go, for good or ill.

- I see Gefion ("Giver") as being the Love Goddess aspect, the one who will give her own body for what she wants, and whose sex makes the recipient feel a love like no other, but also to hold off if the time or person is not right. To be embraced by Gefion, the Giver, is to be embraced by pure Love itself, that sees the beauty and divinity inherent in all creation. Indeed, it is Gefion's vitality born in love, that gives all good things.

A word should be said about Gefn, as there is mention in the lore of a goddess named Gefion, who I believe to be one and the same as Freya.

King Gylfi ruled the land that men now call Sweden. It is told of him that he gave to a wandering woman, in return for her merry-making, a plow-land in his realm, as much as four oxen might turn up in a day and a night. But this woman was of the kin of the Aesir; she was named Gefjun. She took from the north, out of Jotunheim, four oxen which were the soils of a certain giant and herself, and set them before the plow. And the plow cut so wide and so deep that it loosened up the land; and the oxen drew the land out into the sea and to the westward, and stopped in a certain sound. There Gefjun set the land, and gave it a name, calling it Selund. And from that time on, the spot whence the land had been torn up is water: it is now called the Logr in Sweden; and bays lie in that lake even as the headlands in Selund. Thus says Bragi, the ancient skald:

> Gefjun drew from Gylfi
> gladly the wave-trove's free-hold
> Till from the running beasts
> sweat reeked, to Denmark's increase;
> The oxen bore, moreover,
> eight eyes, gleaming brow-lights,
> O'er the field's wide: booty,
> and four heads in their plowing.
> **-Gylfaginning I.**

Here, we see that Freya-Gefion mated with a giant, and her sons were turned into oxen, ploughing land which was for her and her people. That we are dealing with a

Vanic goddess is indicated by the number four (oxen), and in exchange for "merry-making"(obviously, a night of sex), permission to plough Land - ploughing being a Vanic activity par excellence.

Gefion moreover seems to be connected with virginity and a woman's right of refusal, as seen in the *Volsa Tattur*:

> I swear by Gefjun
> and the other gods
> that against my will
> do I touch this red proboscis.
> May giantesses accept this holy object,
> but now, slave of my parents,
> grab hold of Volsi.

It would seem that the daughter here is repulsed by the thought of a phallus and Freya-Gefion is being called upon in protest for not wanting to participate in what is essentially a sex magic ritual, and Freya does know when to say no to such things.

Finally, in *Lokasenna*, Gefion is mentioned as having sold herself for a necklace (probably Brisingamen):

> Gefjun spake:
> "Why, ye gods twain,
> with bitter tongues
> Raise hate among us here?
> Loki is famed
> for his mockery foul,
> And the dwellers in heaven he hates."
> Loki spake:
> "Be silent, Gefjun!
> for now shall I say
> Who led thee to evil life;

The boy so fair
gave a necklace bright,
And about him thy leg was laid."
Othin spake:
"Mad art thou, Loki,
and little of wit,
The wrath of Gefjun to rouse;
For the fate that is set
for all she sees,
Even as I, methinks."

It seems likely that Gefion is Freya's "sovereign" face, keeping women "pure" from unwanted sexual attention (remember Freya's refusal to be sold into marriage with a Jotun), but giving herself for the right price. Odin himself speaks of Gefion seeing even as he does, which would indicate equal power, and that Freya has for certain, having taught Odin at least some of his magic.

I have seen all four of Freya's faces, and have worked most closely with her as Gefn/Gefion/Gefjun, the Giver, the sex and love goddess who teaches the mysteries of sacred sexuality used for healing and transformation: healing your own spirit, the person you are making love to, and the Tree itself... and how to withhold sexuality when it would do more harm than good, to be whole in oneself. It is through understanding Vanic sexuality that I have been able to start the process of knowing myself, knowing what I want for myself, owning my own sovereignity and personal power, and working to make my life a more sacred place. Freya knew her sexuality was worth the most beautiful and magical necklace in the Nine Worlds – indeed, Brisingamen is a tool, empowered by sex rites, forged by four dwarves, embodying the four aspects of Freya, the four seasons of Vanaheim, and the four directions of Midgard.

Brisingamen is not just a tool, but is symbolic of Freya's own beauty, not just her outward physical beauty, but the beauty within her soul, as a person. Her spirit is fire, there is ecstatic joy she feels in the beauty of the world, the Divinity within plants, animals, and people; the sun and the sky, the ocean, fire and smoke, the wind; things made by human hands. Likewise she feels grief and wrath deeply. She is passion. And it is knowing the depth of Freya's emotions – her grief for Odr, her determination to find him, and her joy in the beauty of the World/s and their beings – that we are able to know wholeness, feeling alive in ourselves, and not numbed by the overstimulation of today's world.

Freya shed her own tears over the great grief of losing her soulmate, Odr, but the tears became amber and gold - in the amber that is her tears, you see the light of her essence. She honors our tears, our emotions, our feeling, and can help us make something beautiful out of our pain. She can show us that even as there is tragedy and sorrow, there is also joy and ecstasy to be had in this world. As Lady of the Vanir, she with her brother is connected to the Land, and the beauty within her reflects the beauty within us all.

Gullveig

The fire never completely goes out.

- Leto Atreides II (**Dune**, *Frank Herbert*)

Gullveig is a powerful witch, so much so that the Aesir burned her in fear, which caused the Vanir to rise up and avenge one of their own. She is often thought by modern heathens to be an "evil" goddess not worthy of worship, and often conflated with Freya or Angrboda.

The war I remember, | the first in the world,
When the gods with spears | had smitten Gullveig,
And in the hall | of Har had burned her,
Three times burned, | and three times born,
Oft and again, | yet ever she lives.
Heith they named her | who sought their home,
The wide-seeing witch, | in magic wise;
Minds she bewitched | that were moved by her magic,
To evil women | a joy she was.
On the host his spear | did Othin hurl,
Then in the world | did war first come;
The wall that girdled | the gods was broken,
And the field by the warlike | Wanes was trodden.
Then sought the gods | their assembly-seats,
The holy ones, | and council held,
Whether the gods | should tribute give,
Or to all alike | should worship belong.
-Voluspa, v. 21-24 (Bellows translation)

While I believe that certain portions of *Voluspa* were heavily influenced by Christianity (e.g. the account of Ragnarok) and should be read with a grain of salt, I am not ready to reject the whole text especially as it gives a tantalizing glimpse into the history of the Vanir.

Gullveig, whose name means "Gold-Way" or "Gold-Thirst", has been hypothesized to be Freya by some scholars, Angrboda by others (most notably Rydberg). It is my personal gnosis that Gullveig-Heid is neither Freya (another Vanir) nor Angrboda (a Jotynja) but is very much her own goddess, one who is "more Vanir than Vanir".

Gullveig is associated with gold, which is an indicator that she is Vanic: Frey and Freya also have strong associations with gold, as does Sif, and gold is one of the "official colors" of Vanaheim, signifying not just material wealth (gold itself) but the gold of grain and honey and various fruits and vegetables that grow, the gold of sunshine symbolizing happiness.

Gullveig was also a worker of strong magic: it is said in Ynglinga Saga that Freya practices *seiðr*, an art known to all the Vanir, and so we can assume that Gullveig was some sort of master-sorceress, enough for the Aesir to decide she was not a valuable asset (in the way that Freya was), but too dangerous to be allowed to live. Odin is mentioned here in his *heiti* of Har, the wise man who worded *Havamal*, and it is probable that Gullveig had come to Odin for an initial exchange of information, a dialogue between magicians.

What is most telling of Gullveig's Vanic nature is the war between the Aesir and Vanir began after Gullveig was burned in Odin's hall; the Vanir acted in vengeance to right a wrong done to one of their own. To all accounts the Vanir were winning the war, but decided to not decimate the Aesir, rather settling for a truce including an exchange of hostages. The passage "Whether the gods | should tribute give, Or to all alike | should worship belong" is telling as we know of only three named Vanir and have to speculate as to the rest, and I believe at this point the ruling Vanir (at that time Njord, Frey, and Freya) yielded to the Aesir, reflecting in both marriages and priesthood in Asgard, and the Aesir cult supplanting the Vanic cult in Europe.

Gullveig carries the Vanic gift of witchcraft, both as a seer and a spellworker, but is just as capable of using her magic for harm as well as for help, as evidenced by Odin's decision to burn her as well as the reference to "evil women" enlisting her aid. Gullveig did not die even burned three times, which would suggest strong regeneration powers -- and perhaps her baleful magic going forth as a counter-attack. Clearly the act was offensive enough for the Vanir to go against their peaceloving nature and make an act of war. For those who would dismiss Gullveig as an evil goddess or irrelevant, the Vanir would not waste their time on a being worth nothing; it is likely that Gullveig was extremely important to them, more likely when you consider that it seems that Odin learned magic from Gullveig and when he learned what he could decided to have her neutralized as a threat. He underestimated what he was dealing with, as well as how her people would react.

The first thing to remember when dealing with the gods is there is no "black/white" or "good/evil". Gullveig is a bright light, the gold of the Vanir, and very precious in their sight; she is also the bearer of a great shadow, for to light a flame casts a shadow. While the world can be a beautiful place and there is no reason to be separate and forsake "worldiness" in the Vanic faith, that also means putting aside glorified notions of utopia. The elements can create and destroy. Plants can be pretty, or useful for healing, or good to eat, or potent killers. Animals are companions and/or food and they themselves feed off life, whether plants or smaller animals... sometimes humans if hungry and angry enough. People can do great things, noble things... humans have also committed atrocities. It is often necessary to destroy and kill to stay alive, and this works on a magical level as well as in the mundane world. Many people fear what they do not understand, and then act out of their fear.

From corroborated gnosis, Gullveig seems to take a particular pleasure in teaching "recovering Good Samaritans" who need to learn how to get dirty if it is called for, rather than just lying there and taking it. By civilized standards it is considered "not nice" to assert oneself past a certain point, no matter how much one might be justified in doing so. There's a modern saying, "Nice guys finish last," and for Gullveig and those she speaks to in the modern day, this is very true. Being "nice" may get you killed.

For those who were expecting a book on the Vanir to be all about peace and fertility rituals, it will come as a shock to hear that the Vanir are intimately tied to Death as well as Life. Life feeds on Death, and what goes to Death is recycled out again. Death is the ultimate equalizer, and it is because of our mortality that we need a connection to Something bigger than ourselves, to put life in perspective. If you never go out of your way to pray to Gullveig or offer to her, at least take the message that the gods are not inherently good or evil just as humans are not inherently good or evil, and her way is to find the grey areas when white light meets black shadow, and dance within.

Ullr

The archer sees the make upon the path of
the infinite, and He bends you with His
might that His arrows may go swift and far.
-Kahlil Gibran

Ullr is a god of the hunt, and was noted in lore as a powerful wizard. He is associated with snowshoes and skis, and some modern pagans pray to him for snow. While there is not much lore on him, there are some bits and pieces that suggest he was a very important god at one time and could be so again.

XXXI. "One is called Ullr, son of Sif, step-son of Thor; he is so excellent a bowman, and so swift on snowshoes, that none may contend with him. He is also fair of aspect and has the accomplishments of a warrior; it is well to call on him in single-combats.
-Gylfaginning

Ullr's father is unnamed. Rydberg (whose theories are not generally accepted) think Ullr and Idunna are siblings and the offspring of Ivaldi, one of the elves. It is my personal gnosis that Sif is one of the Vanir, and that Ullr is Njord's cousin and "shield-brother".

Ullr has many Vanic attributes. This verse in the Prose Edda deals with Ullr's role as a warrior, specifically that of single-combat dueling. As a Vanir deity, Ullr would be along the same warrior current as Njord and Frey who are skilled but more defensive than offensive-aggressive. Any medieval martial artist worth their salt knows there are rules for single-combat dueling, which would fit into that Vanic current. Since it is noted that Ullr probably had a much larger cult prior to the Viking/Lore Era, when much of his information was lost (example: there are place-names for Ullr in Norway and Sweden, with names Ulleraker (Ullr's Field) and Ullevi (Ullr's Shrine) surviving to this day), it has been suspected by a few that the cult of Ullr may have survived under the Christian gloss of chivalry.

For starters, his name means "glory" (Proto-Germanic *Wultuz), which is often an attribute given to the Christian God. It may be that the chivalric code and seven knightly skills (riding, swimming, archery, boxing, hawking, chess, and verse writing) were remnants of the training of an earlier Ullr warrior cult.

How should Ullr be periphrased? By calling him Son of Sif, Stepson of Thor, God of the Snowshoe, God of the Bow, Hunting-God, God of the Shield.
-Skaldskaparmal

Here Ullr's hunting nature is emphasized over the warrior nature, although the shield is mentioned. Ullr is a "civilized" hunter, which would make him fit in better with the Vanir (primarily agricultural, with supplemental hunting) than the Jotnar (primarily hunting, more brutal/primal).

There are also some brief but tantalizing clues in the Eddas that there might indeed be an earlier cult of Ullr.

Ullr's and all the gods'
favor shall have,
whoever first shall look to the fire;
for open will the dwelling be,

to the Aesir's sons,
when the kettles are lifted off.
-Griminirsmal, v. 42

Here Ullr is mentioned before "all the gods", which suggests that Ullr has a special position of granting favor. This verse may also allude to fire-scrying, which might be part of the Ullr-cult and along the current of Freya's high-seat *seiðr* and Frey's mound-sitting *utiseta*.

"So be it with thee, Atli!
as toward Gunnar thou hast held
the oft-sworn oaths,
formerly taken -
by the southward verging sun,
and by Sigty's hill,
the secluded bed of rest,
and by Ullr's ring."
-Atlakvida, v. 30

Ullr's ring is probably a reference to an oath-ring, which incidentally in Iceland was sworn on in the names of Frey and Njord (*Landnamabok* Part 4). This may, then, be another hint that Ullr is a Vane, continuing a Vanic custom, and along the same current of Frey and Njord of deities who can be trusted to hear and solemnize oaths taken on the ring, symbolic of the circle of life, actions and reactions.

But the gods, whose chief seat was then at Byzantium, (Asgard), seeing that Odin had tarnished the fair name of godhead by divers injuries to its majesty, thought that he ought to be removed from their society. And they had him not only ousted from the headship, but outlawed and stripped of all worship and honor at home; thinking it better that the power of their infamous president should be overthrown than that public religion should be profaned; and fearing that they might themselves be involved in the sin of another, and though guiltless be punished for the crime of the guilty. For they saw that, now the derision of their great god was brought to light, those whom they had lured to proffer them divine honors were exchanging obeisance for scorn and worship for shame; that holy rites were being accounted sacrilege, and fixed and regular ceremonies deemed so much childish raving. Fear was in their souls, death before their eyes, and one would have supposed that the fault of one was visited upon the heads of all.

So, not wishing Odin to drive public religion into exile, they exiled him and put one Oller (Wulder?) in his place, to bear the symbols not only of royalty but also of godhead, as though it had been as easy a task to create a god as a king. And though they had appointed him priest for form's sake, they endowed him actually with full distinction, that he might be seen to be the lawful heir to the dignity, and no mere deputy doing another's work. Also, to omit no circumstance of greatness, they further gave his the name of Odin, trying by the prestige of that title to be rid of the obloquy of innovation.

For nearly ten years Oller held the presidency of the divine senate; but at last the gods pitied the horrible exile of Odin, and thought that he had now been punished heavily enough; so he exchanged his foul and unsightly estate for his ancient splendour; for the lapse of time had now wiped out the brand of his earlier disgrace. Yet some were to be found who judged that he was not worthy to approach and resume his rank, because by his stage-tricks and his assumption of a woman's work he had brought the foulest scandal on the name of the gods. Some declare that he bought back the fortune of his lost divinity with money; flattering some of the gods and mollifying some with bribes; and that at the cost of a vast sum he contrived to get back to the distinction which he had long quitted. If you ask how much he paid for them, inquire of those who have found out what is the price of a godhead. I own that to me it is but little worth.

Thus Oller was driven out from Byzantium by Odin and retired into Sweden.

Here, while he was trying, as if in a new world, to repair the records of his glory, the Danes slew him. The story goes that he was such a cunning wizard that he used a certain bone, which he had marked with awful spells, wherewith to cross the seas, instead of a vessel; and that by this bone he passed over the waters that barred his way as quickly as by rowing.

-The History of Saxo Grammaticus, Book Three

While I do not like the euhemerized "gods are really humans" worldview of the Christian author Saxo Grammaticus, this does give an account of Ullr ruling Odin for ten years while Odin is away. It would be probable that this "substitute kingship" would be best given to a Vanir, particularly after the Aesir had been at war with the Vanir and traded hostages.

At the end of this account Odin drives Ullr out of (most probably) Asgard and Ullr goes to Sweden, which is notable for being Frey's country, and much more Vanic-oriented than other parts of Scandinavia. We can assume Ullr had adapted the form of the snowshoe into something like magical water skis, which he marked with "awful spells", most likely runes. This would make him a competent runester, and he may well teach a Vanic side of runes to those who call on him now.

The last bit of history I have found directly relating to Ullr is the Thorsberg chape, dating from roughly 200 C.E., which also suggests someone related to Ullr in the context of a god-slave. The chape – a metal piece of a scabbard -- has one of the earliest known runic inscriptions, which reads:

owlþuþewaz / niwajmariz

The first part of the first word is *owltu*, for *woltu-*, means "glory", "glorious one", and would directly point to Old Norse Ullr, Old English Wuldor. The second part of the first word is *-tewaz*, which means "slave, servant" (which is cognate with *theow*). When that word is put together it translates as "servant of the glorious one", or (more likely, being a scabbard) "servant/priest of Ullr". The second word has *ni-* as a negative particle and *waj*corresponds to "woe or ill". The next part is *-mariz* "famous" (Old English *maēre*), the second word thus translates to "not ill-famous", viz. "famous, renowned" or "not of ill fame, not dishonored".

The translation of the inscription is thus either "Wolthuthewaz is well-renowned", or (more probably, taken in context) "the servant of Ullr, the renowned".

There has been at least one person who has seen the inscription and thinks the O is for "Odal" and therefore the chape can be taken to read "inherited property of Wulthuthewaz, the renowned". However that is taking one letter as a separate word, and clearly the runic letters are spelling out a phrase with a name on it, so I generally dismiss this theory.

In 2007 there was much ado made among heathens when the town of Aspen, Colorado, threw a large party in Ullr's honor, specifically giving him a burnt offering of old skis and snowshoes, asking Ullr for snow[7]. Many heathens had a problem with non-heathens doing this, and saying things such as "Ullr is not a snow god." I truly feel that if this had been at an Asatru moot, there would have been

---

[7] http://www.wildhunt.org/2007/12/ullr-comes-through.html

less contention about Ullr "not being a snow god", and the bottom line is that Ullr got more attention and offerings from the people of Aspen than he has probably gotten in the whole 40-odd years heathenry has been around in the United States. Is it a coincidence that the residents of Aspen got what they asked for, with the second-highest recorded snowfall in Aspen's history? It didn't matter to Ullr that most of these people were not Asatru or even some other kind of pagan -- what mattered was the intent and the deed.

And this is the true nature of chivalry, to be helpful to others when they ask, not turn around and ask them twenty questions about whether or not they have the right "worldview". Ullr may not be a snow god, but he is tied to skiing, which... needs snow. I'm sure that the people of Aspen remembered Ullr as they enjoyed the snow for skiing, and this is what counts after all.

In modern times, Ullr calls few people. One would think Ullr would be a natural patron for martial artists, but while Ullr may look like a bad-ass warrior, like any good martial artist he knows several things:

- It takes training, with a lot of patience, self-discipline, and humility, to get to a place of competence with handling weapons. You do not just pick up a sword and think because you've seen *Star Wars* or *Dragonball Z* that you know everything about martial arts. It literally takes years of practice to be fit for combat.

- When one has warrior skills, there needs to be a level of responsibility that comes with it, including self-control. One should not seek to become a warrior for the domination and conquest of others, but rather the service and protection of others. Ullr has little tolerance for fools who would swing their weight around and brag about being tough or being part of a "warrior religion" when they don't know what they're talking about, and don't realize that being a warrior is far more than skill with a weapon.

Ullr may probably never have a large following, as much of his lore has been lost, and much of his ways are not understood by moderns. He is rather big on personal responsibility, and remains a "silent god" because to come under his guidance is to work hard, and to live a cut above the rest. To come under his guidance is to serve, to hunt and fight for one's people. He doesn't mind receiving offerings, and helping those who call to him. But for patronage, he expects certain things that are beyond the grasp of most of us today, though there may be some he calls now, and there may yet be hope for future generations.

Holda

Never put your faith in a Prince. When you
require a miracle, trust in a Witch.
-*Catherynne M. Valente*, **The Night
Garden**

Holda is not mentioned in the Eddas or Sagas but
there is a fair amount of folklore on her, enough that it is
clear she was a very important deity in continental
north/central Europe, and with enough Vanic traits that it
is likely she is Vanir, and indeed corroborated gnosis says
she is.

There was once a widow who had two daughters - one
of whom was pretty and industrious, whilst the other was ugly
and idle. But she was much fonder of the ugly and idle one,
because she was her own daughter; and the other, who was a
step-daughter, was obliged to do all the work, and be the
Cinderella of the house. Every day the poor girl had to sit by a
well, in the highway, and spin and spin till her fingers bled.

Now it happened that one day the shuttle was marked
with her blood, so she dipped it in the well, to wash the mark
off; but it dropped out of her hand and fell to the bottom. She
began to weep, and ran to her step-mother and told her of the
mishap. But she scolded her sharply, and was so merciless as to
say, "Since you have let the shuttle fall in, you must fetch it out
again."

So the girl went back to the well, and did not know what
to do: and in the sorrow of her heart she jumped into the well to
get the shuttle. She lost her senses; and when she awoke and
came to herself again, she was in a lovely meadow where the
sun was shining and many thousands of flowers were growing.

Along this meadow she went, and at last came to a baker's oven full of bread, and the bread cried out, "Oh, take me out! Take me out or I shall burn; I have been baked a long time!" So she went up to it, and took out all the loaves one after another with the bread-shovel. After that she went on till she came to a tree covered with apples, which called out to her, "Oh, shake me! Shake me! We apples are all ripe!" So she shook the tree till the apples fell like rain, and went on shaking till they were all down, and when she had gathered them into a heap, she went on her way.

At last she came to a little house, out of which an old woman peeped; but she had such large teeth that the girl was frightened, and was about to run away. But the old woman called out to her, "What are you afraid of, dear child? Stay with me; if you will do all the work in the house properly, you shall be the better for it. Only you must take care to make my bed well, and to shake it thoroughly till the feathers fly - for then there is snow on the earth. I am Mother Holle." (Thus in Hesse, when it snows, they say, "Mother Holle is making her bed.")

As the old woman spoke so kindly to her, the girl took courage and agreed to enter her service. She attended to everything to the satisfaction of her mistress, and always shook her bed so vigorously that the feathers flew about like snowflakes.

So she had a pleasant life with her; never an angry word; and boiled or roast meat every day. She stayed some time with Mother Holle, and then she became sad. At first she did not know what was the matter with her, but found at length that it was homesickness; although she was many thousand times better off here than at home, still she had a longing to be there.

At last she said to the old woman, "I have a longing for home; and however well off I am down here, I cannot stay any longer; I must go up again to my own people." Mother Holle said, "I am pleased that you long for your home again, and as you have served me truly, I myself will take you up again." Thereupon she took her by the hand, and led her to a large door. The door was opened, and just as the maiden was standing beneath the doorway, a heavy shower of golden rain fell, and all the gold remained sticking to her, so that she was completely covered with it.

"You shall have that because you are so industrious," said Mother Holle; and at the same time she gave her back the shuttle which she had let fall into the well.

Thereupon the door closed, and the maiden found herself up above upon the earth, not far from her mother's house.

And as she went into the yard the cock was standing by the wellside, and cried – "Cock-a-doodle-doo! Your golden girl's come back to you!"

So she went in to her mother, and as she arrived thus covered with gold, she was well received, both by her and her sister. The girl told all that had happened to her; and as soon as the mother heard how she had come by so much wealth, she was very anxious to obtain the same good luck for the ugly and lazy daughter. She had to seat herself by the well and spin; and in order that her shuttle might be stained with blood, she stuck her hand into a thorn bush and pricked her finger. Then she threw her shuttle into the well, and jumped in after it.

She came, like the other, to the beautiful meadow and walked along the very same path. When she got to the oven the bread again cried, "Oh, take me out! Take me out or I shall burn; I have been baked a long time!" But the lazy thing answered, "As if I had any wish to make myself dirty?" and on she went. Soon she came to the apple-tree, which cried, "Oh, shake me! Shake me! We apples are all ripe!" But she answered, "I like that! One of you might fall on my head," and so went on.

When she came to Mother Holle's house she was not afraid, for she had already heard of her big teeth, and she hired herself to her immediately. The first day she forced herself to work diligently, and obeyed Mother Holle when she told her to do anything, for she was thinking of all the gold that she would give her. But on the second day she began to be lazy, and on the third day still more so, and then she would not get up in the morning at all. Neither did she make Mother Holle's bed as she ought, and did not shake it so as to make the feathers fly up. Mother Holle was soon tired of this, and gave her notice to leave. The lazy girl was willing enough to go, and thought that now the golden rain would come. Mother Holle led her too to the great door; but while she was standing beneath it, instead of the gold a big kettle of pitch was emptied over her. "That is the reward of your service," said Mother Holle, and shut the door.

So the lazy girl went home; but she was quite covered with pitch and the cock by the well-side, as soon as he saw her, cried out –
"Cock-a-doodle-do! Your pitchy girl's come back to you!"

But the pitch stuck fast to her, and could not be got off as long as she lived.

-Mother Holle, **Grimm's Household Tales**

There was once a peasant who daily left his wife and children in the valley to take his sheep up the mountain to pasture; and as he watched his flock grazing on the mountain-side, he often had opportunity to use his cross bow and bring down a chamois, whose flesh would furnish his larder with food for many a day.

While pursuing a fine animal one day he saw it disappear behind a boulder, and when he came to the spot, he was amazed to see a doorway in the neighbouring glacier, for in the excitement of the pursuit he had climbed higher and higher, until he was now on top of the mountain, where glittered the everlasting snow. The shepherd boldly passed through the open door and soon found himself in a wonderful jewelled cave hung with stalactites, in the centre of which stood a beautiful woman clad in silvery robes, and attended by a host of lovely maidens crowned with Alpine roses. In his surprise, the shepherd sank to his knees, and as in a dream heard the queenly central figure bid him choose anything he saw to carry away with him.

Although dazzled by the glow of the precious stones around him, the shepherd's eyes constantly reverted to a little nosegay of blue flowers which the gracious apparition held in her hand, and he now timidly proffered a request that it might become his. Smiling with pleasure, Holda, for it was she, gave it to him, telling him he had chosen wisely and would live as long as the flowers did not droop and fade. Then, giving the shepherd a measure of seed which she told him to sow in his field, the goddess bade him begone; and as the thunder pealed and the earth shook, the poor man found himself out upon the mountain-side once more, and slowly wended his way home to his wife, to whom he told his adventure and showed the lovely blue flowers and the measure of seed. The woman reproached her husband bitterly for not having brought some of the precious stones which he so glowingly described, instead of the blossoms and seed; nevertheless the man proceeded to sow the latter, and found to his surprise that the measure supplied seed enough for several acres.

Soon the little green shoots began to appear, and one moonlight night, while the peasant was gazing upon them, as was his wont, for he felt a curious attraction to the field which he had sown, and often lingered there wondering what kind of grain would be produced, he saw a misty form hover above the field, with hands outstretched as if in blessing. At last the field blossomed, and countless little blue flowers opened their calyxes to the golden sun. When the flowers had withered and the seed was ripe, Holda came once more to teach the peasant and wife how to harvest the flax--for such it was--and from it to spin, weave, and bleach linen. As the people of the neighbourhood willingly purchased both linen and flax-seed, the peasant and his wife soon grew very rich indeed, and while he ploughed, sowed, and harvested, she spun, wove, and bleached the linen.

The man lived to a good old age, and saw his grandchildren and great-grandchildren grow up around him. All this time his carefully treasured bouquet had remained fresh as when he first brought it home, but one day he saw that during the night the flowers had drooped and were dying. Knowing what this portended, and that he too must die, the peasant climbed the mountain once more to the glacier, and found again the doorway for which he had often vainly searched. He entered the icy portal, and was never seen or heard of again, for, according to the legend, the goddess took him under her care, and bade him live in her cave, where his every wish was gratified.

-Holda and the Gift of Flax
Source: A German tale quoted here from "Myths of the Norsemen," by H.A. Guerber.

In popular legends and nursery-tales, Frau Holda (Hulda, Holle, Hulle, Frau Holl) appears as a superior being, who manifests a kind and helpful disposition towards men, and is never cross except when she notices disorder in household affairs. ...From what traditions has still preserved for us, we gather the following characteristics. Frau Holle is represented as a being of the sky, begirdling the earth: when it snows, she is making her bed, and the feathers of it fly. She stirs up snow, as Donar does rain...

The comparison of snowflakes to feathers is very old; the Scythians pronounced the regions north of them inaccessible, because they were filled with feathers. Holda then must be able to move through the air, like dame Herke.

She loves to haunt the lake and fountain; at the hour of noon she may be seen, a fair white lady, bathing in the flood and disappearing; a trait in which she resembles Nerthus. Mortals, to reach her dwelling, pass through the well. ..Another point of resemblance is, that she drives about in a wagon. She has a linchpin put in it by a peasant whom she met; when he picked up the chips, they were gold. Her annual progress, which like those of Herke and Berhta, is made to fall between Christmas and Twelfth-day, when the supernatural has sway, and wild beasts like the wolf are not mentioned by their names, brings fertility to the land. Not otherwise does 'Derk with the boar,' that Frey of the Netherlands, appear to go his rounds and look after the ploughs. At the same time Holda, like Wuotan, can also ride on the winds, clothed in terror, and she, like the god, belongs to the 'wutende heer.' From this arose the fancy that witches ride in Holla's company; it was already known to Burchard, and now in Upper Hesse and the Westerwald, Holle-riding, to ride with Holle, is equivalent to a witches' ride. Into the same 'furious host,' according to a wide-spread popular belief, were adopted the souls of infants dying unbaptized; not having been christain'd, they remained heathen, and fell to heathen gods, to Wuotan or to Hulda.

The next step is, that Hulda, instead of her divine shape, assumes the appearance of an ugly old woman, long-nosed, big-toothed, with bristling and thick-matted hair. 'He's had a jaunt with Holle,' they say of a man whose hair sticks up in tangled disorder; so children frightened with her or her equally hideous train: 'hush, there's Hulle-betz (-bruin), Hulle-popel (-bogie) coming.' Holle-peter, as well as Hersche, Harsche, Hescheklas, Ruprecht, Rupper is among the names given to the muffled servitor who goes about in Holle's train at the time of the winter solstice. In a nursery-tale she is depicted as an old witch with long teeth; according to the difference of story, her kind and gracious aspect is exchanged for a dark and dreadful one.

Again, Holla is set before us as a spinning-wife; the cultivation of flax is assigned to her. Industrious maids she presents with spindles, and spins with reels full for them over night; a slothful spinner's distaff she sets on fire, or soils it. The girl whose spindle dropt into her fountain, she rewarded bountifully. When she enters the land at Christmas, all the distaffs are well stocked, and left standing for her; by Carnival, when she turns homeward, all spinning must be finished off, and the staffs are now kept out of her sight; if she finds everything as it should be, she pronounces her blessing, and contrariwise her curse; the formulas 'so many hairs, so many good years!' and 'so many hairs, so many bad years!' have an oldworld sound. Apparently two things have been run into one, when we are also told, that during the 'twelve-nights' no flax must be left in the diesse, or dame Holla will come. The concealment of the implements shows at the same time the sacredness of her holiday, which ought to be a time of rest. In the Rhon mountains, they do no farm-work on Hulla's Saturday, neither hoe, nor manure, nor 'drive the team afield'. In the North too, from Yule-day to Newyear's day, neither wheel nor windlass must go round.

...

Of still more weight perhaps are the Norwegian and Danish folk-tales about a wood or mountain wife Hulla, Huldra, Huldre, whom they set forth, now as young and lovely, then again as old and gloomy. In a blue garment and white veil she visits the pasture-grounds of herdsmen, and mingles in the dances of men; but her shape is disfigured by a tail, which she takes great pains to conceal. Some accounts make her beautiful in front and ugly behind. She loves music and song, her lay has a doleful melody and is called huldreslaat. In the forests you see Huldra as an old woman clothed in gray, marching at the head of her flock, milkpail in hand. She is said to carry off people's unchristened infants from them. Often she appears, not alone, but as mistress or queen of the mountain-sprites, who are called huldrefolk.

In Iceland too they know of this Huldufolk, of the Huldumenn; and here we find another point of agreement with the popular faith of Germany, namely, that by the side of our dame Holde there are also holden, i.e., friendly spirits, a silent subterranean people, of whom dame Holde, so to speak, is the princess.

For this reason, if no other, it must be more correct to explain the Norse name Hulla, Huldra from the ON. hollr [[faithful, loyal]] which is huld in Dan. And Swed., and not from the ON. hulda [[cover, veil; secrecy, hiding]] as referring to the subterranean abode of the mountain-sprites. In Swedish folk-songs I find 'huldmoder, hulda moder' said of one's real mother in the same sense as kara (dear) mother ; so that huld must have quite the meaning of our German word.

It is likely that the term huldufolk was imported into the Icelandic tongue from the Danish or Norwegian. It is harder to explain the R inserted in the forms Huldra, Huldre; did it spring out of the plural form hulder (boni genii, holler vattir)? Or result from composition?

The German Holda presides over spinning and agriculture, the Norse Hulle over cattle-grazing and milking.

-Grimm's Teutonic Mythology, Chapter 13, 4.

There has been some speculation about what "tribe" of gods that Holda belongs to, and many who think Holda is a late (Christian) addition to the folklore of the Continent, or an earlier non-demonized form of Hela, or perhaps another face of Frija (Frigga/Freya). As you see, I have put her in with the Vanir; I do not feel that Holda is Frija or Hela but a goddess separate unto herself both etymologically and by the traits listed which speak (at least to me) of having Vanic qualities:

- stirring up snow from her featherbed
- connection with lakes
- driving about in a wain (the most obvious commonality of the Vanir)
- helping peasants, and rewarding the hard-working
- ruler of the land-wights (nature-spirits)
- being a psychopomp, in this case, for dead children
- ruling over the cultivation of flax, used to make rope and clothing, a healthy food (seeds), and all around very useful
- associated with witchcraft

That being said, Holda feels very, very old. While some heathens have said Holda was likely a Christian-era superstition, Lotte Motz speculates Holda predates Christianity, and I am inclined to agree. In fact, the gnosis of myself and several colleagues is that Holda may have connection to the Jotnar, at a time when the Jotun cult was giving way to the Vanic cult in prehistoric Europe, born during a time when the Vanir and Jotnar were still one people. Moreover, corroborated gnosis says Holda and Frodi are brother and sister (and at one time reigned

Vanaheim as king and queen, directly following the usurpers who overthrew the first king and queen) and that Holda is, by him, the mother of Njord and Nerthus, which would give weight to the successive consanguineous marriages that preserve the fertility of the Vanir. It would truly make her "Granny" in that case!

I find Holda can be a very helpful Goddess for those of us who have problems with "executive function" particularly in the area of organization. She can be persuaded with a nice offering (she loves home-baked cookies!), and helps cheerfully, again, if your intent is there. She seems to understand this does not equal "lazy", and sometimes people need a little extra help. Incidentally, when I think of Holda I see the face of my paternal great-grandmother, who was a jolly but no-nonsense lady, fond of cookies and very active into old age.

Holda is the Goddess who exemplifies the path of the hedgewitch, one who works with the Otherworlds to cause change in this world but serves individuals rather than a tribe. Unlike Frigga's neatness and order which is meant for hosting in her hall, Holda's neatness and order is for the coziness and cheerfulness of home as well as the principle of "everything in its place", so magical items can be found and used properly, and put back for future use. I have traveled to Holda's home, which is a neat little cottage with herbs drying, various knicknacks that look innocent but vibrate with intensity, and I've noticed that indeed things are neat, but there is also a feeling of comfort and of home. Holda knows that it is the intent rather than "the show" that determines whether or not something is effective, and she can use that to hex as well as to heal.

While Holda can be the kindly grandmother-type offering you cookies, do not overestimate her patience and try her temper; you may find yourself on the receiving end of something not so nice!

Holda seems sympathetic to women who want to conceive, as well as women who have a difficult time with menses and/or may probably not want to have children. She has a close connection to the plant mugwort, which can be used for inducing calm focused trance states as well as abortion.

In some folklore Holda is said to ride the Wild Hunt with Odin, and I believe she may have been one of the first Vanir that he was introduced to, as well as Gullveig. Holda is definitely a match for Odin between wisdom and temper. I suspect Holda (with Horn Father and the Lord of the Black) leads the procession to collect the souls of the ones meant to go to the mounds of the Vanir in Vanaheim during the time the Hunt rides. She also collects dead children, which would include those dead by exposure (being unwanted by their families) and in modern times I see her as taking in people who were broken by their families not wanting them/not taking care of them, and teaching empowerment, even if her discipline can at times be harsh.

It seems that Holda is sympathetic to personal hardship, but still feels at the end of the day the clothes must be washed, the floors must be swept, the bread must be baked, and there is no time to contemplate regret. Indeed, when experienced with frightening teeth and shrieking cackles, Holda has no tolerance for what she deems laziness, and plenty about our convenient 21st century strikes her as worthlessness. Even then, Holda teaches that one must nurture oneself, and one's kin, in some way, preferably with a lot of hard work and magical intent behind it.

Sif

The wise ones fashioned speech with their
thought, sifting it as grain is sifted through a
sieve.

-Gautama Siddhartha

Sif is a wife of Thor and the mother of Thrud and Ullr, and often overlooked as a minor goddess, her importance only seen as who she is wife and mother of. Yet if we take a closer look, there is more to her than meets the eye and she is a lot more significant than too many give her credit for.

Then he (Thor) went forth far and wide over the lands, and sought out every quarter of the earth, overcoming alone all berserks and giants, and one dragon, greatest of all dragons, and many beasts. In the northern half of his kingdom he found the prophetess that is called Sibil, whom we call Sif, and wedded her. The lineage of Sif cannot be told; she was fairest of all women, and her hair was like gold.
    -Gylfaginning, Prologue (III).

How should Sif be periphrased? By calling her Wife of Thor, Mother of Ullr, Fair-Haired Goddess, Co-Wife of Jarnsaxa, Mother of Thrudr. ...
    How should gold be periphrased? Thus: by calling it... Hair of Sif...
    -Skaldskaparsmal, XXI-XXXII.

Why is gold called Sif's Hair? Loki Laufeyarson, for mischief's sake, cut off all Sif's hair. But when Thor learned of this, he seized Loki, and would have broken every bone in him, had he not sworn to get the Black Elves to make Sif hair of gold, such that it would grow like other hair. After that, Loki went to those dwarves who are called Ivaldi's Sons; and they made the hair, and Skidbladnir also, and the spear which became Odin's possession, and was called Gungnir.

-Skaldskaparsmal, XXXV.

Then Sif came forward and poured mead for Loki in a crystal cup, and said:
"Hail to thee, Loki, and take thou here
The crystal cup of old mead;
For me at least, alone of the gods,
Blameless thou knowest to be."
He took the horn, and drank therefrom:
"Alone thou wert if truly thou wouldst
All men so shyly shun;
But one do I know full well, methinks,
Who had thee from Hlorrithi's arms, -
(Loki the crafty in lies.)"

-Lokasenna (Bellows)

Sif, as the mother of Ullr, is very, very old, and indeed, one of the eldest Vanir (in my gnosis, the younger sister of Frodi and Holda, and the aunt of Njord and Nerthus), yet she appears young and stunningly beautiful.We can see from the surviving lore that Sif is the wife of Thor and mother of his daughter Thrudr, as well as the mother of Ullr by a previous marriage. While the lore of Sif may be scanty and even seem to be lacking, just from these small pieces of information we can infer that she must have had some importance and perhaps even her own cultus.

Sif lives in Thor's hall in Asgard, however, she is not bound to Asgard as a hostage like Frey, Freya, and Njord. Having seen Sif and Thor interact, I again perceive the great age of Sif, and Thor seems relatively young by comparison (and when you are dealing with very, very old deities, this gets disconcerting). However, they do seem to love each other very much, and are warmly affectionate if not presenting in the same "perpetual honeymoon" way of Frey and Gerda nor the "old married couple" way of Frigga and Odin. Naturally I wanted to know how they met, and the story behind their love, and in listening to Sif, I found out more about her, as well.

Apparently (according to what Sif told me at times when I visited her) Sif and Thor met and fell in love prior to the war between the Aesir and the Vanir, and so Sif left Vanaheim to live with him. Sif accepts that her home is in Asgard and her place is among the Aesir, but at her core she is still Vanic. A corresponding analogy would be that I am a New England native and moved to Oregon in 2013. I will likely be spending the rest of my life in the Pacific Northwest and have come to appreciate my new home. However, I am still a Yankee at heart.

Indeed, there are certain aspects of Thor that seem downright Vanic - he drives a wain pulled by goats, and his hammer was used to hallow crops as well as the bride's lap in weddings. Thor has a far more "rough-and-tumble" or "down-home" attitude than the other Aesir. It seems that Sif's Vanic nature may have influenced the way Thor deals with people, albeit for the positive.

Njord can teach us peace based on his knowledge of wyrd through the waters of life – that the tides ebb and flow and life is always changing, yet still remains constant – and Njord can also teach us responsibility in our words and actions as it impacts our wyrd and that of ours around us. Sif is also one who teaches peace and responsibility, but in a different way. Sif's main duty in Asgard (besides her role as the lady of Thor's hall) is to hallow sacred spaces with flame and song[8].

Sif is respected as a frithweaver, and seems to never have anything bad to say about anyone. This is not the same thing as letting the world walk all over you, but it does seem that Sif is a master of "taking the high road", especially when you consider that she is married to a god whose temper – and strength of force – is legendary throughout the Nine Worlds. If Sif were to speak badly of anyone, it would be giving Thor *carte blanche* to kill whoever she spoke ill of.

But also, I feel that Sif is the epitome of *noblesse oblige*, that being the attitude that if one is of a noble/ruling class, one is obligated to set an example; you cannot be nasty or treat others as being "beneath" you. Beyond the fact that Sif's husband is the Thunderer, the wielder of Mjollnir and Asgard's defender, it does not look well for Sif herself – especially as one who is Vanir, came to Asgard of her free will, and is raising a blended family – to be anything less than gracious. But Sif does take her graciousness seriously, and seems to truly feel that even when others have done wrong it is better to take "the high road". Even when Sif's hair was cut off by Loki, she graciously accepted Loki's *scyld* of golden hair, and often prefers to wear the golden hair at official events, from what I have seen. She offered Loki a cup of mead at Aegir's feast even when he lashed out at the other Aesir, trying to smooth things over until the very end.

Sif has been an example to me in my dealings with the public in my pagan career. Not only can your words be used against you, but it will be your attitude towards others in general. There is a time to rant and to point out

---

[8] Corroborated gnosis.

injustice, and a time to lead by example – to put the proverbial blinders on, continue to perform one's duties, and be the change you wish to see in the world. It is often better to focus on issues than specific people (while there is a time and a place to call others out).

Sif is not a warrior like Freya and Skadhi. Nor is she a strategist like Frigga. Sif is a hallower, one whomakes sacred. Sif's hair is representative of the grain in the field, and burning grain was known to the Heathens of Anglo-Saxon England as a sacred rite. Burning grain is frequently found in ceremonies in my travels through Vanaheim. Sif has a duty to hallow and cannot do her duty if she is poisoned by negative thinking. So, it is not that Sif is oblivious to things wrong in the world and needing to right those wrongs - Sif focuses her energies on being the example, being what is right and good and holy. I am sure that Sif does not agree with one hundred percent of the attitudes, behaviors, and customs found among the Aesir in Asgard, but she is still there, and lives among them peaceably.

Sif's name is closely cognate with the Old High German *sippe* (family unit) and the Middle English *sibbe* (relate by blood), which would suggest that she is all about the family, and in this case hers is Thor of the Aesir, her son Ullr of the Vanir, and Thrud who is of both Aesir and Vanir descent, as well as extended family in Vanaheim and Asgard. The most important thing, to Sif, is family and keeping it together. To have a strong family unit it is necessary to put that family first, and we can see how this would translate into our own personal *innangeard*, into our kin both blood and by choice. Rather than finding fault with everyone else, it is best to find what is good where we are at.

It is my hope that someday, Sif will be more valued by the Northern Tradition, seeing her as a goddess worthy of worship in her own right rather than merely "Thor's wife" or "mother of Thrud and Ullr". These things are worthy and important, yes, but she is so much more.

Idunna

Idunna is the keeper of the golden apples that keep the Aesir young, and the wife of Bragi, the giver of poetic inspiration, the Skald of Skalds.

One is called Bragi: he is renowned for wisdom and most of all for fluency of speech and skill with words.... "His wife is Idunn: she guards in her chest of ash those apples which the gods must taste whensoever they grow old; and then they all become young, and so it shall be even unto the Weird of the Gods."
Then said Gangleri: "A very great thing, methinks, the gods entrust to the watchfulness and good faith of Idunn." Then said Harr, laughing loudly: "'T'was near being desperate once; I may be able to tell thee of it, but now thou shalt first hear more of the names of the Aesir."
-Skaldskaparmal

...three of the Aesir, Odin and Loki and Hoenir, departed from home and were wandering over mountains and wastes, and food was hard to find. But when they came down into a certain dale, they saw a herd of oxen, took one ox, and set about cooking it. Now when they thought that it must be cooked, they broke up the fire, and it was not cooked.

After a while had passed, they having scattered the fire a second time, and it was not cooked, they took counsel together, asking each other what it might mean. Then they heard a voice speaking in the oak up above them, declaring that he who sat there confessed he had caused the lack of virtue in the fire. They looked thither, and there sat an eagle; and it was no small one. Then the eagle said: "If ye are willing to give me my fill of the ox, then it will cook in the fire." They assented to this. Then he let himself float down from the tree and alighted by the fire, and forthwith at the very first took unto himself the two hams of the ox, and both shoulders.

Then Loki was angered, snatched up a great pole, brandished it with all his strength, and drove it at the eagle's body. The eagle plunged violently at the blow and flew up, so that the pole was fast to the eagle's back, and Loki's hands to the other end of the pole. The eagle flew at such a height that Loki's feet down below knocked against stones and rockheaps and trees, and he thought his arms would be torn from his shoulders. He cried aloud, entreating the eagle urgently for peace; but the eagle declared that Loki should never be loosed, unless he would give him his oath to induce Idunn to come out of Asgard with her apples. Loki assented, and being straightway loosed, went to his companions; nor for that time are any more things reported concerning their journey, until they had come home.

But at the appointed time Loki lured Idunn out of Asgard into a certain wood, saying that he had found such apples as would seem to her of great virtue, and prayed that she would have her apples with her and compare them with these. Then Thjazi the giant came there in his eagle's plumage and took Idunn and flew away with her, off into Thrymheimr to his abode. But the Aesir became straitened at the disappearance of Idunn, and speedily they became hoary and old. Then those, Aesir took counsel together, and each asked the other what had last been known of Idunn; and the last that had been seen was that she had gone out of Asgard with Loki.

Thereupon Loki was seized and brought to the Thing, and was threatened with death, or tortures; when he had become well frightened, he declared that he would seek after Idunn in Jotunheim, if Freya would lend him the hawk's plumage which she possessed. And when he got the hawk's plumage, he flew north into Jotunheim, and came on a certain day to the home of Thjazi the giant. Thjazi had rowed out to sea, but Idunn was at home alone: Loki turned her into the shape of a nut and grasped her in his claws and flew his utmost.

Now when Thjazi came home and missed Idunn, he took his eagle's plumage and flew after Loki, making a mighty rush of sound with his wings in his flight.

But when the Aesir saw how the hawk flew with the nut, and where the eagle was flying, they went out below Asgard and bore burdens of plane-shavings thither. As soon as the hawk flew into the citadel, he swooped down close by the castle-wall; then the Aesir struck fire to the plane-shavings. But the eagle could not stop himself when he missed the hawk: the feathers of the eagle caught fire, and straightway his flight ceased. Then the Aesir were near at hand and slew Thjazi the giant within the Gate of the Aesir, and that slaying is exceeding famous.

-Gylfaginning

Ithun spake:
"Well, prithee, Bragi, | his kinship weigh,
Since chosen as wish-son he was;
And speak not to Loki | such words of spite
Here within Aegir's hall."
Loki spake:
"Be silent, Ithun! | thou art, I say,
Of women most lustful in love,
Since thou thy washed-bright | arms didst wind
About thy brother's slayer."
Ithun spake:
18. "To Loki I speak not | with spiteful words
Here within Agir's hall;

And Bragi I calm, | who is hot with beer,
For I wish not that fierce they should fight."
-Lokasenna

How should Idunn be periphrased? Thus: by calling her Wife of Bragi, and Keeper of the Apples; and the apples should be called Age-Elixir of the Aesir. Idunn is also called Spoil of the Giant Thjazi, according to the tale that has been told before, how he took her away from the Aesir.
-Skaldskaparmal

Idunna is best known as the keeper of the apples that preserve the health and well-being of the gods, keeping them from becoming frail and infirm in their old age. These are definitely "some apples", and require a lot of care to produce. Idunna sees it as her sacred duty to grow the apples that keep the gods healthy. She is far more reserved and even humble than the other goddesses, preferring to work in her orchard than preside over a great hall. She presents as a "dirty" farmgirl who is not too proud to get her hands dirty. While Eir is the physician to the gods, it is Idunna's apples that keep them hale and only in occasional need of Eir's services (thus freeing her to work for

Mengloth and as a Valkyrie). However, we can see from Idunna herself being kidnapped by Thjazi that the apples don't "work" without Idunna herself working her charms upon them. If you happen to be in Vanaheim and travel to Idunna's orchard, eating an apple will not make you immortal. Idunna does occasionally give apples to humans as a sign of good will and for healing purposes, this is true, but without her magic, they are just unusually delicious apples, maybe with a bit more life force energy, vitality-giving power, and nutritional value than regular apples, but not inherently immortality-giving.

Gnosis corroborated by several people says that Idunna is the same goddess as Ostara/Eostre, who was celebrated as the bringer of spring, and whose customs survive in modern-day Easter, with bunny rabbits and eggs (obvious symbols of fertility, and fertility is a primary domain of the Vanir). Idunna as Eostre "cleans up" well, and I see this as the time when she transforms into a radiant, beautiful goddess, adorned in pastels and glowing with the sunlight itself, dancing across the fields and awakening them to bloom wildflowers. The ability that she holds to infuse her orchards with the life force energy that produces apples which keep the Aesir hale, is the same ability she uses to awaken the Earth in splendor and glory.

The Vanir all exude a certain vitality that is not even seen among the mightiest Jotun or the noblest Ase, a deep life force energy directly tied to the sea and the soil. Vanaheim is the most fertile world of the Nine, and it is on the flow of energy through Vanaheim that the other Worlds receive sustenance, particularly Midgard with humans who "build bridges" to the Vanir through their worship, and give offerings to all of the Beings of the Nine Worlds. The Vanes all manifest this vitality differently, but even in the eldest Vanir such as Frodi and Holda, there is the sense that they are very healthy, strong, and truly do enjoy life. Idunna has no less of this vitality, if anything she gives her energy to the orchard, producing the apples of life, and gives her energy to the land itself during springtime, her exuberant joy causing the Earth to awaken and bloom with beauty.

Beyond the obvious factor of Idunna's apples, and the customs of the Eostre celebrations, we know from the

Eddas that Idunna is the wife of Bragi, the son of Odin and Gunnlod, conceived during Bolverk-Odin's "visit" to Gunnlod to get the mead of poetry (incidentally made from Kvasir, "born" from the combined spit of the Aesir and Vanir to seal their truce).

While the "lore" regarding Idunna carving runes into Bragi's tongue is actually not found in any of the primary sources, it is accepted by many as a personal gnosis of Idunna's relationship to her husband as muse. Bragi clearly has poetic abilities in and of himself, being the son of Odin and Gunnlod, conceived under the influence of the mead of poetry. However, all poets require something to compose poetry about, and the greatest poets of the ages have been inspired by a muse, from Petrarch's Laura to Dante's Beatrice, to Matilde Naruda (wife of Pablo). I see Idunna as being Bragi's muse.

The lesson of skaldcraft that Bragi teaches is that through the magic of words, stories are told, whether past history, current events, or hopes for the future. Everyone from the lowliest thrall to the highest king loves a good poem or a good song, and the skalds of old were often shown the best hospitality by kings, paid and gifted for entertaining. To weave words well is to inspire others. Not everyone is a poet, and not everyone can handle the "Divine madness" that creates poetic fire. However, for a little while, as the songs are sung and the stories told, even the most common and inarticulate people can taste a little of the poetic fire, and feel connected to something larger than themselves.

Idunna as Bragi's muse made an already good poet great, renowned through the Nine Worlds. Idunna says of Bragi that "all living things love him" (*Lokasenna* 18). It is with first flyting Bragi, a skald well-versed in this genre, that Loki's verbal attacks on the Aesir at Aegir's feast begin. Idunna does not attack Loki in turn, but tells Bragi not to speak harshly. Clearly, she would have some influence over Bragi's poetry, and indeed when he was to keep silent.

Idunna as a Vane serving the Aesir would be a natural wife for Bragi, conceived as the mead of poetry, made from Kvasir's blood, was won. The Vanes adopted into the Aesir tribe were representative of the best of Vanaheim, and the combination of the Vanic nature-cult with the Aesic "civilization"-cult would be a likely explanation for poetry as an art form and even as a class, as poetry and song celebrates beauty, whether of nature or of people. While Bragi is usually depicted as much older than Idunna, I get the sense that Idunna (rather like Sif) is in fact "older" but as with all the Vanir, looks young for her years. Indeed, the mystique of "the older woman" has been a subject of erotica since time immemorial, and is perhaps a contributing factor to Bragi's muse as well.

Idunna, for all of her brief mention in the primary sources and being a goddess who has only called few both then and now, is one of the most powerful goddesses, holding not only the magic to keep the gods strong, but the mystery to inspire the greatest poetry. For a "dirty farmgirl" who would rather tend to the trees than rule over kingdoms, who transforms into Eostre, goddess of spring, once a year, in beauty and radiant glory - one has to wonder just how powerful this quiet, unassuming goddess really is. Maybe it is better that we don't know.

Eir

The wish for healing has always been half of
health.

-Lucius Annaeus Seneca

Eir is the physician of the Aesir, and her pantheon of origin is not explicitly named in lore, but there is a good case to be made for her being Vanir.

Svipdag spake:
"Now answer me, Fjolsvith, the question I ask,
For now the truth would I know:
What call they the mountain on which the maid
Is lying so lovely to see?"
Fjolsvith spake:
"Lyfjaberg is it, and long shall it be
A joy to the sick and the sore;
For well shall grow each woman who climbs it,
Though sick full long she has lain."
Svipdag spake:
"Now answer me, Fjolsvith, the question I ask,
For now the truth would I know:
What maidens are they that at Mengloth's knees
Are sitting so gladly together?"
Fjolsvith spake:
"Hlif is one named, Hlifthrasa another,
Thjothvara call they the third;
Bjort and Bleik, Blith and Frith,
Eir and Aurbotha."
Svipdag spake:
"Now answer me, Fjolsvith, the question I ask,
For now the truth would I know:
Aid bring they to all who offerings give,

If need be found therefor?"
Fjolsvith spake:
"Soon aid they all who offerings give
On the holy altars high;
And if danger they see for the sons of men,
Then each from ill do they guard."
-Fjolsvinnsmol, Bellows translation

Then said Gangleri: "Which are the Asynjur?" Harr said:
"...The third is Eir: she is the best physician."
-Gylfaginning XXXV, Brodeur translation.

There are yet others, Odinn's maids, Hild and Gondul,
Hlokk, Mist, Skogul, Then are listed Hrund and Eir, Hrist, Skuld.
They are called Norns who shape necessity...
-Skaldskaparsmal, Chapter 75

In corroborated personal gnosis, Eir is one of the
healers of Lyfja Mount under Mengloth (Mengloth is
mentioned in lore to live among the etins), *as well as* one of
Frigga's handmaidens, *as well as* one of the Valkyries. I
believe she is the same Eir mentioned in these three
accounts. I see her going back and forth between the three,
and one of the reasons why I believe her to be a Vane is
indeed this going back and forth; as one of the Vanir, she
would have "neutrality" to work both for the Aesir and
among the Jotnar.

I also suspect that Eir is a Vane because of her
obvious domain of health and healing. It is said she is "the
best" physician - not merely "a really good" physician, but
"the best". Corroborated gnosis says there are two tribes
within Vanaheim that specialize in healing – the Frogs for
more common ailments and preventative medicine, as well
as midwifery, and the Serpents for more serious cases.

136

There is a shared gnosis that Eir may be affiliated with the Serpent tribe and have trained with them.

We can see that Eir probably revealed herself in days of old to those with a certain inclination towards healing. We know that the medical innovations and technology, such as medications, equipment, and procedures, have only been with us rather recently in comparison to the scope of human history. I believe that Eir is a patron of those working with alternative medicine, but also more "conventional" methods. It does happen that many herbs will treat physical conditions as well as improving mood, concentration, etc. For example, aspirin is actually made from a synthesized form of the bark of a willow tree. We would not have known that if it were not for the old-time healers using herbs and figuring out what worked and what didn't. I personally believe many of these ancient healers were spirit-taught by Mengloth and Eir (even if they did not know these were the entities they were dealing with), and the information has been lost to the sands of time as generally such lore was kept between the healer and their guides.

I see Eir as being one of the more "subdued" Vanir. Since she has to work both under Frigga and Mengloth, she is generally not around her people, and thus comes off as a bit closed-off and not very social, and in any event carries herself with a no-nonsense demeanor because she is very much her job. In working with Eir I have found her to be matter-of-fact: she asks questions, but when she gives diagnoses or advice she is not wordy in her response, and seems to spend more time listening and observing than talking. She also communicates a good deal through touch, and I have found her touch to radiate love and warmth and compassion.

Eir is indeed a goddess with a great reserve of compassion, but it only goes so far. It is Eir who inspires "do no harm", and if you go to her for healing, She is not the type to prescribe and mask what is really going on, she will prescribe but also work on treating the root of the illness or injury. It does seem that Eir understands that sickness and injury is not just a body thing, but that mind, body, and spirit are truly connected. She may be willing to help remedy your condition especially if there is an emergency, but you cannot go back to an unhealthy lifestyle afterwards. If you go to her for help and then you return to things like abusing drugs, workaholicism, or certain other dysfunctional behavior patterns, and then ask her for help a second time, she will refuse.

It should be noted that when I work with Eir for personal healing, it is always when she is under Mengloth at Lyfja Mount. I have seen Eir in Asgard and it seems that there, she specifically heals the Aesir gods. While one might wonder how gods can be healed, we do know that they needed Idunna's apples to stay young and hale, and we see from the death of Baldur that gods can indeed be killed. They are stronger than humans, but still have their own susceptibilities, and I believe it is Eir who checks in on their health and treats as needed.

When Eir is in "Valkyrie mode", I believe she is there on the battlefield tending to the wounded, and will help to transition those who can't be healed. It is through this side of Eir that we know sometimes death is the ultimate healer, when a body or spirit is so broken that it must transition, rest, and eventually be recycled out again with a blank slate. I have seen some of Eir's pragmatic attitude towards death when praying to her on behalf of others. She thinks death is just as much a part of the life cycle as living, and indeed, death is necessary. We as a society are not only too quick to "fix up" rather than treat what is wrong, but we are all terrified of death and have gone to great lengths to prevent it even at the expense of quality of life for ourselves and others. Eir does not approve of this, and indeed, praying to Eir for healing if one is "terminal" may result in a hastening of the inevitable, so work with her at your own risk.

Ultimately, I believe working with Eir helps one to realize that connection with the Divine and the Otherworlds is very helpful to maintain proper health, and working with her is, indeed, working. It involves action, not merely going to her, but carrying out what she prescribes, even if she guides your mind and your hands. She is the best physician not because she tells you everything you want to hear, but because her way is best for the whole of what you are experiencing, as well as how it relates to the whole of your world - where you live, the people you care about. The phrase *Waes þu hal* in Anglo-Saxon literally translates as "Be thou whole". The words "healing" and "whole" are cognate. We cannot have healing unless it is total healing, and Eir helps us to remember that and begin that process of wholeness.

Nehelennia

Twenty years from now you will be more
disappointed by the things that you didn't do
than by the ones you did do. So throw off the
bowlines. Sail away from the safe harbor.
Catch the trade winds in your sails. Explore.
Dream. Discover.
-*Mark Twain*

Nehelennia – a regional Dutch goddess - is another
that is not explicitly named in lore as Vanir, but is
suspected by some to be Vanir, both due to what is known
about her, and shared personal gnosis.

We must also allude briefly to the Belgian or Frisian
Nehalennia, about whose name several inscriptions of like
import remove all doubt; but the word has also given rise to
forced and unsatisfying interpretations. In other inscriptions
found on the lower part of the Rhine there occurs compounds,
whose termination (-nehis, -nehabus, dat. plurals fem.) seems to
contain the same word that forms the first half of Nehalennia;
their plural number appears to indicate nymphs rather than a
goddess, yet there also hangs about them the notion of a mother.
-Grimm's Teutonic Mythology, Chapter 13

More than 160 votive altars, almost all discovered
in the Dutch province of Zeeland, have been found
dedicated to the goddess Nehelennia. (There are two altars
in Cologne, which was the capital of Germania Inferior.)
Most of these altars were found by Dutch fishermen in the
17th and 19th centuries CE and can be dated back to the

2nd and 3rd centuries CE; they depict a young female figure, sitting on a throne between two columns, holding a basket of apples (or sometimes bread) on her lap; there is almost always a wolf dog at her side, and sometimes she is holding a scepter in her hands. On some of the altars, the woman is standing next to the prow of a ship.

In many (but not all) cases, the votive altar was placed to show gratitude for a safe passage across the (often-treacherous) North Sea. Many of these altar stones have the Latin inscription; "Votum solvit libens merito", which is literally translated as "Prayer to loosen with good will deserving", but essentially means the one who erected the altar stone fulfilled a promise to do so after safe passage.

There was also a temple dedicated to Nehelennia near Walcheren, destroyed by Christian missionaries in 694 CE; as well as near the coast to the west of the city of Domburg.

While it has been speculated by some scholars that Nehelennia may be one and the same as Nerthus, it does not sit well with me for two basic reasons: 1. the names are not cognate, 2. anyone who looked upon Nerthus' face was subject to death (often by drowning); all of the altar stones of Nehelennia have her face visible, and Nehelennia is associated with safe passage rather than drowning. (I also, having encountered both goddesses, can say they feel very different.)

Nehelennia appears to be a Germanic goddess and not a Celtic or Roman deity, even though there is some overlap between cultures. Obviously there is no extant folklore of Nehelennia, and we cannot definitively say to what tribe of gods she belongs. That being said, there is a strong argument for Nehelennia as a Vanir Goddess.

- According to the personal gnosis of some who have journeyed to Vanaheim (myself included), Nehelennia does have a hall there, which is said to be "next door" to Njord's, made of branches in the shape of a cornucopia.

- There is a shared personal gnosis that Nehelennia is one of Njord and Nerthus's siblings (Njord and Nerthus are twins, but SPG says they were not the only children born of their parents).

- Nehelennia is associated with ships (Frey and Njord come to mind) and food, specifically apples and bread (the domain of Idunna and Frey respectively), and her domains of prosperity, abundance and protection in travel for commerce (as opposed to protection in battle) would be very apt for a Vanic deity.

I have only encountered Nehelennia a few times in the years I have been working with the Vanir. She usually appears as a young woman (in her twenties by standards of human age and appearance, though she is much much older), but as mentioned before in this book the Vanir seem much younger than they actually are. Also, you can see that despite the appearance of youth, she is calm, poised, dignified, and wields much power and authority. Like all of the Vanir, she chooses her words carefully, and radiates brightness: she is pleasant to be around if not necessarily "nice". She will be gracious to those who visit her, making sure there is enough food, and no harm befalls them while in her hall. I have had the opportunity to see

Nehelennia sit on the council of Vanaheim among its leadership, representing the Salmon tribe (though she is of Boar lineage).

In the 21st century Nehelennia can be called upon for protection in travel, especially for business: most of us do not have to cross the North Sea to earn a living, but many of us fear flying, and even staying in your own town or state and going back and forth between work and home can be fraught with dangerous possibilities. Nehelennia can also be invoked for abundance, especially if one is having financial difficulties or may want to improve one's lot in life. In my experience Nehelennia can also be petitioned if you are stuck in your life and need a "sea change" (though do not be surprised if you wind up travelling long distances as a result), and she can also be petitioned for safe passage during life transitions, especially following situations that might make one feel unsafe (such as leaving an abusive relationship).

If presented with an offering -- usually with a promise to preserve her worship in some way, especially by building an altar and promoting her cultus -- she seems to be eager to please; Nehelennia's desire for worship is not out of ego as humans would perceive it, but to have her presence bring peace to the land and its people. One could conceivably make an altar stone out of concrete, making an image and inscription while the concrete is still soft, letting it harden, and then, once hard, you would periodically leave gifts there. For those who do not have the ability to make an altar stone, finding a cornucopia would be just as well, placing it on a table, and periodically dropping offerings into it.

Many pagans in the Netherlands have resurrected the cultus of Nehelennia, re-creating a temple in her honor[9], and holding rites in her worship. I think this is good, and important, and those wishing to have a special relationship with Nehelennia may offer to travel to the Netherlands as a pilgrimage, while still noting her presence can be felt anywhere in the world, if one calls to her. Deities are generally capable of being multiple places at once, and she is a goddess involved with travel at that.

[9]http://www.nehalennia-tempel.nl/;
http://www.boniface.demon.nl/rel_2.html

Wayland

Of the four elements, air, earth, water, and
fire man stole only one from the gods. Fire.
And with it, man forged his will upon the
world.

-Anonymous

Wayland is a smithing god and one of the few
Northern deities to have almost equal mention in English,
German, and Scandinavian lore. He is mentioned in Das
Heldenbuch, as well as in several of the Anglo-Saxon
poems:

No need then
to lament for long or lay out my body.
If the battle takes me, send back
this breast-webbing that Weland fashioned
and Hrethel gave me, to Lord Hygelac.
Fate goes ever as fate must."
-Beowulf, Heaney translation

.   . . she encouraged him eagerly: 'Surely the work of
Weland will fail not any of men, of those who can hold stout
Mimming.
-Waldhere

Welund tasted misery among snakes.
The stout-hearted hero endured troubles
had sorrow and longing as his companions
cruelty cold as winter - he often found woe
Once Nithad laid restraints on him,   .
supple sinew-bonds on the better man.

That went by; so can this.
-Deor, Pollington translation

Wayland is also seen on the Franks Casket and the Ardre image stone VIII. The Ardre stones are a collection of ten stones with runes and images on them, dating from the 8th to 11th centuries CE. They were used as paving under the wooden floors of the church in the Ardre 241 parish of Gotland, Sweden, and re-discovered when the church was restored around 1900. They are now preserved in the Swedish Museum of National Antiquities, Stockholm.

The Franks Casket is a small whalebone chest, carved with narrative scenes in flat two-dimensional low-relief and with Anglo-Saxon runes. The casket is dateable to the mid-seventh century CE, reckoned to be of Northumbrian origin. The front panel of the Franks Casket depicts elements from the legend of Wayland Smith on the left panel, and the adoration of the Magi on the right. Around the panel, runs the following inscription in Anglo-Saxon runes:

> hronas ban
> fisc flodu / ahof on fergenberig
> wart gasric grorn / tar he on greut giswom

The two alliterating lines constitute the oldest piece of Anglo- Saxon poetry, and the verse may be interpreted as:

> whalebone
> fish flood hove on mountain
> The ghost-king was rueful when he swam onto the grit

Also from Anglo-Saxon England there is a finding of cross shafts, particularly from Leeds, depicting a smithy with tools, a beheaded body and "shape-changer" (a human being in bonds), grasping a female and growing wings.

Wayland's Smithy is a Neolithic long barrow and chamber tomb site located, near the Uffington White Horse and Uffington Castle, at Ashbury in the English county of Oxfordshire (historically in Berkshire). Wayland's Smithy is one of many sites associated with Wayland. The name was seemingly applied to the site by the Saxon invaders, who reached the area approximately four thousand years after Wayland's Smithy was built. According to legend, a traveler whose horse has lost a shoe can leave the animal and the smallest silver coin (a groat) on the capstone at Wayland's Smithy. When he returns next morning he will find that his horse has been re-shod and the money gone. It is thought that the invisible smith may have been linked to this site for many centuries before the Saxons recognized him as Wayland.

Finally, we come to the Eddaic lay which tells Wayland's story: *Volundarkvida*. At the beginning of *Volundarkvida*, his lineage is noted:

There were three brothers, sons of a king of the Finns, one was called Slagfid, the second Egil, the third Volund. They went on snow-shoes and hunted wildbeasts.

It is thought that where "Finns" appears in the lore it is a gloss for the Vanir (such as a mention in the sagas that *seiðr* was practiced by the Finns). In addition to this, Wayland's connection to the elves is noted several times in *Volundarkvida*:

On the bearskin sat,
his rings counted,
the Alfar's companion:
one was missing.
He thought that Hlodver's
daughter had it,
the young Alvit,
and that she was returned.
Then cried Nidud,
the Niarars' lord:
"Whence gottest thou, Volund!
Alfars' chief!
our gold,
in Ulfdal?"
"Tell me, Volund,
Alfars' chief!
of my brave boys
what is become?"

The phrase "Alfars ljodi" is translated as "Alfars' chief" although it is more accurately "Alfars' leader". As we will explore later in this book, "Vanir" and "elves" seem to be used fairly interchangeably in the lore, and corroborated gnosis says that Vanir are in fact elves and that the other elven groups noted in lore (e.g. Ljossalfar) are descended from the Vanir. The Vanir also seem more likely candidates for marriage to Valkyries or swan-women.

Smithing would be important to the people of the Vanic era, and from the perception of the Vanir, to construct tools which are useful as well as aesthetically pleasing. As mentioned in the *Northern Tradition Timeline* earlier in the book, tools were constructed since the Paleolithic era, but continually evolving in terms of function and look. Weapons were important to hunters, and the earliest farmers still used instruments albeit primitive. Kings and chieftains liked having status symbols. Smiths had a valuable role in the service of the community even before "civilization".

As further possible evidence, the snowshoes and archery mentioned in Wayland's lore would make a connection to Ullr, and Egil (Wayland's brother) has been hypothesized to be one and the same as Aurvandil (Earandel), the father of Ullr by Sif, which would make Wayland the uncle of Ullr.

To summarize the *Volundarkvida*, and not have to put the entire poem in the book, Wayland and his two brothers lived with three Valkyries: Olrun, Hervor-alvitr and Hladgudr-svanhvit. After nine years, the Valkyries left them. Egil and Slagfidr followed, never to return. Hervor left Wayland with a ring. Later in time, Wayland is captured in his sleep by king Nidud (literally, "bitter-hater") in Nerike who orders him hamstrung and imprisoned on the island of Savarstod, forced to forge items for the king. Hervor's ring was given to the king's daughter Bodvild, and Nidud wore Wayland's sword. In revenge, Wayland killed the king's sons when they visited him in secret, fashioning goblets from their skulls, jewels from their eyes, and a brooch from their teeth. He sent the goblets to the king, the jewels to the queen, and the brooch to Bodvild. When Bodvild took her ring to him to be mended, he impregnated her and escaped on wings he had made.

Thidrekssaga – a collection of sagas linked with 'Dietrich von Bern' and a relatively young source, dating from the thirteenth century – has a slightly different variation of the story. Here Wayland is mentioned as a human. Wayland's brother Egil is a deus ex machina here, who shoots birds and collects the feathers to help Wayland build a flying device. As he plans to escape he has his brother test the flying device, and when he leaves the island, Egil is forced to shoot him down. However, it was arranged beforehand, so Egil just hits a bladder filled with blood and everyone assumes Wayland is mortally wounded. But he is not, and years later returns to join his wife and son.

Egil is depicted on the Franks Casket as well as the Pforzen buckle, shooting arrows against attacking troops. In *Thidrekssaga* besides assisting in Wayland's escape, Nidud forces him to shoot an apple from the head of his son. He does it but there are no evil consequences, neither for the marksman nor for the king. He readies two arrows, but succeeds with the first one. Asked by the king what the second arrow was for, he states that had he killed his son with the first arrow, he would have shot the king with the second one.

In both cases Egil is seen as protecting his land and family (his wife, Ailruna or Olrun), rather than fighting for the glories of war itself, which is the trait of a Vanic warrior as opposed to an Aesic warrior. Moreover, archery seems to be a recurring theme with Vanic warriors (i.e. Ullr) and "elf-shot" is well-known in folklore as consequence for angering elves in some way. So, Egil gets a mention here, even though there is not enough information to give him an entire chapter, it may be that he was important to the pantheon at one time and should at least be given a nod.

Wayland's myth more than anything else illustrates that the gods are distinct individuals who feel joy and pain just as we do, who have experienced love and loss just as we do. Mythology is very much "as above, so below". We feel less alone in being able to relate to the experiences of our gods. Despite being imprisoned and hamstrung, Wayland finds a way to escape as well as to exact justice on those who wronged him. Wayland suffered greatly, yet his ingenuity got the last laugh in the end. Necessity is the mother of invention, and in Wayland's trial, he invented wings to fly, symbolic of his spirit soaring and outperforming his broken body.

I think the legend of Wayland has endured throughout the ages because we can look at his story and know no matter what befalls us, so long as we keep our wits about us, we can find a way through somehow, and perhaps even find greatness.

Wayland's cult endures with offerings given and even a feast day reported in November around the same time as American Thanksgiving. In appreciating Wayland's skill and cleverness, we not only give him worth, but worth that within ourselves.

Frodi

There is no escape - we pay for the violence
of our ancestors.
- From "Collected Sayings of Muad'Dib"
by the Princess Irulan (Dune, Frank
Herbert)

No pantheon is without their "bad guys", and Frodi ("the Fruitful") is one of the most problematic figures in the Vanic pantheon. It is a corroborated gnosis that Frodi is one of the elder Vanes, twin of Holda, the father of Njord, Nerthus, Nehelennia and others, and grandfather of Frey and Freya.

While this story (from certain editions of the *Poetic Edda*) is presented elsewhere as an historical account by Saxo, he also euhemerized all of the gods, ergo I feel that it may also have been one of the few surviving pieces of explicitly Vanic lore:

> Now then are come to the king's high hall
> the foreknowing twain, Fenja and Menja;
> in bondage by Frodi, Fridleif's son,
> these sisters mighty as slaves are held.
> To moil at the mill the maids were bid,
> to turn the grey stone as their task was set;
> lag in their toil he would let them never,
> the slaves' song he unceasing would hear.
> The chained ones churning ay chanted their song:
> "Let us right the mill and raise the millstones."
> He gave them no rest, to grind on bade them.
> They sang as they swung the swift-wheeling stone,
> till of Frodi's maids most fell asleep.

Then Menja quoth, at the quern standing:
"Gold and good hap we grind for Frodi,
a hoard of wealth on the wishing-mill;
he shall sit on gold, he shall sleep on down,
he shall wake to joy; well had we ground then!
Here shall no one harm his neighbor,
nor bale-thoughts brew for others' bane,
nor swing sharp sword to smite a blow,
though his brother's banesman bound he should find."
This word first then fell from his lips:
"Sleep shall ye not more than cock in summer,
or longer than I a lay may sing."
Menja said: "A fool wert, Frodi, and frenzied of mind,
the time thou, men's friend, us maidens did buy;
for strength did you choose us, and sturdy looks,
but you didn't reck of what race we sprang."
"Hardy was Hrungnir, but his sire even more;
more thews than they old Thjatsi had.
Ithi and Aurnir are of our kin:
are we both born to brothers of jotuns!"
"Scarce had Grotti come out of grey mountain,
from out of the earth the iron-hard slab,
nor had mountain-maids now to turn the mill-stone,
if we had not first found it below."
"Winters nine we grew beneath the ground;
under the mountains, we mighty playmates
did strive to do great deeds of strength:
boulders we budged from their bases.
"Rocks we rolled out of jotun's realm:
the fields below with their fall did shake;
we hurled from the heights the heavy quernstone,
the swift-rolling slab, so that men might seize it."
"But since then we to Sweden fared,
we foreknowing twain, and fought among men;
byrnies we broke, and bucklers shattered,
we won our way through warriors' ranks."
"One king we overthrew, enthroned the other.

To good Guthorm we granted victory;
stern was the struggle ere Knui was struck."
"A full year thus we fared among men;
our name was known among noble heroes.
Through linden shields sharp spears we hurled,
drew blood from wounds, and blades reddened."
Now we are come to the king's high hall,
without mercy made to turn the mill;
mud soils our feet, frost cuts our bones;
at the peace-quern we drudge: dreary is it here."
"The stone now let stand, my stint is done;
I have ground my share, grant me a rest."
Fenja said: "The stone must not stand,
our stint is not done,
before to Frodi his fill we ground."
"Our hands shall hold the hard spearshafts,
weapons gory: Awake Frodi!
Awake Frodi!, if listen thou wilt
to our olden songs, to our ancient lore."
"My eye sees fire east of the castle
battle cries ring out, beacons are kindled!
Hosts of foemen hither will wend
to burn down the hall over thy head."
"No longer thou Leire shall hold,
have rings of red gold, nor the mill of riches.
Harder the handle, let us hold sister;
our hands are not warm yet with warriors' blood."
"My father's daughter doughtily ground,
for the death of hosts did she foresee;
even now the strong booms burst from the quern,
the stanch iron stays -- yet more strongly grind!"
Menja said: "Yet more swiftly grind: the son of Yrsa
Frodi's blood will crave for the bane of Halfdan --
Hrolf is hight and is to her
both son and brother as both of us know."
The mighty maidens, they ground amain,
strained their young limbs of giant strength;

the shaft tree quivered, the quern toppled over,
the heavy slab burst asunder."
Quoth the mighty maiden of the mountain giants:
"Ground have we Frodi, now fain would cease.
We have toiled enough at turning the mill!"
-Grottasöngr

This piece of lore would suggest that there was a time when those who were of the Jotnar had a history of walking among men and giving victory to certain ones, fighting alongside others, which suggests they were probably worshiped at some point, and in any case this was not censored completely in the *Grottasongr*.

In corroborated personal gnosis, the Vanir and Jotnar originally started off as one species, and split apart from each other approximately 10,000-9000 years ago. Later on, the Boar tribe wrested control from the Serpents and a civil war commenced, and the Boar tribe was the ruling tribe of Vanaheim until recently. At this point, Vanaheim began to make a transition in its culture, wherein certain individuals within the realm were elevated above others to be revered as gods in our realm. This story directly mentions that Frodi took the Jotun-women Fenja and Menja as slaves, grinding at a mill, but what is ground at this particular mill is actually *frid*, or peace. It would seem that the symbolism behind the story is the aggressive nature of the Jotnar being "ground" into work - and very hard work at that - to keep the peace of the land, including keeping the prosperity (because when food is scarce and one is just surviving hand-to-mouth, people get ugly).

And thus, Frodi is a problematic figure, forcing these women to work against their will, and when they were exhausted, and "grinding down" their Jotun nature, which in turn "ground down" the influence of the Jotun cult (or more specifically, the time when the Vanir and Jotnar had more in common) in favor of the rising cult of the Vanir gods. For all that the Aesir have blood on their hands with regards to an act of war upon the Vanir, the Vanir are not wholly innocent. Not only was Frodi in the wrong for enslaving Jotnar and having them perform the magical work of diminishing the influence and power of the Jotnar (not dissimilar to the implications of Odin outlawing consanguineous marriage amongst the Vanir in Asgard, knowing perfectly well that much Vanic magic is performed via the twinbond).

In the previous edition of this book, I justified Frodi's actions by saying "one of the drawbacks of leadership is oftentimes doing things that seem 'wrong' or at the very least distasteful, but are necessary for keeping law and order." I regret saying this. At the time that I wrote this, I was associating with some people who held some very problematic points of view, including the attitude that the gods are always right, and that enslaving and subjugating humans was OK because it was "necessary for the deity's purpose" and we should be happy to be their bootscrapes and just suck it up. It has been (at the time of this writing in 2014) five years since I disassociated from said people, and re-evaluated my attitudes towards religion and the way their own viewpoints influenced mine. I am ashamed that I put something in the original edition of *Visions of Vanaheim* condoning Frodi's actions; I had considered leaving this section out entirely from the re-write of the book, but I decided that this subject needed to be touched upon for reasons.

It is true that leaders often have to make unpopular decisions, and oftentimes decisions made on the lesser of two evils. It is also a fact that the Western world has engaged in colonialism and cultural imperialism for a very long time now; America was built on the backs of those conquered and enslaved, doing the grueling labor that the rich who bought them would not do for themselves, and indeed white European-descended people became a majority in power in this country because they fought and conquered other peoples who would oppose them, such as the Native Americans. Conquest and Dominator Culture has been a fact of European society since prehistory, with tribes battling, conquering, and taking slaves and forced spouses from other tribes.

This is true of their gods as well. Just as the Aesir came into power through an unfair "truce" with the Vanir, the cult of the Vanir gods came into power through a bloody split with the Jotnar and an even bloodier civil war where the new power dynamic became the Boars lording it over the rest of Vanaheim, and individual Vanir coming into power to be regarded as gods in Midgard, as opposed to the previous system of more equal power amongst the tribes and more personal deities/spirits amongst individuals (a relationship between a tribal member and single human, or small group of humans). One could argue that the reason why Njord (who made the "truce" with the Aesir on behalf of the Vanir, ordering his people to stand down and not completely annihilate the Aesir) bent over backwards in the "truce" with the Aesir, and his own people (the Vanir) got the proverbial shaft in favor of the Aesic cult, is because Njord is the child of Frodi and saw his father's mistakes and did not want to enslave and subjugate the Aesir, and the Vanir were in turn colonialized by the Aesir.

Things are what they are. My own blood family came to America more recently (20th century) compared to others, though I have family that were on the wrong side of World War II. My blood ancestors did not take slaves, but I cannot deny that I experience privilege (even as I experience systematic oppression in other areas of my life, being disabled, queer, etc) because of my white skin and European heritage. I will not kill myself in guilt for what my cultural (if not blood) ancestors have done, that would not accomplish anything, but I can be mindful of my privilege and do what I can to promote change towards equality.

Likewise, I am not telling anyone to not worship the Vanir (in case that weren't painfully obvious in a book talking about the Vanic cultus and Vanic paganism), even if the rise to power of the Vanir considered gods was based in oppressing others. Those Vanir gods who have come after Frodi – Njord, Frey, Freya, and others – make it a point of helping humanity regardless of the color of their skin, ethnic origin, sexual and gender orientation, status of health and ability – and there has been an effort to build bridges with Jotunheim (particularly among the tribes the Vanir and Jotnar have in common, such as the Serpents and Ravens), to try to right the wrongs done, and have also used their power to begin changing things so that there is a more equal share of power and influence in this realm (which we can see in the rise of Rokkatru and other forms of Jotun worship, as well as more bio-regional paganisms such as Waincraft where large local entities [that could be considered Jotnar in Northern Tradition-speak] are revered).

There is an important lesson to be had of Frodi – he who was fruitful because others were forced to grow and pick the proverbial fruit – and the way that Vanaheim and Vanic culture has changed since he left the throne.

Frodi was in the wrong for enslaving Jotnar and making them work against their own people, in the supposed "interest" of the Vanir (which ultimately went against the interests of the Vanir, as the wild has given way to ever greater taming at the cost of the health of the land and people), but he eventually realized his wrong, abdicated in favor of his son (who then abdicated much later due to the destructive influence of Asgard on Vanaheim), and lives a more reclusive life amongst his orchards, keeping lore, giving cautionary reminders about the abuse of power. The Vanir have taken steps to undo the damage done thousands of years ago, and we can see that unfolding before us.

Here in this realm, we can recognize that having privilege in and of itself does not make you a bad person, but it does mean that when you become aware of your privilege and the way society benefits others like you at the expense of others who are not like you, that you are obligated to try to change that in the ways you can. In an ideal world, there would be no privilege, everybody would be equal regardless of race and ethnicity, sexual and gender orientation, class, and so on. In an ideal world, people would be decent and respectful to other people by default, all non-criminals would have the same rights, and everybody would have a contributing place in society doing what they could do. We do not live in that world. But those of us who society favors for one reason or another, we can help create that world, and we can ally with those who are oppressed by the way the world is now, and make sure their voices are heard, stand with them as they fight for their rights.

As above, so below.

The Fair Bright Queen

And the day came when the risk to remain
tight in a bud was more painful than the risk
it took to blossom.

-Anaïs Nin

The Fair Bright Queen is an epithet given to the current Queen of Vanaheim. His job (yes, he) includes (but is not limited to) diplomatic relations with other realms, and having ritual sex with his twin for the fertility of the land; the Fair Bright Queen is the embodiment of the land. The Fair Bright Queen is not a dictator, his power is checked by a Prime Minister and Parliament. Nonetheless, the Queen wields a tremendous amount of influence in the realm.

It should be noted that the Queen is not Nerthus, or Freya, but a different person unnamed by the primary sources. Nerthus reigned in previous generations; this is a new generation.

The Queen was assigned female at birth, and for a long time she accepted this, even though there was a quiet longing to be like her brother. She was, in general, a quiet person, though there was a hidden passion when she worked on her crafts, or sang.

When the Queen came of age, she was kidnapped and taken far away, and badly abused. She eventually fought her way out of captivity and began the journey home, running into monsters in the forest and battling them, and getting wounded, picking herself back up to continue, even though she was so far out she was going only by what her intuition told her, and at times she wondered if she was getting more and more lost. That hidden fire that had come out in her art was now applied to surviving, and fighting.

Her brother tracked her, and found her, and carried her back home, through storm and fire, fending off monsters himself, and getting wounded himself. However, he knew the way home, and they found their way there after a long journey.

There was much rejoicing, but the celebration was not to last long, for Vanaheim tasted war, and the land was scarred, and the Queen wondered if anyone would ever be safe again. The Queen, in her pain, began to fall apart. She was no longer able to suppress the male form that had been held back because Vanic custom was for the Queen to be female and the King to be male.

When the Queen's male form came out, he was afraid, afraid of being rejected by his people, afraid of being rejected by his own twin, the love of his life. The Queen ran, or tried to run, and his twin chased him down, through the dark forest, through storms and fire. And when there was no place left to run, the King found his twin and said, "You are who you are, and you are no less beautiful to me, and if anything I love you more and find you even more beautiful for becoming more yourself, your true self."

The King brought his Queen home once more, and the Queen decided to face full life consequences and let the people see who he really was. They lay together, and instead of the fertility magic in their union growing weaker as the Queen had feared, it was even stronger, giving their seed to a hungry, scarred land and watching it bloom. As the Queen had become his true self, the fog that had hung over the land lifted, and the land healed, and the people rejoiced.

The King took to himself other lovers – the outlander who had healed his wounds, and her husband, who had become a dear friend. The Queen tried to be happy, but the old insecurities came roaring back. The Queen fought against them as he had fought his whole life, busying himself in his hobbies and with warrior training.

When the Queen decided that he didn't need anyone else to be happy, and that being wrapped up in the King to the exclusion of all else was unhealthy and he needed to let go and he owed his twin that much after all he'd done – he owed himself, as Queen, as one who wyrd had seen fit to rule with or without his twin - he met the twin brother of the King's wife-to-be, a beautiful man who charmed him. They greatly enjoyed each other's companionship, as well as making love together. The Queen tried to resist falling in love, not wanting to be hurt, but gave in, and found his love was returned, the greatest, deepest love the Queen had ever known.

As the Queen was able to fight his fear and take a risk and trust in this love, so Vanaheim came out of a long period of being isolated following an invasion from the Aesir and a truce gone wrong, and was able to make new alliances with other realms, creating mutually beneficial exchanges of culture and wealth. And as the Queen found joy with his new love – his sweetest love, his true soulmate, who had chosen him, and who he chose - Vanaheim had the most beautiful spring in its history, the land coming to life, the growing season the most abundant the realm had ever seen.

As the Queen and King had sacrificed themselves as the Serpent Twins and trusted in the power of their love to bring them back together, they trusted that their love was big enough to share with others and still have room for each other, and they were rewarded for that trust, and their land and people blessed in that reward.

-Eshnahai myth

The Queen is transgendered and a gay male; non-heterosexual people and transgendered people are sacred to him. The Queen also honors transgendered folk who are not strict conformists to roles of masculinity and femininity, such as trans men who are "pretty boys", being one himself.

The Queen is a lover and patron of art, and indulging and pampering oneself, making oneself beautiful however you see fit. When he lays with his brother for the fertility of the land and prosperity of the people, it is also for the beauty of the land, and for people to have beauty within themselves and their lives, and the joy that comes from it.

The Queen is also a patron of finding love after a broken heart, being able to risk and trust in love.

The Queen has a reputation for being quite charming and cordial, but the saying "beware the nice ones" exists for a reason; the Queen has a hidden predatory side that will come out if he feels his home and family are threatened, that makes Nerthus look tame.

The most noteworthy qualities of the Fair Bright Queen are his willingness to be his true self even though it was unprecedented in terms of Vanic custom – his willingness to change custom as the land and people needed to heal – his willingness to fight, his willingness to risk, and to trust, and to love.

If you would honor the Fair Bright Queen, honor your true self as best as you can. If you are having a hard time with self-expression and self-acceptance, viewing yourself as an art project can be helpful. Remember that wyrd made you who you are, and there is no shame if you were born in a body different than what your soul's truth is, and no shame in becoming yourself. Keep fighting, and you will find your way home.

The Lord of Plenty

Love, love is a verb
Love is a doing word
Fearless on my breath.
-*Massive Attack*

The Lord of Plenty is an epithet given to the current King of Vanaheim. His job includes (but is not limited to) diplomatic relations with other realms, having ritual sex with his twin for the fertility of the land, and leading the realm in battle if called for. The Lord of Plenty is not a dictator, his power is checked by a Prime Minister and Parliament, and his twin, the Queen, is a higher authority than he is and executive decisions must be cleared by the Queen first. Nonetheless, the King wields a tremendous amount of power and influence.

The King is not Njord, or Frey, but a different person unnamed by the primary sources. Njord reigned in previous generations, but abdicated in favor of his grandson due to the destructive influence of Asgard on Vanaheim.

The King, when he was young, loved his sister above all else, and when she was kidnapped, he was devastated, and dedicated his life to finding her. While he worked to find her, he helped many others, feeding the poor, giving them little boons as he could, and sometimes training warriors, companions in an otherwise solitary life.

Eventually he did find his sister, and brought her home, carrying her because she was too badly injured to walk. Along the way he too fought monsters and was wounded, and was burned in the fires at the boundary between worlds.

Their time of rejoicing in finding each other again was cut short when the realm experienced war. When the war was over, the Queen fell apart in grief, and the King did also. The King began to bleed from his wounds, and could not stop bleeding. He was taken to the Serpent healers, but there was only so much they could do for him.

An outlander came, with the knowledge of how to heal the King, but it would require ripping him apart and putting him back together piece by piece. The King was afraid, and yet he knew that his wounds were not just hurting him, but his twin, and his land and people as well.

So the King decided to face full life consequences and trust the outlander to lay hands and heal him. And even as being broken piece by piece and remade was torture like nothing he'd experienced, and even as he was afraid of what would come of it, he went through it willingly, for the greater good, and when he came out on the other side he was even more beautiful and strong than he was before. As importantly, he had fallen in love with the outlander who had compassion on him and touched the innermost depths of his soul, and he asked her to marry him; it was no longer he and his twin against the world now. He fell in love with the outlander's husband as well, who had become his best friend and confidante, who had pulled him back from the edge of despair, with whom he had a great many things in common, such as a passion for justice and punishing evildoers.

The Vanir often have many loves, and the King's love for his Queen was no less, even if his time was now shared between his loves and his time with his Queen was less. But, the Queen was no longer able to suppress the male form that he had kept secret since childhood for sake of custom. The Queen was afraid that the King would find him repulsive, especially now that he had new loves, and ran. The King chased his twin until they could run no more, and he told him the truth - "You are who you are, and you are no less beautiful to me, and if anything I love you more and find you even more beautiful for becoming more yourself, your true self."

The King brought the Queen home once more and the Queen let the people see his true self. The people also found him beautiful, and as they lay together, the land was healed in the joy of their union, loving each other as they truly were.

The Queen came to accept the King's outlander bride and groom - that he was not being replaced, the love he and the King shared for each other was great enough that they could have others and still love each other as much as they did - and the Queen benefited from having someone to talk with about him, and tease his sibling with, and they both benefited from expanding their family and having more people around to love and support them in different roles. As they found joy, the realm increased in peace and prosperity.

-Eshnahai myth

The King is a warrior and a hunter, so martial arts and hunting are sacred to him. He is also the Law within Vanaheim, so the profession of law and respectable enforcement is sacred to him as well. The King upholds the Law and does not tolerate lying or other transgressions of the Law in his presence. He has a reputation for being too honest with people, blunt enough to wound. He has a bit of a temper. While not necessarily disturbing per se, people who are expecting a calm, graceful Elvenking will be surprised to find someone loud and boisterous and temperamental.

The King is a real "salt of the earth" type person, generous and friendly, does not put on airs, does not think himself above his people because he is King. While temperamental, he is generally kind, warm and good-natured, the sort of person who will give you the shirt off his back if you need it. He firmly believes in protecting the weak and helping them to become strong. He does not tolerate bullying or abuse in his presence, and his wrath towards bullies and abusers is fearsome indeed.

The Lord of Plenty is sacrificed at Lammas and resurrected later that day, echoed in the surviving John Barleycorn practice at Harvest Home. He gives himself yearly to feed the people – not just their bodies, but also their spirits. Regardless of whether they are rich or poor, just or unjust, the King gives himself without complaining, and those who come to know him will also learn of sacrifice - what is of most benefit, the highest good, even if it demands a high cost.

I most admire his perseverance, his dedication to his twin, his willingness to sacrifice himself for the greater good, his humility and generosity.

If one would honor him, one can best do so by being willing to face your fears, be open-handed with others, and trust in wyrd.

The Lord of the Black

If a thing loves, it is infinite.
-William Blake

      The Lord of the Black is an epithet given to a man who is both the face of Death and of Life within Vanaheim. He is present when people in Vanaheim die (though Vanir live long and thus death is rare), and he is present at baby naming ceremonies (when Vanir babies are nine days old; birth is also fairly rare, as the Vanir control their fertility) to bless children. He is a psychopomp and healer.

      There once was a boy who was old for his years. He remembered a life lived before, a life that ended in horror, his people massacred and his children killed in front of him, before he was killed himself. These memories haunted him and he grew up with a passion for justice, and also for vengeance - for punishing those who sought harm to his realm, his people, and most of all those he cared about.

      The boy became a man and became a fierce warrior, his reputation known throughout the realm and also outside of it. He fought valiantly in the Aesir-Vanir war – he was the one who would fought Odin himself and would have killed Odin if he had not been ordered to stand down - wanting to protect his people from invasion.

      And yet, war was not enough. Bloodlust was not enough. He wanted love. He wanted a home, a family. And even as he tried, all that he loved was taken away from him, and this too was its own horror, its own death. He tried to build, and it was taken away a piece at a time.

      He threw himself into his work, into teaching others the art of war, and of history for the realm to never repeat its past mistakes. He taught severity, but longed for mercy.

When he'd lost everything, he found the one who had loved him in that previous life, and they reunited, and in their love, he began to learn mercy and compassion. He and his love were taught by the White Ravens - one was killed and brought back, then the other, and then they both flew into the void of Star Mother herself, coming back with the light of the stars in their wings.

-Eshnahai myth

The Lord of the Black is still a fierce warrior who will fight for his family and his people, but only when necessary, and with great sorrow that it is needed at all. As one who has killed and has been killed and reborn, he wields the power to end suffering and help a soul cross the threshold, as well as the power to give the spark of life and renewal. He is a warrior but he is also a healer, a creator. In the black darkness of the Void, there he found light, and he is Lord of the Black, of the darkness where souls go beyond, and from where they return. He holds both severity and mercy in his grasp.

He is a consort, companion, and advisor to the King and Queen.

The Lord of the Black is quiet, and tends to not go out of his way to interact with humans. He can be called upon in matters of birth and death, or to assist with a large life changing ordeal that is like a death and rebirth experience. He is not to be invoked for trivial matters. However, he is kind-hearted and enjoys being helpful when his help is needed.

The Lord of the Black, with the White Ravens, leads the ceremony of the dead performed once a year, where those who have died in the realm – or those who have died from outside the realm, who have loved ones in the realm – are named, and candles lit in their memories, and their souls honored, the veil between living and dead sundered for a time so people may speak with their beloved dead.

The Lord of the Black also (with Holda and Horn Father) leads Vanaheim's procession of the Wild Hunt in its seasons, guiding Ravens, Wolves, and Cats to collect the souls of the dying and guide them to peace, as well as perform "cleanup" with neutralizing any threats to Vanaheim and/or Midgard. The Wild Hunt embodies both mercy and severity, and the Lord of the Black is a living microcosm of this ride.

I most admire his compassion, his wisdom, his willingness to surrender to wyrd and allow wyrd to guide him from the flaming wreckage of a life he tried to cling to even as it was being smashed apart, into something new and beautiful.

The Lord of the Black is homoflexible, and has had partners of many genders, including transgendered and non-binary partners. As one who wields both Death and Life, souls are sacred to him regardless of sexual orientation or gender orientation or expression.

If one would honor him, one can best do so by living. Be grateful for your life. Try to make a difference in your corner of the world; be the change you wish to see in the world. Feel the wounds that have made you who you are, and know that we are all wounded at heart.

The Question of Heimdall

There are some who identify as Vanatru who feel very strongly that Heimdall is one of the Vanir, and some who feel that Heimdall is not Vanir at all. In a Vanic practice it is important to identify who is Vanir and who is not. So, we will explore who Heimdall is, and what it means for being counted among the Vanir:

Heimdallr is the name of one: he is called the White God. He is great and holy; nine maids, all sisters, bore him for a son. He is also called Hallinskídi (Bent Stick) and Gullintanni (Gold-Teeth); his teeth were of gold, and his horse is called Gold-top. He dwells in the place called Himinbjörg (Sky-Mountain) hard by Bifröst: he is the warder of the gods, and sits there by heaven's end to guard the bridge from the Hill-Giants. He needs less sleep than a bird; he sees equally well night and day a hundred leagues from him, and hears how grass grows on the earth or wool on sheep, and everything that has a louder sound. He has that trumpet which is called Gjallar-Horn, and its blast is heard throughout all worlds. Heimdallr's sword is called Head. It is said further:

> Himinbjörg 't is called, where Heimdallr, they say,
> Aye has his housing;
> There the gods' sentinel drinks in his snug hall
> Gladly good mead.

And furthermore, he himself says in Heimdalar-galðr:

> I am of nine mothers the offspring,
> Of sisters nine am I the son.
> **-Gylfaginning**

It is noted by H.R. Ellis Davidson that Þrymskviða 15 says "Then Heimdall spoke, whitest of the Æsir | Like the other Vanir he knew the future well." From this, we can infer a possible connection with the Vanir. There are also certain qualities Heimdall has that can be described as Vanic.

It's worth noting that one of Freya's names is Mardoll, which is similar to Heimdall, "Heim" means "home" and "Mar" is "sea", and the -doll/-dall suffix seems to mean "bright", so Mardoll would be "bright sea" and Heimdall would be "bright home". The connection with the sea in and of itself would also connect Freya to Heimdall. Indeed, Heimdall at one point fought with Loki for Freya's Brisingamen necklace, which is something a brother, relative, or close friend would do. And to further connect these deities with the sea, and possibly by blood, it is stated in Lokasenna that Njord had kinky sex with the nine daughters of Ran and Aegir, who are Heimdall's mothers:

> Be silent, Niörd!
> Thou wast sent eastward hence,
> a hostage from the gods.
> Hýmir's daughter had thee
> for a utensil,
> and flowed into thy mouth.
> **-Lokasenna**

Moreover, Heimdall has gold teeth, and the Vanes do indeed have a connection with all things gold, evidenced by Frey (boar, crops), Freya (Brisingamen), Sif (hair, crops), and Idunna (apples). Finally, his senses are noted as being the most acute of any deity, and the Vanir are not only very sensual but seem to notice the fine details in the bigger picture. He wields a sword, which is a weapon also wielded by Frey prior to giving it as Gerda's bride-price.

However, even with these characteristics present, there is also a case to be made that Heimdall is wholly of the Aesir. Here is more on Heimdall, from the Prose Edda:

> How should one periphrase Heimdallr? By calling him Son of Nine Mothers, or Watchman of the Gods, as already has been written; or White God, Foe of Loki, Seeker of Freya's Necklace. A sword is called Heimdalir's Head: for it is said that he was pierced by a man's head. The tale thereof is told in Heimdalar-galdr; and ever since a head is called Heimdallr's Measure; a sword is called Man's Measure. Heimdallr is the Possessor of Gulltoppr; he is also Frequenter of Vágasker and Singasteinn, where he contended with Loki for the Necklace Brisinga-men, he is also called Vindlér. Ùlfr Uggasòn composed a long passage in the Húsdrápa on that legend, and there it is written that they were in the form of seals. Heimdallr also is son of Odin.
> **-Skaldskaparsmal VIII.**

It explicitly states here that Heimdall is son of Odin. Of course, Snorri is also the same author who said the Norse gods are from Troy, and promoted the Adam and Eve creation story, and in one of his accounts Odin is Thor's father, in another Thor is Odin's father. So Snorri is not necessarily the most reliable source on lineage of deities, however it is noted in the Poetic Edda poem *Rigsthula*:

In ancient Sagas it is related that one of the Æsir named Heimdall, being on a journey to a certain sea-shore, came to a village, where he called himself Rig.

Rig is Heimdall, not Odin as some have erroneously claimed, and it makes sense that the warder of the Bifrost Bridge, between Midgard and Asgard, would be especially invested in humanity. Rig-Heimdall contributing to the societal structure strikes me as very Aesic, as the Vanir seem more egalitarian, when the population was a lot smaller and there was less diversity in what people did. Also, Heimdall's primary job as the warder of the Bifrost Bridge is also not characteristically Vanic, as it is not directly tied with the land or elements in some way but indeed is completely outside of them.

I don't get the "feeling" that Heimdall is Vanic, although I'm willing to concede a strong argument can be made either way for or against, and I'm also of the opinion that even if Heimdall is not one of the Vanir, he is well-loved by them, especially Freya. So, to call Heimdall with the Vanir in a Vanic-specific ritual, he gets along well with them, his general good will is compatible with Vanic energies and workings, and it is not as big of an issue as mistaking, say, Odin or Baldur as one of the Vanir.

Thoughts on the Thunderer

While Thor is typically classified as one of the Aesir, and many of his traits fall into what could be typed as Aesic functions, a number of Vanatruar still feel close to him and there is a school of thought in Vanatru that Thor was originally one of the Vanir. There is a lot of plausibility to this theory, and we shall explore this here.

While imagery of Aesic gods such as Odin and Tyr did not show up in the North until relatively late into its history, imagery associated with Thor has been in the North since the Neolithic period. This would be during the time when artifacts have been found pointing to an earlier "Vanic" religion - a religion of horticulture (small-scale farming) supplemented heavily by hunting and fishing, where society seemed more tribal and egalitarian, and known Vanic customs such as mound burials, wain processions, and sacrifice by bogging were done throughout northern and central Europe.

Most of the Vanir known to humans as gods are based in some form or phenomenon of nature. Nerthus is the Earth Mother, Njord is connected with the sea. Frey and Freya are connected with the birth, life death cycles of the land, plants as well as animals (and by extension, human animals). Thor is connected with thunder and lightning, which itself seemed to be a thing of reverence to ancient, animistic people. Those who grow crops for food know that the nitrogen in lightning strikes is one of the very best things for the soil.

There is yet more evidence that Thor may have originated as one of the Vanir. His mother is Jord, a name that literally means "Earth", and is related to "Nerthus", and is likely one and the same as Nerthus. While Jord is said to be a giant, Nerthus seems to be in that grey area between giants and Vanir (dating from a time when the Vanir and Jotnar were one species) and could conceivably be considered both. However, Snorri's account of Thor's parentage is suspect as he contradicts himself (giving one account of Thor as son of Odin, but also listing Odin as son of Thor).

Something a bit more concrete pointing to Thor as Vanir is that out of all of the Aesir, Thor is the only one to drive a wain, and have connections with domestic livestock animals (the goat) to boot. His wife, Sif, has golden hair symbolic of grain crops, and is herself thought to be one of the Vanir. Thor was the only one of the Aesir to have goðar (there are no accounts of Odin, Tyr, Baldur, or Heimdall having goðar in the primary sources, but Vanic deities like Frey did).

Finally, while the Vanir are often thought to be Indo-European fertility gods, there is much historical and archaeological evidence that points at their being pre-Indo-European, and the original gods of the Northlands, indeed with god-forms and customs spread throughout Europe. To further corroborate a pan-north/central European pre-Indo-European religion, all of the northern European (Celtic, Germanic, and Slavic/Baltic) pantheons have entities that look like the Vanir under different names pertaining to the language of the tribe. This includes Thor, who who was known to the Slavs as Perun and to the Celts as Taranis. Conversely, deities resembling Odin, Tyr, and Heimdall do not show up in other northern European pantheons; they are exclusive to the Germanic pantheon. After the Indo-European migrations, artifacts show the religion and its practices changed.

So, for all effective purposes, we can see that Thor had his origins with the Vanir. Why, then, are so many of his functions Aesic, and why is he killed with the other Aesir at the Ragnarok?

In the theory of this author, the proto-Germanic people, migrating westward from the Caucasus, had their own thunder god, originally known as Indra, and taking on new names/new features as there was migration and resulting changes to their culture. When the proto-Germanic people came to the Northlands, and gradually conquered this region, there were some elements of the original "Vanic" religion they did not stamp out, whether because there was resistance, or they thought it boonful to keep such practices for their new way of life (or both). The worship of the Thunderer was likely quite popular then as it is now, and it seems that the proto-Germanic invaders grafted elements of their thunder god onto the original thunder god, thus resulting in the new "improved" Asa-Thor – typified by his tool Mjolnir rather than his element, and made into a Divine policeman - and it was Asa-Thor who met the Vanic Sif, and she reminded him of home. It is the case that by his lot being thrown in with the Aesir, he will go down with them at the end of days.

It is probable that the original, pre-Aesic version of Thor was more of a general protector and helper, and the conflict with the giants came later (as there is no ongoing conflict between the Vanir and etins like there is between the Aesir and giants). Indeed, Slavic Perun and Celtic Taranis are not fighting against giants themselves.

Because of Thor's "Aesic functions", many Vanatruar have a hard time connecting with him as they do with other of the Aesir. However, for those Vanatruar who wish to honor Thor as one of the Vanir, it can be done, looking less at his role of "Divine policeman" towards the etins, and more of a personal protector, as well as a helper and friend, hallower, and luck-giver. In this way, Thor can be remembered as "part of the family".

Vanic Symbols

This is a quick reference for the construction of altars, websites, a choice of jewelry, design for artwork or even tattoos. One could even have a "Vanic Yule Tree" hung with ornaments of these symbols.

- **boar** - the primary sacred animal of Frey, Freya, and Nerthus.
- **wain** - Frey, Freya, Nerthus, and Holda were all said to have wagons or chariots.
- **ship** - Frey and Njord have ships, and Nehelennia is associated with ships also.
- **stag/antler** - Frey carries an antler, Ullr is associated with hunting, and Herne is antlered.
- **sunwheel** - for the changing of the seasons, and Frey, Freya, Njord, and Nerthus
- **Ing rune** - for Ing-Frey
- **Jera rune** - to symbolize the year and the cycles of growth and harvest
- **Fehu rune** - for prosperity, particularly as given by Frey and Freya
- **Wunjo rune** - for joy, and the fruitfulness and plenty of the Vanir
- **Uruz rune** - for Eir, or Nerthus; healing and strength as given by the Vanir
- **acorn** - The acorn, having a phallic shape, and being a seed, can be seen as a Frey "lingam".
- **walnuts/other nuts** - associated with Frey's fertility.
- **phallus** - Associated with the Frey cult.
- **seagull, albatross** - Njord's sacred birds.

- **footprint/s** - Njord's feet.
- **cats of all kinds** - a sacred animal of Freya.
- **cow/cattle** - a sacred animal of Nerthus.
- **wheat sheaf** - sacred to Frey and Nerthus, and possibly Sif, also to the Lord of Plenty.
- **fish, dolphins/porpoise** - sacred to Njord.
- **flax** - sacred to Holda.
- **goose** - sacred to Holda.
- **white feather** - associated with Holda.
- **corvid feathers** – associated with the Lord of the Black.
- **snowflake** - for Holda and Skadhi
- **dog** - sacred to Nehelennia.
- **wolf** - associated with Ullr and Skadhi.
- **bear** - some associate the bear with Ullr. The mount of the Lord of Plenty.
- **elk/stag** – The mount of the Fair Bright Queen.
- **cornucopia** - sacred to Nehelennia, and a general Vanic symbol of abundance.
- **swan** - sacred to Njord.
- **shells** - sacred to Njord and possibly Freya (as Mardoll).
- **bow** & arrow - Ullr's weapon of choice.
- **oath ring** - associated with Frey, Njord, and Ullr.
- **axe** - Njord's weapon of choice.
- **boar helm & shield** - symbolic of the Vanir as protective gods, and worn by tribes dedicated to Ing and Nerthus.
- **rowan tree** - sacred to Sif.
- **briar-rose** - associated with Holda.
- **white rose** – associated with the Fair Bright Queen.
- **corvid** - associated with Holda.

- **skull** - associated with Holda, also with the Lord of the Black.
- **apples** - sacred to Idunna.
- **eggs** - sacred to Eostre.
- **hares** - sacred to Eostre.
- **goldenrod** - sacred to Sif
- **various berries, especially blackberry/elderberry** - associated with Holda, and possibly Nerthus.
- **bees** - associated with Frey through Byggvir and Beyla.
- **snowshoes** - worn by Ullr and Skadhi.
- **yew tree** - sacred to Ullr.
- **mountains** - Skadhi's preferred place of residence.
- **ocean wave** - Njord's element.
- **flame** - for Gullveig.
- **sword** - carried by Frey before giving it up to carry an antler. Weapon of choice of the Lord of Plenty.
- **spear** - associated with Gullveig.
- **wand** - for Frey or Gullveig.
- **trident** – weapon of choice of the Fair Bright Queen.
- **pine tree** - associated with the Vanir and the most common tree in Vanaheim ("Eshnahai" means "evergreen"), and shared UPG also connects it with Frey and Ullr
- **oak tree/leaf** – sacred to the Fair Bright Queen. Also several Vanatruar associate Frey with the oak tree.
- **ash tree** – sacred to the Lord of Plenty.
- **horse** - horses were traditionally kept in Frey's honor.
- **bells** - bells were traditionally worn by Frey's priests.

- **anvil** - associated with Wayland Smith.
- **sickle** - associated with Nerthus.
- **birch** - sacred to Nerthus (and possibly Holda).
- **broom or rake** - associated with Holda.
- **scales** - associated with the Lord of the Black as Keeper of Time.
- **hourglass** - also associated with the Lord of the Black.
- **sun** - for Sunna or Dagr
- **moon** - for Mani or Nott
- **star** - for Nott or Star Mother
- **vegvisir** – the personal seal of the Lord of Plenty
- **aegishjalmur** – the personal seal of the Fair Bright Queen

Vanic Deity Correspondences

The following is a list of correspondences for specific deities counted as Vanir by modern Vanic pagans; the items on this list have been corroborated amongst a few who work with the Vanir. These things can be gifted a deity and/or placed on their altar, or worn, or carried, etc.

Items marked with an asterisk * are dangerous or deadly and should be handled carefully, kept out of reach of children and pets, and never ingested.

Star Mother
Colors: black, silver, dark blue
Minerals: meteorite iron, moonstone, silver
Food: the heart organ, particularly a meal of hearts made from different kinds of food animals
Drink: Milk, water, jasmine tea
Incense/Oils: myrrh
Plants/Herbs: all night-blooming flowers* (datura and mandrake are poisonous)
Items: stars, planets, sky-discs
Deeds: teach a child about space, adopt a star, watch a meteor shower, sit out overnight (in a safe place) and meditate

Horn Father
Colors: black, dark greens, brown
Minerals: petrified wood, jet, smoky quartz, black tourmaline, flint, obsidian, green jasper
Food: game (particularly venison)
Drink: spring water
Incense/oils: musk, patchouli, dragon's blood

Plants/herbs: aconite*, clove, sage, valerian
Items: antler, bone, fossils
Deeds: adopt a wild place and take care of it, be yourself free of expectations, nurture the wildness/innocence within, hunt an animal you would use for food

Nehelennia
Colors: blue, green, brown
Minerals: labradorite, iolite, lodestone
Food: Fish (Atlantic cod, sole, haddock, flounder, plaise, eel, whiting, Pollock; native fish to Europe or your bioregion), fruit (particularly those in season during June/July), honey, exotic/traded spices
Drink: Fresh water, honey drinks, ale, cider, apple and orange juices
Incense/Oils: ambergris, pine, apple
Plants/herbs: horehound, elecampane
Items: compass, miniature/model ship, statue/artwork of a dog, stone/concerete altar with inscription, corncucopia, basketry
Deeds: build a concrete or stone altar with an inscription in her honor, care for a dog, clean up a roadway/highway

Gullveig
Colors: gold, red, black
Minerals: pyrite, mahogany obsidian, hematite
Food: red apple, pomegranate
Drink: red wine, aquavit, Goldschlager
Incense/oils: dragon's blood
Plants/herbs: wormwood, belladonna*
Items: wand, sword, spear, magic books, feathers (especially swan feathers), gold coins or objects made of gold (especially jewelry)

Deeds: help an abuse victim, rescue animals, learn defensive magic or martial arts, mentor

Holda
Colors: white, blue, purple, black
Minerals: kyanite, jet, amethyst, onyx
Food: apple, elder/goose/black/raspberries, cakes and pies, herring, porridge, goose
Drink: milk, spring water, Black Haus, German beers/ales (artisan), elderberry juice/elderflower pressé
Incense/Oils: Myrrh, copal, rose, vetivert, musk
Plants/herbs: Cinquefoil, mandrake*, broom, vervain, flax, nettle, Monk's Hood*
Items: miniature brooms (made the old way), textiles, sugar skulls
Deeds: clean your home, cook food, practice fiber arts, walk in the snow, make an ancestor altar, help an orphan, practice witchcraft

Idunna/Eostre
Colors: pale green, red, gold, brown, orange
Minerals: pearl, red tourmaline, watermelon tourmaline, carnelian
Food: eggs, apples, pears, chicken, rabbit, edible flowers
Drink: milk, honey wine, apple juice or cider
Incense/oils: jasmine, vanilla, lilac
Plants/herbs: lilac, tulip, daffodil, lily of the valley, apple blossom (Idunna), poppies (Habondia)
Items: rabbits (statues/art), sunrises (pictures/art), flowers, cornucopia, basketry, wreaths
Deeds: plant or harvest a garden, feed others, make people smile, share resources, adopt/care for a rabbit, help the old feel young again

Nerthus
Colors: white, dark green, brown, black, earth tones
Minerals: obsidian, jet, jade, serpentine, gold, moss agate, chalcedony
Food: beef, pork, fish, duck or goose, bread, root vegetables, "bog" berries (cran, blue, bil, etc.), pomegranate
Drink: milk, spring water, stout, brandy, blood*
Incense: patchouli, frankincense, kyphi, sandalwood, musk, clove, water/forest blends
Plants/herbs: birch, mugwort, lavender, myrtle, cattails, reeds
Items: reed/rush/corn dolls, pottery, landscape art, cows
Deeds: clean up a natural place, set up a shrine/altar outdoors, donate to environmental causes, become a "nature" activist, protect the weak/less fortunate

Njord
Colors: blue, white, green, grey, gold
Minerals: ocean agate, ocean jasper, sodalite, amazonite, glass, petrified wood
Food: fish, seafood, biscuits, exotic/traded spices and delicacies
Drink: rum (particularly spiced)
Incense/oils: "ocean", rain, lavender, pine, cedar
Plants/herbs: seaweed, salt-water reeds, driftwood
Items: fishing net, boathooks, miniature/model boats, starfish, shells, sea glass, stones smoothed by the sea
Deeds: help clean up the beach, play with dolphins, go fishing, teach a child about the ocean

Sif
Colors: gold, green
Minerals: citrine, jade

Food: bread, pork, goat, root vegetables, gourds, wheat berries
Drink: ale, beer, honey wine
Incense/oils: amber, sweetgrass
Plants/herbs: goldenrod, St John's Wort, sunflower, wheat, rowan, corn
Items: flail & scythe; hair brush, comb (especially an ornate comb of bone or silver), veil, cauldron, fan
Deeds: help a farmer harvest his crop, connect with family/loved ones, learn divination or oracular work

Skadhi
Colors: white, blue
Minerals: howlite, flint
Food: game, all pickled foods
Drink: Jagermeister, brandy, scotch, vodka
Incense/oils: pine, spruce
Plants/herbs: evergreen needles
Items: wolves (statue/art), warm clothing (boots, gloves, etc.)
Deeds: hunt, learn about wild foods and forage, hike in the woods

Ullr
Colors: black, green, brown
Minerals: jasper, obsidian, bloodstone
Food: game, all pickled foods
Drink: Jagermeister, brandy, scotch
Incense/oils: pine, musk
Plants/herbs: evergreen needles, yew*
Items: arrowheads, bones
Deeds: hunt, learn about wild foods and forage, hike in the woods, keep an oath

Wayland

Colors: red, orange, grey
Minerals: iron, glass, ceramics, hematite
Food: anything beautifully put together
Drink: scotch
Incense/oils: dragon's blood
Plants/herbs: Nettle, Elm
Items: art, handicrafts, anvil/hammer, constructed wings (especially if wrought from gold, or golden in color)
Deeds: make something, learn blacksmithing, overcome a near-insurmountable obstacle

Eir

Colors: white, grey, beige
Minerals: fluorite, clear quartz
Food: fresh fruit and vegetables
Drink: spring water, milk, white wine
Incense/oils: myrrh, bergamot, mint, eucalyptus*
Plants/herbs: marshmallow, any herb that can be used for healing
Items: mortar and pestle
Deeds: care for a sick person, learn herbalism/energy healing, watch own health

Gerda

Colors: burgundy, eggplant, dark green, brown, black
Minerals: amethyst, garnet, obsidian
Food: She will eat whatever Frey eats.
Drink: She will drink whatever Frey is given, though she has a preference for vodka.
Incense/oils: lavender, chamomile, mint, rosemary
Plants/herbs: lavender, mugwort, vervain, catnip, mint, ivy
Items: cat statues, stones

Deeds: grow an herb garden, reduce the amount of words you use in a day and listen more, spend time with oneself

Frey

Colors: gold, green, brown
Minerals: amber, bloodstone, citrine, smithsonite, moqui marbles, agate, horn
Food: pork, root vegetables, bread, cherries
Drink: ale, honey wine, Goldschlager, metheglin (herbed mead), cider
Incense/Oils: amber, patchouli, musk
Plants/herbs: lemon verbena, cinnamon, sunflower
Items: gold coins, boar and horse figurines, an oath ring, phallic symbols, greenery, a sword
Deeds: plant a tree and/or garden and tend to it, spend time outdoors in nature, spend time with animals, compost, recycle

Freya

Colors: gold, red, green, purple
Minerals: amber, bloodstone, jade, lapidolite, moonstone, pearls, rose quartz
Food: strawberries, peaches, chocolate, fish, pork, pastries, edible flowers
Drink: chocolate liqueur, honey wine, cognac, punch/lemonade, rose hip tea
Incense/Oils: rose, jasmine, orange blossom
Plants/herbs: rose, violets, hemp, saffron, catnip
Items: necklace, amber, cat statues
Deeds: spend time with cats, help cats in some way, teach magic

Frodi

Colors: green, yellow, orange, lavender

Minerals: citrine, moss agate

Food: fruit and vegetables (especially that which you have grown yourself, or grows in your locale), pies, bread, pork, fish

Drink: melomels (fruit mead), wine, lemonade or other fruit drinks

Incense/Oils: lemongrass, orange blossom

Plants/herbs: orange blossom, apple blossom, cherry blossom

Items: tree branches

Deeds: plant trees, brew mead, bake bread, do something kind for one's elders

The Lord of the Black

Colors: Black, purple, white, silver

Minerals: obsidian, onyx, jet, black kyanite, smoky quartz, black tourmaline, blue tiger's eye, bone

Food: dark chocolate, bread, sea salt, raw meat and/or the blood, the eyes of a butchered/hunted animal

Drink: wine, water

Incense/Oils: dragon's blood, frankincense, "opium"

Plants/herbs: tobacco, sage, lavender, sandalwood, frankincense, myrrh

Items: raven or crow feathers, corvids (statue/art), skulls, bones, urns, glass vials filled with curious objects, quill pen and ink

Deeds: honor ancestors, remember the dead, visit hospices

The Fair Bright Queen

Colors: White, silver, indigo, plum

Minerals: selenite, moonstone, pearls, aquamarine

Food: sweets, pastries, fruit
Drink: mead, buttered rum, vodka + juice
Incense/Oils: lavender, violet, rose, copal
Plants/herbs: oak trees, white or deep purple roses, lavender, lilies, violets, lilacs, magnolias
Items: keys, ceramic pottery, chalices and cups, beautiful glass objects, hats, scarves, jewelry
Deeds: make art, express love for loved ones, queer/trans activism, gardening, communing with nature, personal growth/healing (especially rejecting the conformity of society and becoming more yourself)

The Lord of Plenty
Colors: green, gold, red
Minerals: amber, peridot, emerald, orange calcite, labradorite, citrine
Food: bacon, cheese, lamb, venison, fish, root vegetables, grain
Drink: Scotch whisky is preferred, mead is acceptable
Incense/Oils: sandalwood, vanilla, sage, juniper
Plants/herbs: ash trees, holly, heather, thistle, juniper, cinnamon, clove, grain crops, vegetables especially phallic-shaped (e.g. zucchini)
Items: swords, knives, gold coins or gold objects, ornate chests for holding precious things, lamps and lanterns, torcs, crowns, dragons (statue/art), bells
Deeds: gardening, taking care of family (by blood or by choice), martial arts, standing up for what you believe in, hard work (especially to help friends or loved ones with a task)

Beyond the Powers: The World of Vanaheim

As mentioned at the beginning of this book, the Vanir are more than the Big Name Deities, such as Frey, Freya, Njord, and Nerthus. Vanaheim is an entire realm, full of people, the overwhelming majority of whom were never named by lore. This doesn't mean they're unimportant, as we will revisit in a moment. I also understand the Vanir to be elves (corroborated by others), and in private conversations I prefer referring to them as elves (or Eshnahai, which is their own name for their people, "Vanir" is an outlander's term), though they are not the same entities as the Ljossalfar and Dokkalfar (who are related, but ultimately their own people).

While much has been made about these entities as fertility-oriented, this is oversimplifying them at best. These wights oversee and influence life and death cycles. That includes fertility - the birth and healthy development of land and what lives upon it - but it also means taking tribute. "The Lord giveth and taketh away" is not just a concept limited to monotheistic religion. Life feeds on life.

CULTURE AND BIOLOGY

Vanic elves tend to be on the tall side (with notable exceptions), with expressive eyes and pointy ears, and are usually very beautiful to look at, and move gracefully, even and especially during combat (whether with weapons or magic). These beings relate to us as kin, and have said they had a hand in shaping this world, and continue to influence this world, as we influence them. Their realm is inextricably tied to and superimposed upon this realm. In some ways, it is like a parallel version of Earth, but without the dramatic regional and biological diversity. Most of the realm resembles northern continental Europe with regards to terrain, flora and fauna, and seasonal changes. It is heavily forested (albeit with some "highlands" and "plains" areas), and there is ocean to the east and south, and in the upper northwest. The population is in the tens of thousands.

There are a series of menhirs and stangs (tall poles) across the landscape, which other visitors have concurred. The standing stones serve as portals into the realm from elsewhere, but are also empowered to affect the energy of an area. The stangs serve as portals within the realm, such as going from one tribal territory to another. One can usually tell what tribal territory they are in by looking at how the stang is decorated. Most of the stangs are also watched by a tribal guardian, even if the traveller is never aware of their presence lurking in the area.

The most important feature of culture within the realm is that it is organized tribally. The tribal structure operates rather like a large eco-system, with each tribe and clan important to the health of the realm as a whole - each tribe has its own special purpose, as well as its own particular form of magic. Some tribes have villages, some are more scattered through their territory.

In addition to the work that they do within the realm for their own land and people, Eshnahai usually have ties to specific human families/people for various reasons (often, due to having taken human consorts and keeping track of those family lines of wyrd and incarnation); some of them do "walk between worlds" and serve as genius locii here, guardians/keepers of specific patches of forest, rivers, waterfalls, fields, etc, some of them do both; some of them moved here permanently and visit home occasionally.

With regards to the different tribes of Vanaheim, the tribes each have an animal totem, and people within that tribe can take the form of that tribe's totem at will. Thus, Cat folk can shapeshift into cats, Ravens into ravens, Wolves into wolves, and so on. In addition, each tribe has a specific "look" to it, in terms of preferred hairstyle, dress, and accessories, and it is common for someone's appearance to start changing as well - for example, the Ravens are pretty universally black-haired, but not everyone who gets sorted into that tribe looks like that initially; the Fox tribe tends to have reddish/auburn hair regardless of skin color; the Wolves have locks.

There are 24 main tribes, which most people are sorted into when they come of age. These tribes are: Serpent, Raven, Wolf, Cat, Hare, Bear, Bee, Bull, Deer, Fox, Ram, Salmon, Spider, Swan, Squirrel, Horse, Eagle, Owl, Seal, Frog, Goose, Crane, Otter, and Boar. There are also several mystery cults, which are much more select in their membership, and much more secretive about their activities, mostly involving the magic they work on behalf of the realm and/or to "push the wheel of the year" along. The White Ravens are a mystery cult hosted/sponsored by the Ravens, and the Dragons are a mystery cult hosted/sponsored by the Serpents, as two notable examples.

There is a fair amount of interaction and intermarriage between the tribes - for example, a number of Wolves tend to marry Hares. A child is typically raised in the tribe of their mother, but otherwise seen as a "blank slate" and not sorted until they come of age. Some children do wind up being sorted into one of their parents' tribes, but not everyone does. The one tribe that seems to consistently marry among its own and produce offspring that belong to the same tribe is the Serpents, who are notoriously insular and secretive.

All the tribes are represented at a parliament by two members from each tribe elected by the tribe, and the government is headed by a prime minister and secretary of state; they also have a secretary of defense and a military. The role of the king and queen of the realm is purely sacral/religious in nature, mating for the fertility of the land as the wheel turns. The parliament meets at the realm's capital, which also has a marketplace, a ritual space, temples (sacral brothels), inns and pubs, and some other spaces, many of which are maintained by people who chose to live outside of their tribal territory for one reason or another. The capital is probably the safest place for an outlander to journey, if they wanted to.

HISTORY

I was told by my Vanic spirit companions and other Vanic contacts that initially, elves and giants used to be the same species, and there was a split, mainly disagreeing over how to deal with humanity – those who became "Jotnar" saw the humans as prey, those who became "Vanir" saw the humans as kin and felt compelled to help them.

Following the split, energy modifications were made in both species, which is why (as one example) elves tend to be allergic to iron/steel (with exceptions) and giants regard it as a power source (i.e. the Iron Wood). There are a few elven tribes which have counterparts in the giants' Otherworld, such as the Wolf, Raven, Eagle and Serpent tribes, and serve as a reminder of when they were one people, even if the tribes have differing customs (and perspectives) now. A couple of the Vanic tribes, such as the Serpents and Ravens, have cordial relations and an exchange with their Iron Wood counterparts.

There have been two civil wars in Vanaheim: the first was approximately 10,000-9000 years ago, following the split from the Jotnar and when the Boars took control from the Serpents following the split, wherein a large number of Vanic elves exiled, and the entire Squirrel tribe was slaughtered.

The biggest group of exiles came to be known in mythology as Ljossalfar; they made some modifications to their culture, biology, and so on (they did away with the animal tribes, and replaced the animal tribal system with seasonal courts - the Summer Court, the Spring Court, etc). The Vanir and Ljossalfar are on friendly terms and allies to an extent, but nobody wants a reunification, they are content with being separate realms and separate ways of doing things.

The "Svartalfar" is a catch-all term which a lot of people think means "dark elves", but the Eshnahai interpret this less literally and more as "dark" in the sense of "elven exiles they lost track of, and thus have 'gone dark'". Most of them went out to make new realms or live as immigrants in extant realms connected to Midgard (this world), which accounts for some of the elven population here that's not members of the "core realm" in Vanaheim. So "Svartalfheim" is less of a singular realm, and more like a multitude of different realms of elven exiles, most of whom have business in Midgard. One of the groups of elves did retain the name Eshnahai, and according to the personal gnosis of a few individuals, settled near the Silver

City, the land of the Abrahamic angels, and some of the Eshnahai and angels intermarried and produced offspring, but the Eshnahai and half-Eshnahai encountered some racial prejudice among the angels.

The Dokkalfar or drow are a notable group of exiles, who were approximately 90% Ravens (with some other tribes, most notably the Spiders), then bred with dragons, and once exiled, got a very bad reputation as baby-thieves and sexual predators, however this reputation is undeserved and is only true of a small segment of their population (and there is an undesirable criminal element among any species); the same rumors were told of the Eshnahai among the Dokkalfar for a long time! Currently both groups are working on improving relations and possibly forming an alliance. The Dokkalfar are certainly a bit more "warlike" than the Eshnahai and those who choose to work with them should proceed with caution, but are not evil as rumor has it.

The second civil war took place in 2012 and was a long time in coming, where there was an attempt at genocide with the tribes who dealt more in death (especially Ravens and Wolves) to "clean up reputation and public relations". Following a truce, the realm temporarily (for approximately a year and a half) split into East and West. The West side of Vanaheim was more of an equal share of power while the East side of Vanaheim was ruled by the Boar and Eagle tribes.

Following the split in the realm, some of the Bulls and Rams went to the West side and some remained allied with the East side and the Boars; the Cats and Deer were originally allied with the West, but a small handful of Cats and Deer went to the East due to allegiance to the Boar crown, leaving the rest of the tribe behind in the West. While the West side had more tribes, the East side was more numerous in population (several of the tribes in the West are very small).

In July 2013, a year after the end of the second civil war and the split in the realm, the Owl tribe decided they wanted neutrality. After being given an assurance by the West that the West would defend a neutral zone if the East side threatened it in any way, five other tribes of the East joined the Owls in declaring intent to build a neutral zone - Owl, Crane, Frog, Goose, Otter, and Seal. Meetings were set up on the East and West sides to discuss the formation of a neutral zone; in addition to six unarmed diplomats from the southeastern tribes, one member of the Western government went to represent the West with a bodyguard, and members of the Bear, Bee, Salmon, Fox and Deer tribes also went from the West as observers, unarmed, and members of the Eagle and Horse tribes of the East also attended the Eastern meeting as observers. While multiple precautions were taken, the East side meeting still ended badly, with Boars and East-aligned Bulls murdering the six southeastern diplomats, attacking the West side observers, and assaulting the West side representative and his guard. Action was taken, and a military strike threatened on the East side if a formal apology and weregild to the families of the deceased and injured was not offered, as well as demanding that the Boars and Bulls who participated in the attack and the one/s who orchestrated it be delivered for capital punishment by the West.

Not only did the Owl, Crane, Frog, Goose, Otter and Seal tribes decide to dispense altogether with the notion of neutrality and join the East, but the Horse and Eagle tribes - who had been closely allied with the Boars during the second civil war, and the Eagles had a position of authority in the East – said "enough" and also defected to the West save a number of Boar loyalist diehards. The balance had tipped and the East was now outnumbered, and the west also has multiple inter-pantheon allies who were willing to intervene in a military strike, so the East recognized it was in their best interests to comply. Many of the Boar tribe were disgusted by the actions of their fellow tribesmen and also defected to the West.

As of August 2013, all tribes were represented on the West side; the East side retained some of the Boars, Cats, Eagles, Horses, Bulls, and Rams, but not the entirety of these tribes. In late 2013 peace talks began between East and West and a treaty and reunification was achieved.

Currently Vanaheim has a parliamentary government, where all tribes are represented by two delegates from every tribe that are elected by the tribe; the Prime Minister (who is elected by the parliament) can be from any tribe, in addition to the Secretary of State and Secretary of Defense (appointed by the Prime Minister). The current King and Queen are Serpent and Dragon affiliated, and while their opinion on official affairs holds some weight and they engage in diplomacy with other realms, their role is mostly ceremonial in nature, and it would be erroneous to call the Serpents or any other tribe within Vanaheim the "ruling tribe" at this point in time.

In addition to the civil wars, the realm has been invaded once, during the notorious Aesir-Vanir war, and there has also been an influx of problematic tourists since that time, most particularly post-conversion-era and with the modern resurgence of paganism.

Because of this, Eshnahai tend to be suspicious of outlanders as a rule, and this includes humans. This is not universal - the younger generation is a bit more trusting (that doesn't mean naive, gullible, or completely trusting and not suspicious, however), whereas the older generation (especially those who were there at the Aesir-Vanir war) is a bit more wary. Most elves will warm up to an outlander given time, and hospitality is a rule of the Vanir regardless. Eshnahai are particularly likely to be more welcoming if they know you want to respectfully learn of their culture and ways, and help re-weave and strengthen bonds between our people and realms.

THE HEART OF THE PEOPLE

Sex and relationships in general are a primary concern to the Vanic elves, most of whom are bisexual and polyamorous and have large families (however there are heterosexual and homosexual Eshnahai, monogamous Eshnahai, asexual Eshnahai and those who choose celibacy for whatever reason). Most elves are fond of their extended families and regularly visit with cousins and other relatives, and certain clans are known for having certain aptitudes, even if people within a clan are sorted into different tribes. Elves love children and to hurt a child is seen as one of the greatest crimes a person can commit. For all that the elves are open about their sexuality, it is within strong boundaries. Sex crimes are virtually unheard of - elves believe strongly in consent and free will and the right and ability to choose, and respect the autonomy of other people's bodies and space.

The Eshnahai have what could be considered their own religion on their plane, where they do celebrate the moon tides and seasonal cycles, and do workings to bless their land, and push that blessing out into the human realm, to their kin and to places in the human realm they are fond of. They do not have any Higher Powers that are worshiped among them as gods, but do casually revere Star Mother and Horn Father, the creators of all; in addition, they are animists and reverent of the terrain and flora and fauna, the sun and moon and the elements, and often express gratitude for these things, and exchange energy with them. There are entities such as Frey, Njord, and Nerthus who hold important jobs in maintaining ties with this realm, but they are seen more as royal family or government, rather than being worshiped by their fellow elves.

Ultimately, the line between a god and an elf is very thin as to be nonexistent - beings who were named in lore as gods are certainly very powerful, with many followers giving them energy, but "mere" elves have ability to manipulate wyrd, they have agency in this world, and most of them serve as guardians/keepers of regions in this realm, or as personal guardian or companion spirits, in addition to having their lives in the Otherworld.

What seems to characterize the elves more than anything else is an awareness and reverence of interconnectedness. Even those who deal more with death energy still understand the role of death within the life cycle, how a death of a creature impacts the world around it, and that life necessarily feeds on life. The sexual intensity of most of the Vanir could be said to be a sort of lust for life itself, being fully alive and feeling connected with all things, each sexual act seen as a microcosm of the unfolding of the Universe, and of the living, dying, and rebirth cycles of the land. It should be pointed out however that there is more to the Vanir and Vanaheim than sex, and so asexuals and others should not feel that there is no place for them with the Vanic elves - they are understanding of others' boundaries and differences.

Again, what characterizes the Vanir most is a general lust for life and a sense of interconnectedness, and so while sex is a way to honor and commune with them, they can also be fellowshiped with in other ways - art, poetry, stories, song and dance, enjoying the beauty of nature, sharing good food together, laughter, non-sexual sensuality and intimacy. A *joie de vivre* and appreciating the pleasures of life is just as "Vanic" as anything sexual.

The Tribes of Vanaheim

THE BEAR TRIBE

The Bear tribe occupies a forested territory in south-central Vanaheim and are a clan of warriors and hunters, working both solitary and in groups. Bears are part of Vanaheim's military, and have sometimes assisted the Wolves with policing duties, particularly with regards to tracking and finding missing people or where extra brawn is needed.

Tribal Structure

The Bear tribe is led by a single Bear, currently a male who will answer to Lord Bear; the leader is chosen by battling every single member of the tribe, and can be ousted if bested in battle. Both men and women have led the Bear tribe; Lord Bear has a large harem and family.

The Bears are nowhere near as hierarchical as the Wolves, and indeed, apart from Lord Bear inspiring warriors and helping to train them, the tribe is fairly egalitarian. Anyone can become the ruler of the Bear tribe if they fight their way there.

Bear Culture

As mentioned above, the Bears tend to be both solitary- and group-oriented. It is common for Bears to train and hunt solitary, as well as work together in groups. The Bears, like the Foxes, are very family oriented and tend to have extremely large families. It is very common for a Bear household to have spouses from different tribes and many offspring who are themselves sorted into different tribes.

Bears tend to favor cabins to live in. Bears are not nearly as friendly and approachable as the Foxes, preferring to keep to themselves and their families. Bears can also be territorial even with their other tribesmembers. Within their space Bears are as particular as the Hares about food, and as prone to enjoying sweet and savory food. They are, like the Hares, fond of creature comforts and coziness.

Making Allies with Bears

It is generally inadvisable to approach Bears, and instead better to have them make contact with you. They are everything from surly to outright aggressive if you are in their space and you don't have a prior appointment or invitation.

When Bears do work with humans, it is usually to train them as warriors, not just physically but psychologically. The Bears are fond of humans who they see as having potential but that potential has been broken by society; they make these folk into their pet projects, challenging them and getting them stronger.

If you work with a Bear, they are fond of honey, rare meat (and especially game/venison), whisky, pipe tobacco, and warm fires (candles are acceptable). They enjoy sparring, and are fond of rough sex if one becomes that way with them.

THE BEE TRIBE

The Bees are the closest thing to a monastic community that Vanaheim has. They live in a large hive structure in south-central Vanaheim, bordering Bear territory.

Tribal Structure

The Bees live and work together with a Queen and spend their time chanting, making the threads of wyrd hum, making the surrounding threads resonate. They are also "conductors", carrying messages to the Powers, and from the Powers to the people (when the Powers are busy). The Bees are not hierarchical; all serve the Queen Bee and are otherwise considered equals from newest to eldest.

Bee Culture

The Bees tend to work in shifts - working within the Hive to chant and work magic upon the threads of wyrd, and out in the open in Bee territory to transmit messages back and forth.

The Bees sometimes mate with their own tribesmates, sometimes intermarry with other tribes. In the case of inter-tribal marriage, the Bee partner tends to live with the other Bees at the Hive and will visit their partner and family during "down time"; the Bee will usually trade custodial responsibilities with an outside partner.

The Bees are very fond of adornment, and are among the most elaborately dressed Vanir.

The Bees are masters of group ritual and the entire Hive (which is one of the largest tribes within Vanaheim) has often worked together on the seasonal holytides for blessing of the tribe as well as the realm as a whole.

Beyla (one of Frey's assistants, and the one who transmits messages directly to and from Frey when he is busy) is Bee tribe, and loves all of Frey's people.

Making Allies with Bees

The Bees are one of the friendliest tribes within Vanaheim, and love being helpful. The Bees are good at teaching the art of meditation as well as chant/vocal magic, and the art of magical prayer.

The Bees appreciate offerings of honeyed alcohol, honey itself, flowers (especially edible flowers) and fruit. They also love receiving jewelry as gifts, and are fond of fine incense and pretty lights.

The Bees are busy, so if you have a Bee guide it may be awhile between visits. This is normal and doesn't mean you're doing anything wrong. Bees can be sexual with humans without getting too attached and expecting marriage, though they are less finicky and flighty than the Cats. Bees are fond of orgies, so if you take on a Bee guide and begin sexual relations with them, don't be surprised if they want to add more to make it the merrier. You can always say "no", but the Vanir have a reputation as amazing lovers for a reason!

While the Bees are friendly and love being helpful, do remember that they can sting, so be careful to remain on their good side (general protocol for dealing with the Eshnahai will be mentioned later in this book). Thankfully they are hard to offend and fairly easy-going.

THE BOAR TRIBE

The Boar tribe were, until recently, the ruling tribe of Vanaheim. (The current king and queen have Boar lineage but are not Boar affiliated.) They took control from the Serpents about nine thousand years ago. The Boars are a class of warrior priests, enacting rites of blood, sex, and death for the fertility and healing of the land.

Tribal Structure

The Boar tribe is currently led by Frey, with his father Njord in an advisory position. The Boars have a council of twelve elders who make decisions on behalf of the tribe. The Boars are fairly insular and most people who are born into the Boar tribe stay in the Boar tribe, and very few people are ever sorted into the Boar tribe when they come of age. The Boars are, despite male leadership, fairly egalitarian as the Vanir tend to be, and every man, woman, and child is taught how to read, write, bear arms, hunt, and do magic. The Boars are a mid-sized tribe, not one of the largest but not necessarily a small tribe either.

Boar Culture

The Boars are extremely hierarchical and have an entire set of social codes and honor codes that can seem outright baffling to tribal outsiders never mind outlanders. The Boars are also the tribe, other than Bulls, that an outlander tourist is most likely to encounter if they are just "going to Vanaheim" without a specific destination in mind (which I don't necessarily recommend doing) as the Boars tend to be stereotypical of what people think the Vanir are, right down to dressing in Norse Viking garb and having mead halls and stave buildings. The Boars also tend to have elaborate hairstyles and are especially fond of amber jewelry.

Making Allies with Boars

Like all Vanir, the Boars are fond of good food and good drink. Give them the very best of what you have if you are planning on entertaining them; you may also want to perform song and poetry for them. The Boars can also be gifted with amber, Viking-style jewelry (but no Mjolnirs, that's an Aesir thing), drinking horns, and leatherworked items.

The Boars are very invested in the good of Midgard and helping humanity to grow and evolve, and if they sense potential in you to be a force for good in the world, they may offer to mentor you. The Boars are particularly interested in those of a "warrior priest" type disposition and enjoy training leaders, but you will be tested and challenged past your comfort zones. The Boars have much to teach about sacral leadership, sacrifice, and personal strength and power. Your conduct must be impeccable when you are working with a Boar, or they will really get on your case about it.

If a Boar enters into a romantic/sexual relationship with you, it is not something to undertake lightly. Many of the Eshnahai do casual sex and that's part of the culture; not so much with Boars. Everything for Boars is serious business and if they are sexually interested in you, there are ulterior motives beyond just wanting to get down your pants. Remember that you always have the right to say no.

A final word: the Boars as a tribe spent the better part of nine thousand years abusing their power and are now trying to repair the damage done to both Vanaheim and Midgard. Boars have much to teach and offer, but they are not infallible. It is vitally important if you work with a Boar to be mindful of standing your ground and not allowing yourself to be pushed around or roped into things that you're not 100% sure of what you're getting into. This will in fact be a lesson they will require you to learn if you work with a Boar mentor, and it is important with any spirits, but particularly this tribe. The Boars have a lot of blood on their hands, but they are paying their debts. Another lesson to be had from the Boars is restitution and second chances and making things right, which is not always a lesson people want to learn.

THE BULL TRIBE

The Bull tribe are one of the most numerous tribes of Vanaheim, located in the center of Vanaheim. They are the most like what people's expectations are of the Vanir – a tribe of farmers who are also warriors, living in rich farmland and performing rites of sex and blood sacrifice for the fertility of that land – and indeed, are the Vanir that tourists from Midgard are most likely to encounter when journeying to Vanaheim. Byggvir, one of Frey's servants, hails from this tribe.

With regards to being warrior-priests whose daily lives are bound in agriculture, they are most like the Boars, and work closely with them.

Tribal Structure

Leadership of the Bull tribe is hereditary in nature and is a lifetime position; the current chieftain, Tarron, is the grandson of the previous chieftain, who was chieftain for a great many thousand years and only more recently retired. The chieftain is the official spokesperson of the tribe and consults with a council of twenty-four elders of varying ages and genders on tribal matters. Said elders are elected by their tribe per region of the Bull territory and every four years their position is up for renewal and they have a challenger. In this regard the Bulls feel their tribe is more of a democracy, where everyone has a chance to help govern their tribe, and the leadership is treated with respect but is not an absolute authority, and indeed beyond a few laws, the Bulls are very free.

Bull Culture

As soon as a Bull joins the tribe after being sorted and coming of age, the Bulls enter warrior training. This is true irrespective of gender or levels of physical ability; even those who are disabled in some way have the potential to become great warriors, and indeed one of the most famous of the Bull warriors was blind and learned to rely on his other senses in battle.

All Bulls are required to bear arms, which are only lay down at seasonal rituals as a symbolic gesture of peace, or when they are visiting the temples within Vanaheim where no weapons may be brought in. Many Bulls are proud of their weapons, giving them names, and enjoy showing them off to visitors. A good many weapons carried by Bulls are family heirlooms, such as a spear or sword belonging to one's grandparent or great-great-grandparent. Bulls are also fond of ornate weapons that are as beautiful as they are functional. A Bull brings their weapon "to life" by letting it taste their blood.

The elders and chieftain perform seasonal rituals on behalf of the tribe. There are eight seasonal festivals within Vanaheim where the population as a whole celebrates at the capital with the King and Queen, and then the Bull tribe has their own separate ritual specific to the tribe during that week also. This is also true of the three days of the full moon – as the King and Queen mate in the capital at each full moon for the blessing of land and people, so the elders mate ritually, and also make a blood sacrifice for the land.

In addition to this, families and individuals perform rites for their own pieces of land, such as a family farm. Land is frequently "fed" with blood, usually one's own. The heads of a family, such as a married couple, may also mate to bless the land with their fluids and energy. Land is also sung to, and danced upon, and there are sometimes sacred battles where blood will be shed to feed the land. The first sheaf of grain of the farm's harvest season is sacrificed to the land, and the first loaf of bread made in a household during the dark half of the year is given half to the land and half to the family and any friends from outside the tribe they wish to invite.

The Bulls typically live on large farms, and their households typically consist of multi-generational families. If a Bull marries outside the tribe, the outsider is likely to live in Bull territory with their spouse even if they continue to go outside the territory to participate in their tribe's work and customs.

Said farms are usually rustic but cozy farmhouses, sometimes large estate-type homes. Bulls tend to dress in Viking-style garb, with women (and sometimes men) wearing apron dresses and men (and sometimes women) wearing tunics and leather breeches. The Bulls are fond of braiding their hair; their chieftain has very long hair which he ties into a single braid going down his back to his waist. The Bulls also are fond of jewelry, though they tend to limit this to one or two pieces which are usually family heirlooms or of other sentimental value (such as given by a spouse).

The Bulls pride themselves on hospitality above and beyond usual Vanic hospitality. Those who visit the Bulls will find themselves treated like royalty regardless of who they are or where they come from, given wonderfully delicious food and put up in simple but comfortable quarters, with little touches like sweet-smelling herb sachets in the bed, mint sweets on the pillow.

Making Allies with Bulls

The Bulls are well-known in Vanaheim for being one of the easiest tribes to get along with, "the tribe that nobody hates", and those sorted Bull are often of a kindly, generous disposition. They are real "salt of the earth" type people, even the wealthiest and most noble-born among them do not put on airs and do not consider themselves above hard work or helping others. In the Bull tribe everybody works, there is a place for everyone to contribute to the collective prosperity of the tribe no matter how young or old, able-bodied or infirm. Everybody does something, and the Bulls take much pride in their work, and even more pride in sharing the fruits of their labor with the realm as a whole.

With all of the hard work, the Bull territory is the largest producer of agriculture in the realm, "the breadbasket of Vanaheim". They have hearts to go with it, and thus it is not hard to make friends with a Bull or family of Bulls.

That said, the generosity and hospitality of the Bulls has limits, and one would do well to stay on the right side of those limits.

If a Bull is hosting you while visiting, they typically do not ask their guests to help out with labor. However, they will not refuse offers of help, and it is seen polite to offer your hosts with help of household or farm chores at their place in Vanaheim, and this will earn you respect.

Those who would work with a Bull mentor or have a Bull ally are likely to be observed here in Midgard for a time; the Bulls tend to take time to make decisions and even if they meet you and like you, they want to be sure you are worth an investment of their time, their energy, their work. So you will be watched here in this realm.

In the mundane world, a Bull is more likely to be willing to mentor you or have some other sort of alliance or working relationship with you if you try to be productive and helpful and considerate to others. This does not mean you have to be able-bodied and have a "normal" job, there are plenty of ways to contribute to the world without doing this (and Bulls could argue much about "normal" life in Midgard is destructive and counter-productive). Helping around your home if you live with others, offering a sympathetic ear to those who need it, being courteous, being respectful, being encouraging, are all things the Bulls will notice and approve of.

Bulls are likely to disapprove of those who put on airs and think themselves better than everyone else, those who can only find fault in others, those who are afraid to get their hands dirty and break a sweat. Bulls dislike poor sportsmanship and a cocky attitude, and some Bulls take pleasure in breaking people out of this, making folk learn humility. If one would approach the Bull tribe, be mindful of this.

That said, if one earns the respect and friendship of a Bull, they are steadfast, loyal allies, who will have your back when you need it and help pull strings for you so long as you are also pulling your own weight and trying your best with what you are able to do. Bulls have much patience and can teach much in the way of learning about community and friendship, as well as learning the magic of the land and the fertility thereof. They often speak in metaphors of agriculture, especially seasons and cycles, when they do speak; Bulls are known to be quiet, better listeners than conversationalists, but what they do speak of contains more insight than one would expect from "mere farmers". The Bulls more than anything exemplify the need to not judge a book by its cover, to remember that soil runs deep, and is fed with blood and bone.

THE CAT TRIBE

The Cat tribe is generally responsible for three things within Vanaheim:

- They open the ways for the elven Wild Hunt to ride in its season, and they maintain the portals and pathways in the realm; some Cats are hired as grovekeepers to tend the stangs (transporter devices that are powered by magic, and look like tall poles decorated per tribal territory).

- They are seers and specialize in *seiðr* as well as protective magics. A few Cats are healers.

- They are the tribe officially in charge of the kreshani, the most highly respected profession within Vanaheim, which is essentially sacred prostitution but is a bit more complicated than that.

Tribal Structure

The Cats have a singular leader, a chieftain or chieftess. For a long time the Cat tribe was led by a chieftess named Hael, and prior to that a woman called Laina (both women now deceased); the current Cat chieftain is a man who you can call Ben (short for his Eshnesk name which is long and complicated) who was blinded during the civil war. His second-in-command is a man named Kresh'ele (literally "fucker", the Vanic equivalent of naming your kid Don Juan or Casanova). Both gentlemen are fairly friendly and approachable so long as they are treated with respect.

The Cats have a council of twenty-four elders, and then the kreshani council (people who are dedicated to training kreshani and supervising their employment) is another twelve people. While there is a "pecking order" in the tribe and you will see some Cats defer to others, leadership is fairly informal.

Cat Culture

Of the Vanic tribes, the Cats are the ones who shift into their animal forms most often to hunt, spar, or play. The Cats when in their humanoid elven forms wear as little clothing as possible as clothing restricts movement.

The Cats occupy a large forested territory in west-central Vanaheim between Serpent and Wolf territory. Many Cats choose to live more of a rustic lifestyle in huts (think the proverbial witch's hut but add a few rooms for family members).

Making Allies with Cats

The Cats are one of the friendliest and most approachable tribes within Vanaheim, though one should still exercise caution as these cats have claws.

If you work with a Cat, they are fond of the sorts of offerings most Vanir like - alcohol, milk, cider or tea, bread and honey. Cats are, unsurprisingly, particular to fish and meat, and an offering of catnip tea would be appreciated. Cats like shiny toys and adornments.

Cats are one of the tribes most likely to be sexual with interested humans; the Cats tend to be loose even by Vanic standards. Cat tribe Vanir typically mix business with pleasure. Here is your warning that Cats do not often create bonds like some others who take elf-human sex a lot more seriously; while it is not impossible to have a serious romantic attachment with a Cat, they often have short attention spans and will not always be available for a partner and sometimes may get bored and move onto the next shiny thing. They do not do this maliciously, but this is something to be mindful of; if you're a spirit-boinker who doesn't mind casual sex, the Cats are the tribe for you to get it on with. If you fall hard and expect commitment, don't get involved with a Cat. There are exceptions to this, but don't expect to be the exception.

Cat tribe Vanir can be excellent teachers of seership, *seiðr*, and other magics, however they will call the shots and teach you on their timetable. Cats are not always available when wanted, and sometimes feel like doing a lesson at the worst possible time. Cats also expect fair compensation for lessons (which can, as you may have guessed from above, include sex).

A Cat can be a good ally to have especially if one needs to feel safe. However Cats do not forgive or forget easily, so be mindful of staying on their good side.

THE CRANE TRIBE

The Crane tribe lives in marshlands in southeastern Vanaheim, bordering Seal territory. They are a tribe of priests, focusing on the crafting of ritual, as well as magic, especially vocal magic and with magical writing systems (e.g. runes). They are teachers of the art of poetry and prayer, as well as sacred and magical dance.

Tribal Structure

The Crane tribe is governed by three Cranes, a man, a woman, and a person outside the gender binary. They lead rituals within the tribe, and give advisement on work done by tribal members.

Beyond this the tribe is fairly non-hierarchical. Some deference is given to elders, but apart from this, everyone has their own work to do and business to attend to, and there is not much interaction within the tribe.

Crane Culture

The Cranes tend towards a solitary existence. When two Cranes are seen together, there is usually something important going on. The Cranes spend a lot of time alone working on their craft, and in the contemplation and disciplines that help hone their craft.

The Crane tribe is fairly spread out along the marshes and meadows, living in huts. They tend to be self-sufficient with food, growing individual garden patches, and living mainly on fish and the occasional game.

Cranes favor wearing white clothing and will wear feather pelts to represent their tribe at official functions. They often wear jewelry that is of personal or magical significance, and they also tend to be heavily tattooed, their bodies being marked by different visions they have (which they refer to as the Dreaming), where their creative inspiration comes from.

Cranes are known for not speaking often, only when they have something to say. A proverb within Vanaheim goes: "When a Crane speaks, the Tree listens." Cranes hold their counsel until it is time to be delivered, and what they say is insight, and often magic itself.

Making Allies with Cranes

The Cranes typically do not approach humans, but they are one of the best tribes to have a mentor from if you are approached by one. They are particularly good to work with as teachers of magic and ritual, prayer and poetry, as well as sacred dance and movement. Cranes will also give insights into runes and sigil work.

But as noted above, Cranes do not often approach humans, and they are fairly particular about protocol when dealing with a human. They will come to you, and they will do so on their timetable. It is typical to see a Crane and then not see them again for weeks or even months. This isn't personal; they have things to do and so do you, and they will not breathe down your neck. Cranes prefer to not be asked questions - let them guide the work you do together, and recognize that they don't talk much, preferring to show, not tell. Cranes are also perfectionists, and if you are working with them on magic or artistic disciplines they will be difficult taskmasters, expecting no less than your best effort. That said, they also have a tremendous amount of patience and understanding, and kindness and compassion.

Cranes enjoy offerings of fish, fresh fruit and vegetables, and sweet meads like melomels, or fruit juice. They especially enjoy offerings of art, poetry, or song that you made yourself. They will accept dance as offering.

Cranes are frequently asexual, though this is not true of all Cranes. However when a Crane mates it is usually monogamous and usually for life. If a Crane pursues a relationship with you, they are serious, and they will be extremely hurt and possibly break off contact if they are rejected, which is not to guilt you into doing something you don't want to do, but only advising that there is no "just friends" with a Crane if they have feelings for you. That said, Cranes rarely involve themselves romantically or sexually with humans, as they tend to be "married" to their craft and the disciplines surrounding it.

It is more likely that, if you work with a Crane, they will visit you in this world, rather than you going to their territory, but it is not unheard of; to be let into a Crane's "nest" is a profound act of trust, as this is their sanctuary.

THE DEER TRIBE

The Deer tribe borders Bull territory in the south-central 'part of Vanaheim. They live in a large deciduous forest and lead seekers to their sacred groves, initiating into the dark heart of the forest and the thrill of the chase. They are teachers of passion, pride, and grace.

The Deer tribe has a subgroup, the mystery cult of the White Deer, who are givers of prophetic visions to humans, and train seers.

Tribal Structure

The Deer have a king and queen (their titles being the Stag King and Hind Queen) who are made king and queen through sacred combat - those who want to be the tribal rulers will battle everyone else who wishes for this title, and the last ones standing are raised on their shields. This event happens every thousand years, with the Stag King and Hind Queen reigning for a thousand years and then giving their crowns to their successors. The changeover of the tribal heads usually takes place on the summer solstice.

The leadership within the Deer tribe is taken fairly seriously, with members of the tribe frequently consulting their rulers for advice and suggestions on their tasks and personal lives. The Stag King and Hind Queen also lead ceremonies on behalf of the Deer tribe, usually performing seasonal rites as well as moon rituals to bring about tribal solidarity and ensure prosperity and good will within the tribe.

Beyond the tribal leadership the Deer tribe has a council of twelve elders, who keep the power of the King and Queen in check, as well as supervising the work the Deers do - as one example of how this works, the Deer elders frequently perform reconaissance and let the Deer tribe know of people to watch for and bring in, and will check up on these "charges".

That said, the tribe is fairly egalitarian and there is not much in the way of a hierarchical structure. There is more freedom in the Deer tribe than some others in terms of associations and how one's time is spent.

Deer Culture

The Deer tribe is scattered throughout their forest territory, preferring to live in cabins and sometimes in caverns. Their territory is heavily warded, as are most tribal territories, except the Deer tribe have actually warded their territory so you cannot even get in there without an invite from someone in the tribe, and this extends to the rest of Vanaheim, not just wandering or visiting outlanders. The Deer know how to not be found when they don't want to be, and are masters of re-routing those who approach, as well as cloaking their lands.

The Deer tribe are somewhat insular, though it is not terribly uncommon for Deer to mate with folk in other tribes. Deer do tend to primarily socialize with other Deer, and also tend to segregate themselves by sex, with women socializing mainly with women and men associating with men, and non-binary people going wherever they want to; the Deer tribe has a disproportionately high number of gender-shifters and transgender folk within their ranks compared to the trans/non-binary population of the rest of the realm, and they typically become priests of the White Deer cult, though not all of the White Deer are trans/non-binary, and not all trans/non-binary Deer are White Deer.

The Deer are fond of wearing antlers on their heads, and often these antlers are adorned with greenery and/or beading of some sort. The Deer tend towards elaborate hairstyles and clothing that blends in with the colors of the forest but is beautifully embroidered and trimmed; they are fond of wearing suede.

Pride and nobility are inherent within the Deer tribe's bearing, and they are passionate people, fiery at heart, whether they be of a more gentle or bold personality, they feel things fiercely and live fully.

Making Allies with Deer

It is generally inadvisable to approach the Deer tribe without an invite, mainly because you'll be wasting your time looking for something that isn't there or waiting for a response you'll never get. If a Deer is interested in working with you, they will come to you first.

Deer are all about the chase, and taking you deeper. Working with a Deer can be overwhelming, but it can also teach ever-increasing joy, ecstasy, and wonder, even as there is fear to be faced and you are pushed farther than you think you can go. The ultimate lesson of the Deer tribe is surrender, that the wild cannot be fully tamed, and it is when we stop trying to tame and control everything that freedom is found and wyrd can move freely.

Deer are frequently highly sexual people, and frequently become sexually involved with those they work with. They gain much of their power through sex, and they can teach sex magic, especially with a hunter/hunted struggle/surrender BDSM dynamic. However, a Deer may not necessarily pursue sex with you, and I do not recommend pestering them about it - let them decide if that's something they want to do with you.

As mentioned above Deer are proud people, and it is important to respect their sense of pride and dignity. Deer are also intensely emotional - if they care about you, they will feel strongly about you and often react strongly to you and have strong opinions about your life and its circumstances. Deer can be possessive as well as protective, but there is a gentleness in their strength, a desire to nurture and love.

Deer are quiet, and prefer to teach by doing rather than talking about doing. Their companionship is of the silent type, but they often affirm affection through touch and gesture.

Like most Eshnahai, Deer will graciously accept food and drink offerings - they particularly enjoy things like game meat (e.g. wild boar) and jerky, stews, chowders, as well as lots of greens, root vegetables, and berries. The Deer consume alcohol moderately and the White Deer have a prohibition with consuming alcohol, but fruit juice or cider is a very acceptable drink to them, as is tea.

The Deer also enjoy receiving dance as offering, being invited as a dance partner. They are also good to spend time with in the company of nature, just quietly being together and observing the beauty and wonders of the land.

THE EAGLE TRIBE

The Eagles are a tribe of elite warriors within Vanaheim, dedicated to defending the realm and teaching the art of war with both weapons and magic. The Eagles are more technically warrior-priests, with lots of rituals involving sacred combat and battle training that they perform in secret.

Tribal Structure

For a long time the tribe was led by an elderly Eagle who was called the Eagle King, and he was killed during the second civil war in summer 2012. The Eagles have a new King, and have a hierarchy based on color: White, Black, and Red. The White Eagles are the neophytes and those who do not advance within tribal ranks. Most Eagles fall within the rank of Black. Red is the top cadre, the best of the best.

Once an Eagle is admitted into the tribe, they spend a very long time within the White rank training, before they are deemed good enough to advance to Black and be given warrior duties within the tribe. Most of the Red-ranked Eagles are either very old or very bloodthirsty and ruthless and driven.

The Eagles live in a mountain range in northeast Vanaheim, which is heavily warded and fortified. They are rarely seen outside their tribal territory unless they are going on patrol or are engaged in a battle (which is rare, as Vanaheim's outside conflicts are rare).

Eagle Culture

The Eagle tribe is fairly insular and xenophobic, and does not tend to intermarry. It is not uncommon for most children born of Eagles to be sorted Eagle upon adulthood and those who are not Eagle-sorted are often seen as a "disappointment".

The Eagles are notorious for looking down on other tribes, to the point where they instigated the second civil war in 2012 to attempt to wipe out the Ravens and Wolves, who they saw as "eaters of carrion" and bringing Vanaheim down. This has gotten somewhat better since the reunification in 2013, and the Eagles are actively attempting to work on more inter-tribal sensitivity and better relations. However this is slow going and the Eagles still have a tendency to offend when they go outside their realm for various functions. Their reputation within Vanaheim is "snooty". Another word would be "hardassed".

The Eagles are a large tribe, and the largest insular tribe.

The Eagles are, as noted above, very hierarchical and the most strict of the tribes of following tribal customs and hierarchy, having "their way" of doing things. Even more severe is the mystery cult of the Fire Eagle (mostly populated by Red Eagles, and some Black Eagles on their way to Red), which performs extreme ordeals as a way of gaining power and wisdom.

Making Allies with Eagles

Working with Eagles is generally not recommended unless you are of a warrior disposition and prepared to work very, very, very hard with physical and psychological discipline, and go through ordeals.

If you still think this is the path for you, they accept blood sacrifice. Period. It does not have to be a food animal you kill, you could offer your own blood. But blood needs to be shed as a regular offering to an Eagle guide. Eagles will also, once a relationship is established, accept offerings of alcohol and tobacco, preferably made on a fire. However they will not accept this in lieu of blood, and it really cannot be emphasized enough that they demand regular blood offerings and working with an Eagle means a lot of ordeal and soul-breaking transformation.

THE FOX TRIBE

The Fox tribe are the tricksters of Vanaheim. They are in charge of building traps around the borders to keep away unwanted outlanders. They also confuse and trick outlanders who might be able to get past the border defenses (such as those who are themselves tricksters).

The Fox tribe also provides much of the entertainment within Vanaheim, and at least one Fox is usually present at diplomatic negotiations to help defuse tensions as well as be able to detect trickery or suss out information that the other party might be reluctant to share.

Tribal Structure

The Fox tribe are led by a chieftain and chieftess, a married couple who go by the names Zeldyar and Arissa. The Foxes are very family-oriented and have large families and when not working, are usually found with their families, hunting or just playing. The Foxes are a fairly large tribe and control a large territory within Vanaheim, and spread out in concealed villages. The Foxes are one of the least hierarchical tribes, with Zeldyar and Arissa serving less as tribal leaders and more as representatives of the Fox tribe within the realm or to outlanders.

Fox Culture

The Foxes are not only one of the least hierarchical tribes but one of the friendliest and most easy-going. The Foxes are known for throwing good parties and being especially funny and fun to be around, and they very much enjoy meeting new people and entertaining them.

The Foxes train in illusions and trickery, as well as various forms of entertainment such as song, dance, and wielding fire. It is very common for a child of a Fox to learn magic tricks, pranks, and command of fire from their parent, which will stay with them even if they are sorted into another tribe. The Foxes pride themselves on their abilities to conceal and prank, and frequently hold contests amongs themselves.

The Foxes typically open their territory to other Vanir for the summer solstice and fall equinox, so friends and friendly folk can join in their tribal celebrations, which include fire dancing and games.

The Foxes spend a fair amount of time in their animal forms (though not as much as the Cats), and when in humanoid elven form tend to wear fox pelts (red in the summer, white/grey in the winter) over elaborately embroidered leathers and linens, with moccasins and ornate beaded. It is common for the men to wear their (very long) hair tied back and women to wear some "tails" and the rest of their hair down, with beads threaded into the hair representing their different partners and children. Foxes of all genders tend to wear earrings in both ears (often more than one pair) and usually at least three or four necklaces. They are fond of bartering jewelry, or bartering items for jewelry.

Fox dens are fairly cozy, deceptively simple in their outward appearance but often elaborately decorated on the inside (as well as larger on the inside than they appear on the outside), and often contain hidden rooms that serve as libraries or work spaces, or places to store liquor and food. It is not uncommon for a Fox to have two homes, one for the light half of the year and another for the colder dark half of the year (frequently the latter is underground). It is also not uncommon for Foxes to oath-bond as adopted siblings and share a household with their oath-sibling, where the oath-siblings live together with their spouse/s and children.

Making Allies with Foxes

It's not hard. If you want to build a relationship with a Fox, they appreciate good food, good drink, and fun. They like music, they like being introduced to Midgard culture, they like good conversation. A Fox will especially enjoy your company if you have a good sense of humor. Be prepared for good-natured ribbing, and you really need to have a sense of humor to deal with them. They are fond of trolling. If you take yourself too seriously or you are too wound up and have a problem relaxing, they can help with this, but their way of helping with this may not be something you want to deal with.

If you have a Fox as an ally they may be able to help you with things like wards, but you would need to have a good working relationship with them for awhile and they would need to be able to trust you. While Foxes are friendly and easygoing, this is not to be confused with trust. There is a lot that they do not share with tribal outsiders, or outlanders; they take bonds of trust very seriously, and as mentioned above, they will punish bonds of trust broken rather severely. It is very hard to offend a Fox but if you've managed to do so you can count on having an enemy for life who will make a career out of taunting and complicating things for you.

THE FROG TRIBE

The Frogs specialize in healing - not catastrophic serious healing like the Serpents, but little things. If the Serpents could be compared to surgeons and oncologists, the Frogs would be the general practitioner, giving preventative medicine as well as treating minor ailments and injuries. Frogs also tend to train as midwives and most births in the realm (though not all) are assisted by Frogs.

Tribal Structure

The Frogs do not have a specific leader but rather a council of tribal elders who make decisions when decisions for the entire tribe need to be made, and train the younger members in the arts of healing. The Frogs are a mid-sized tribe and live along the Three Rivers.

Frog Culture

The Frogs tend to have brown or tawny skin, some being lighter or darker in tone. They dress simply, usually favoring browns, greens, and russet tones. They live in huts that are surprisingly comfortable and cozy on the inside, and when not performing healing services, are fond of making clay pottery and weaving baskets. Frog pottery and baskets are beautifully made and highly prized in the realm; the cornucopia for the realm's festival of gratitude is usually made and blessed by the Frog tribe. Frogs are fairly laid-back and good-humored, but also no-nonsense, and can err on the side of being blunt. Frogs enjoy spending time with their families and playing games, and sustain themselves via fishing and community gardens.

They are likely to marry outside the tribe (most commonly to Otters and Deer), and there is an interesting phenomenon wherein Frogs do not often have children sorted Frog, but grandchildren of Frogs are more likely to become Frogs themselves upon adulthood.

Making Allies with Frogs

Like the Salmon tribe, the Frogs are fairly easy to approach and it is not hard to win a Frog over. A Frog will be particularly interested in you if you have an interest in the healing arts, and may spirit-teach you energy work techniques, as well as cleanness of body and mind, and living more simply and having more enjoyment and relaxation in one's life.

Like most Vanir, Frogs will graciously accept food and drink given to them, especially fruit and vegetables, roasted fish, and poultry. They enjoy trinkets made specifically for them, especially pottery and baskets. They do prefer things that are useful as well as beautiful, so unlike most Vanir, jewelry is not likely to impress them much. Frogs enjoy spending time in nature, especially forested ponds, lakes, and streams. Taking a Frog on a fishing trip is likely to be welcomed enthusiastically.

It is highly recommended against lying to a Frog or in a Frog's presence, they are likely to completely cut off contact with you and deem you not to be trusted. While Frogs are kind-hearted and fun-loving and laid-back, do be prepared to hear the unvarnished truth from them; Eshnahai tend to be brutally honest as a rule, but Frogs have a sort of earthy bluntness matched only by Wolves that not everyone can deal with.

THE GOOSE TRIBE

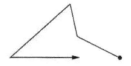

The Geese are to genealogies what the Salmon tribe are to histories of nations and realms what the Ravens are to histories of individual lives what the Serpents are to tracking incarnations and patterns of wyrd. The Goose tribe specializes in keeping genealogical records both of elves within Vanaheim, as well as their descendants among nations. If you suspect you are Vanic-souled or Vanic-blooded, the Goose tribe is the tribe to go to about it.

This is not all the Goose tribe does - the Goose tribe are also educators, many of the finest teachers of literature, arts, and sciences within Vanaheim come from the Geese, and the Geese are, with the Ravens, dedicated to Eshnahai cultural preservation. The Geese believe that a strong society is built on families and honoring one's roots, and they live to do just that.

Tribal Structure

The Geese are led by an elderly woman who is literally known as Mother Goose. She has a council of twelve elders, and then there is an "academy" of forty-eight Geese who oversee tribal education and the general good of the tribe (such as keeping law and order within the tribe, planning marriages, and the like). The Geese are otherwise not particularly hierarchical, and fairly laid-back within their hierarchy, with every voice of the tribe carrying weight, and everyone being seen as having an important job within the tribe.

Goose Culture

One thing that has been strongly corroborated by people who have encountered them within Vanaheim is that the Goose tribe seems to be permanently stuck in the Victorian era, in terms of mode of dress, and with Victorian-type buildings in their villages including a large clock tower resembling Big Ben. The Geese admire humans, with the caveat that they are not fond of the ecological destruction and social ills of modern human society, so while they are friendly with outlanders and will be hospitable to human visitors, they are not fond of technology or urbanization. They also strongly encourage people to make their own families (not necessarily through child-bearing, but through forging bonds with others) if the person dealing with them is more socially isolated.

Making Allies with Geese

The Geese are good at entertaining, and have a keen interest in history and culture, literature, and art, so if this is one of your personal areas of interest you can expect the Geese to enjoy your company.

That being said, it is a good idea to avoid interacting with Geese in very urban areas. This is not to say that they cannot be engaged at all in a city, but you would be best dealing with them in your home or in a very green area. They are somewhat phobic of technology so if they are visiting you at your home and you have any technological devices around them (such as a cell phone or computer) you may either want to hide said device or be prepared to explain to them how it makes your life better and contributes positively to the world.

Geese do not like cars.

The Goose tribe is fond of tea, wine, good food, and good conversation. They are fond of classical music, and can be encouraged to enjoy modern music or literature.

A Goose ally can be helpful with discovering whether or not you are Eshnahai-souled or -blooded, how to integrate this into your day-to-day life, or how to build connections to people and have meaningful family relationships. A Goose mentor can also be helpful if you are pursuing a career in literature, art, or history. Geese do not make alliances lightly but once you have a Goose ally, you have a friend for life, and indeed, adopted family who will look out for you and nurture and protect you as one of their own.

THE HARE TRIBE

The Wolves were the first to reach out to humanity; the Hares are the tribe that deals the least with humanity (next to the Spiders and Cranes). They are, next to the Spiders, the most xenophobic tribe, insular even among other elves; more interested in the health and well-being of the land than its people. In a way, the Hares could be considered the opposite number to the Wolves - the Wolves protect and guide humans, and the Hares could care less except for those few individual humans who endear themselves to a Hare mentor or working partner. The Wolves are violent and put themselves in the path of danger on an everyday basis, whereas the Hares shy from it as much as possible.

The main purpose of the Hare tribe is twofold:

- waking up the land from winter, and ensuring its vitality during the light half of the year

- enchanting places and things – Hares are respected craftsmen.

Tribal Structure

The Hares have a King and Queen. They are a mated pair, both Hares, who are elected by their people; it is a position held for life. When the current King and Queen pass on, the next election will happen. This position can be shortened if the people become displeased with their King and sacrifice him, but this has only happened once in the Hares' history.

The Hare King and Queen are seen more as advisors and guardians, and are not authoritarian in their rule. In general, the Hare tribe is very egalitarian. There are a few positions in the tribe of importance - guildmaster and priest - but these are seen as roles to serve their people, a responsibility. The Hares are otherwise very down to earth and shows of putting on airs are heavily frowned upon.

The Hares are, statistically speaking, the largest tribe with regards to number of people. The Hares are, as noted above, xenophobic and insular. Intermarriage with other tribes can and does happen - a disproportionately high number of Wolves take Hares as mates - but the size of the Hare tribe is such that this becomes only a small percentage. Most Hares are mated with Hares, and most of their children wind up Hares. For a Hare to marry outside the tribe, there is a long, complicated bureaucratic procedure where the Hares want to make sure the mate from another tribe is worth giving their person to, usually because that person will then leave Hare territory and go to their mate's tribal territory (the Hares tend to not let people from other tribes live in their territory), so they will observe the potential mate for at least a couple of years before agreeing to the wedding. This is true even if the mate is the person's twin; considering how respected and valued the twinbond is in elven culture, this gives a clue as to the skittishness and caution of the Hares as a tribe.

There are two subdivisions of the Hare tribe - the House of the Earth and the House of the Moon. They are divided not by territory - it is common to see a House of Earth Hare living next door to a Moon Hare - but rather by affiliation. The Hares of the House of the Earth are the "public" face of the Hare tribe, and more numerous in number. The Hares of the House of the Moon operate almost like a mystery tribe, and indeed, the House of the Moon is home to not one but two tribes, the Hares and the Wolf cult. The House of the Moon performs the seasonal rites to wake up the land from winter, preserve its vitality during the light half of the year, and ensure the tribe's survival and a good rest for the land during winter; at the tides of the moon, the House of the Moon Hares are chased by the Wolves, enacting the dance of predator and prey, hunter and hunted.

Hare Culture

The main purpose and task of the Hare tribe is creation. They are, of the tribes, most stereotypically

"Vanic" in the sense of being true life-givers, averse to conflict, and extremely sexual.

The Hares are very culturally similar to Tolkien's hobbits. Many of them prefer living in mound houses, or underground outright. They have a love of good food, music, and simple pleasures. They tend to be on the shorter and more squat side for elves (though there are exceptions to this), and dress plainly, not dissimilarly to the Amish but with more use of colors and embroidery.

The House of the Earth Hares tend to present with brown hair and eyes and a corresponding brown rabbit form, and the House of the Moon Hares with pale blonde hair and a corresponding silver or white rabbit form. This is also regardless of skin color – there are House of the Moon Hares with dark skin and silver-white hair and silvery eyes, for example.

The Hares tend to raise power one of two ways - through music and dancing, or through sex. With the former, the Hares can "make the world", by leaping and dancing across an open space with intent, terrain and flora and fauna springing up in their trail. With the latter, the Hares can create spirits within objects or places, or give healing energy, as well as channel visions from beyond of things that need to be brought into being.

The Hares are also known as master artisans. Many important landmarks and objects of power - such as jewellry, ritual objects, and weapons - have been made by a Hare, who saw the item in a vision and worked to anchor that vision to form, giving it life with the great magic of their touch. The Hares all have a great love of beauty; the Earth Hares tend to favor more simple and practical constructions, and the Moon Hares more ethereal.

The Hares, finally, have a reputation for making the best food, and nine times out of ten if there is a large event in the capital, or put on by another tribe, it is being catered by Hares. The Hares make simple but hearty fare - bread, soups, grilled meat, platters of fruit and cheese, roasted and fresh vegetables. They are notorious for having sweet tooths, and no Hare banquet is complete without mooncakes, made from the nectar of the moonflower native to Vanaheim, which tastes a bit like buttered rum. The Hares are also fond of sugared flower petals.

Making Allies with Hares

The Hare tribe are skittish as far as dealing with humans, but should a human artist be seeking a Hare as mentor, they may, if approached over a long period of time with proper respect, come to trust the human and send one to teach them how to respect the magic of the body electric and with it, express what they see inside their soul. The Hares enjoy offerings of wildflowers, root vegetables, milk and honey, as well as song and dance, or anything creative made by the human seeking a mentor that comes from a sincere place in their heart.

Once a relationship with a Hare mentor has been established, it is a good idea for the human to deal with them by appointment, scheduling a specific day and time per week, or every couple of weeks, to meet for lessons, or doing some sort of working together. (Some Hares are not adverse to a human working partner for blessing the land in Midgard, or enchanting bio-side places/objects.) The Hares are very much creatures of routine and habit and dislike surprises, so having a regular time for getting together is their preference.

When meeting with a Hare, it should preferably be in some lovely place in nature, or otherwise a comfortable setting indoors, with ambiance such as candlelight. Having a beautiful or at least pleasant and homey surrounding will make the Hare feel more at ease. It is a very bad idea to invoke a Hare into a chaotic place such as a very cluttered or filthy home, or a crowd, and doing so can make the Hare decide to stop dealing with you altogether.

THE HORSE TRIBE

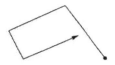

The Horses primarily serve as guides within Vanaheim. They will help assist visitors from other realms, especially Midgard, with getting to and from the realm as well as getting around the realm itself. They are also a sort of welcoming committee within Vanaheim - immigration is handled by them.

Finally, the Horses are teachers of trance, using rhythm and movement to focus the passage between worlds. The drum is sacred to them.

Tribal Structure

The Horses live on the plains of east-central Vanaheim, bordering the Great Forest of the Owls. They are a fairly non-hierarchical group: they are led by a chieftain or chieftess who assigns duties and periodically checks in to supervise that things are going well, but apart from that the Horses have a lot of freedom and everyone from young and old, experienced and new, are seen as valuable members of the tribe and there is something for everyone to do, nobody is seen as more important or worthy of respect than the others.

Tribal Culture

The Horses live fairly nomadically, with few permanent residences, many of them living in yurts or tents. Their territory is large, and they will make a circumnavigation of their territory once a year, making camp in different spots, which they see as a sort of hallowing of their space and "keeping the magic flowing".

The Horses dress fairly simply, usually in earth tones, though some favor bold colors such as red or gold. The Horses are fond of wearing braids in their hair with beads or pieces of silver or gold attached, but unlike the Squirrel tribe these do not represent anything and for adornment only. The Horses wear a lot of leather and suede, and favor braids as trim on their clothing as well as in their hair.

The Horses have moots twice a year, wherein everybody within the tribe gathers to a central location and tribal business is discussed, and there is feasting and fellowship. This is typically done on the summer solstice and at Yule, and lasts approximately a week. This is also a time to bring up any grievances that people might have with others in the tribe and have them arbitrated by the chief/tess; these are sometimes settled by ritual combat and then the wronged party being gifted or given restitution in the presence of witnesses. There is usually at least one animal sacrifice made during the moots, and a ritual done with the entire tribe bathing in the blood and then having an orgy underneath the stars while the food animal cooks, and then there is a grand feast afterwards.

Worth noting is that there is a mystery cult within the Horse tribe, a "tribe within a tribe" if you will, the Black Horses, which is where many of the kelpies from folklore come from, sent by the elves as agents of divine retribution when such is called for, or sometimes to frighten/ward away those who do not belong in the realm.

Making Allies with Horses

The Horses are perhaps the friendliest and most approachable tribe within Vanaheim and if you are looking for an introductory point of contact within Vanaheim, you could not do better than a Horse. They enjoy being helpful, and tend towards easygoing and good-natured temperaments.

That being said, the Horses are not an ideal match for everyone. Horses can be mischievous and teasing, and sometimes like to prank their friends. They are light-hearted, and very playful, and tend to treat their work as play. If you are of a more serious disposition and not terribly social, you may find a Horse guide to be obnoxious company.

The Horses, like most Eshnahai, enjoy good food and drink, and will be pleased with small tokens of affection and friendship such as pretty crystals or little objects; they are particularly fond of items that are both practical and beautiful (with a simplistic beauty), perhaps a leatherworked pouch or a knife you forged yourself or specifically chose for them. Horses are more concerned with sincerity of intent and something given from a place of good will, rather than what the object actually is, being that Horses are fairly nomadic and don't accumulate much in the way of "stuff". Food and drink offerings are the most appreciated by them, and they will usually be glad to have whatever you're having, though if you want to make things special for them you typically can't go wrong with stew, fresh bread, or skewers.

The friendliness of Horses extends sexually and Horses are some of the most likely Eshnahai to become sexually involved with a human they are fond of. They are also pretty straightforward in their intent, they don't do a lot of courtship, so hearing "Hey, want to fuck?" is pretty par for the course. Becoming sexually involved with a Horse may or may not lead to a relationship. If it does, you should be aware that Horses tend to be the most polyamorous of the already poly-tending Vanir; most Horses have at least one or two spouses or life-mates within the tribe, and then two to five other spouses, life-mates or other types of partner outside of the tribe. A romantic relationship with a Horse will be full of quiet moments of enjoying just being together, and lots of play and banter. They are not big on "wining and dining" and generally do not favor strong outward displays of emotion (it is rare to see a Horse cry openly), though they may surprise you with occasional emotional gestures.

Horses are one of the least secretive of the Vanic tribes; they are usually willing to teach so long as they are treated with respect, and they are usually OK with the student "passing on" what they learn with outsiders (though it is always safest to ask).

Horses can be protective of someone they guide, but will not be smothering. If you make bad choices in life, don't expect a Horse to come bail you out, they will want you to learn your lesson.

Horses tend to be blunt. This isn't necessarily meant to cause offense, it's just the unvarnished truth. But it can still hurt sensitive feelings.

As far as avoiding faux pas: don't insult their hair, don't touch their hair without permission, mind your manners, don't be snooty about their simple clothing and abodes and ways of life, be willing to help the Horse with any chores they have if you visit them in their realm at their home, and if a Horse tells you a place or thing is off-limits do respect that (especially because the Horses, as mentioned above, are not very secretive so if there is knowledge of something they think you shouldn't have, it's for a reason). Horses are otherwise hard to offend and usually willing to give a second chance if apologies and restitution are made for an offense.

THE OTTER TRIBE

There are two Otter groups: River Otters and Sea Otters. The Sea Otters border Seal territory on the east coast of Vanaheim, and the River Otters border Frog and Goose territory. They have a balance between hunting and play, with lots of emphasis on community and teamwork. They are an extremely social tribe but also extremely territorial.

Tribal Structure

The Otter tribe is one of the mostly non-hierarchical tribes of Vanaheim. The River Otters have a chieftain and chieftess, and the Sea Otters have a different chieftain and chieftess. However these titles seem to be mainly ceremonial in nature, and are chosen by election; the chieftain and chieftess of each group actively participate in the work of the tribe and there is not much in the way of leadership in terms of directing people to do things. All Otters from young to old are seen as an important part of the tribe and with their own niche within the tribe, and the Otters are fairly self-sufficient which reflects in each Otter with their own work.

Both sets of Otters are fairly large tribes.

Otter Culture

The Otters tend to prefer living in huts that seem rustic but are cozy, comfortable, and richly adorned on the inside and out - the River Otters dress their homes with forest greenery and found shiny objects, the Sea Otters with shells and starfish and woodburned driftwood and knotwork made of dried seaweed.

Otters dress in earth tones and neutral colors such as greys, sometimes black; there is a tendency towards wearing leathers and pelts. The Otters are very fond of jewelry - the Sea Otters are famous for their shell necklaces and wearing little shells braided into their hair. They consume a lot of fish, and the fish market in Vanaheim's capital is vended primarily by Otter tribe folk (with some Salmon and Seals).

The Otter tribe is unique in Vanaheim in the sense that they do not have a specific tribal duty (such as the Geese with genealogies, the Ravens with lore, the Serpents with healing), but rather they are a "jack of all trades" tribe. Some Otters are healers, some are Makers, some are warriors, some are loremasters, and some are mages.

While the profession of *kreshani* is heavily dominated by Cat folk, the Otters are the second most numerous among the *kreshani* ranks. Those Otters who train and work as kreshani use the Otter talent of "going with the flow" to raise and direct energy, and specialize in sexual healing, particularly with providing peace, serenity, and quiet joy. Otter *kreshani* tend towards kink, being playful and willing to experiment.

The Otters are not at all insular and xenophobic, and regularly welcome people from other tribes to their monthly fish feasts (during the full moon), which is an all-night event with storytelling and song. The Otters frequently marry outside the tribe, and are one of the most poly-leaning tribes, where it is common to see an Otter with 1-2 mates within the tribe and then 3-4 other mates from other tribes, and assorted children within different tribal territories. The Otters are also very friendly with humans, though they can be protective of their territory and much more so of their families.

Making Allies with Otters

Otters usually welcome humans wanting to work with them so long as the human is respectful, minding their manners and being willing to give, be a good host as well as a good guest, and so on.

Good offerings for the Otter tribe include (but are not limited to) fish and dishes made with seafood (such as clam chowder), strong drink (they tend to favor rum), and shiny objects - they are particularly fond of jewelry made for them. They enjoy stories and poems and songs, as well as dance. They absolutely adore music, and many Otters are surprisingly good singers. They have a love of communing with nature and the eldest, most serious Otters will still play like big goofy kids.

Otters can be sexual with humans they work with, though whether it is just for fun or means something more serious will depend on Otter. If an Otter is romantically courting you they will be very obvious in their affections, somewhat territorial and possessive, and have what I can only describe as "adorkability. Expect nose boops and shy kisses.

Otters are fun-loving and fairly hard to offend. It is not impossible to offend them - they are proud people and can be sensitive about their work and appearance. They are also, as mentioned, territorial so be mindful of staying within bounds, not just within Otter country but also in dealing with them as people. Otters frequently do not talk about themselves - they are very friendly and interactive with other Vanic tribes as well as humans, but they tend to keep their personal lives private. When an Otter works with a human it is more about what the human is doing and what the Otter can do with them, as Otters are more than anything else playful and inquisitive and enjoy new experiences. If you don't pry, you're willing to fairly exchange time, energy, and gifts, and you are respectful, you should get along with the Otters just fine.

THE OWL TRIBE

The Owl tribe primarily serve as guardians of the liminal spaces where Vanaheim and Midgard intersect - the "thin veil" points - as well as initiators. While the Raven tribe limits its initiatory work to death and rebirth/renewal, the Owls are initiators of all rites of passage: coming of age, marriage, parenthood, and wizening. They are also enforcers of taboos and oaths, testing those who would make vows, and punishing those who break these binds.

Tribal Structure

The Owls live in what has been described by visitors as The Great Tree (but not the World Tree itself) in a heavily forested area in east-central Vanaheim. The Great Tree is an extremely large tree that is even larger on the inside than it is on the outside, hollowed out and made into hundreds of rooms where the Owl tribe lives communally.

The Owl tribe is unique to Vanic tribes in that it does not have a single leader or pair of leaders presiding over the tribe, but has four leaders, called the Ministers, each representing one of the four winds and dressed in a monochromatic scheme: red, gold, green, or blue. The Ministers govern the tribe, advised by a council of twenty-four elders (some of whom are elders in terms of age, some of whom are not elderly but gained a place of respect through experience and work within the tribe).

The Owls are one of the more hierarchical tribes, with different degrees/ranks as one advances within the tribe. Typically an Owl who has been in the tribe for awhile will have at least one to three apprentices (sometimes more) who help them with their particular niche and are trained, and also answers to their own teacher/chief, who answers to their own teacher/chief, with the highest authorities being within the elders and the Ministers themselves. The Owls are fairly strict on protocol and punish harshly for infractions - as an example, an Owl who forgets to greet their teacher properly or sasses them might be made to clean one of the bathrooms. Because the Owls are guardians of the thresholds between Midgard and Vanaheim as well as enforcers of taboos and oaths, they feel it is necessary for their own tribe to be held to stricter standards than the others, less they become lax in their duties.

Owl Culture

The Owls are one of the larger tribes in Vanaheim, and are a middle point between the more insular and gregarious tribes. The Owls are equally comfortable keeping to themselves and interacting with others in Vanaheim and in Midgard.

When one is sorted into the Owl tribe upon coming of age, they are put through an intense training period with long days of work and study, and very few privileges. The initial training period typically lasts a year and a day. Upon graduation, an Owl is usually sent to The Academy, a school within The Great Tree wherein Owls are educated in anything that might be useful to their tribe's purpose, and with their own individual role within the tribe: typically this involves history, geography, cultures and languages, magic, martial arts, and the laws the Owls have created for the thresholds and upholding vows and keeping taboos.

For Owls who show great promise and potential, which is typically determined within 3-5 after joining the tribe, there is an Academy within the Academy, an "elite of the elite" where Owls are given special magical training to go on to special tasks within and outside of the realm.

The Owls are fairly secretive of what is taught in their schools - we know they learn about history and magic and the like, but what specifically is learned and how it is applied is not something the Owls will discuss with tribal outsiders, not even their own families. The Owls are some of the least likely Eshnahai to marry outside their tribe for this reason, and those who do marry outside the tribe are held to keeping tribal secrets and customs. Those who marry outside the tribe are given permission to live outside The Great Tree, in the surrounding forested area, but still within Owl territory; going with spouse to the spouse's tribal territory to live (as some do) results in a ban.

The Owls are one of the most adamant of tribes with regards to respecting the elderly, and the most severe punishments meted within the tribe usually involve perceived or actual disrespect of the old folks. Happily, this does not happen often. Most of the tribe's old folks are headmasters of the Academy or chiefs-of-chiefs, and revered and often consulted for their lifetime (many thousands of years) of experience and lessons learned. However, even as the venerable ones are given the utmost respect, they are not in as large numbers as one might think. Due to the risks involved with their duties, one out of every eight Owls is killed in the line of duty and the sort of magic that they do can shorten the lifespan; the average life expectancy of an Owl is about eight thousand years old, which translates to early fifties in human years. Compare this with average life expectancy within Vanaheim being about fifteen to twenty thousand years old (with some Eshnahai living 30,000+ years).

Making Allies with Owls

Owls are one of the easiest tribes to run afoul of (no pun intended), and it is of extreme importance to remember this if you plan on dealing with them.

First of all, it is inadvisable to approach the Owls on your own because you want an Eshnahai mentor/ally. My advice to you is go seek one of the friendlier tribes. This is not to say that the Owls can't be friendly, but they are harsh, and extremely harsh if they think you are worth their time and investment of working with. To say they are difficult taskmasters is a dramatic understatement.

Owls have approached people for various reasons; one can always decline if an Owl expresses interest in you.

If one wishes to incline an Owl's invitation of working with you, the most polite way to do so would be to make them an offering such as food or drink, tell them "I am honored, but no thank you," and leave it at that. Do not apologize for yourself or they will take that as a sign of weakness and a way in. Do not try to give them excuses like "I'm busy" or "you scare me" even if that's the truth, because they will argue against excuses. Just leave it short and sweet.

If you do plan on working with an Owl for whatever reason, here is what you need to know:

- Owls expect you to be on time. If you're planning on doing a working with an Owl or meeting them/having them meet you at eight o'clock, don't have things start at eight o'five.

- Owls expect you to do what you say you're going to do. If you are given an assignment to complete within an allotted time and this is not done by the due date, they will be most displeased. If you in your mundane life regularly make promises you can't keep, or procrastinate, or make plans that you never get around to, this is going to become a problem with your Owl friend sooner rather than later and will be addressed and probably in a way that you don't like.

- Owls are masters of glamour and may not show you what they actually look like right away. They may come to you initially in bird form, or in shadow form. Even when they drop this and assume a more humanoid elven appearance, you may notice them shifting hair color and eye color in subtle or more dramatic ways.

- An Owl will make it a point to terrify you at least once, and typically early on in your relationship with them. The Owls will strongly dissuade people from working with them even if they have invited you, because they feel only those who can rise up to the challenge and face down the fear and still pursue this relationship, are worthy of it.

- The Owls also believe in testing those they work with. They are masters of ordeal, especially psychological. If you have a lot of fears and skeletons in your closet and truths you will not face, it is not a question of if but when you will be made to deal with them.

- Owls demand protocol. You will probably be asked to address the Owl by a title such as Lord or Sir rather than their name. There are exceptions to this, such as becoming intimate with an Owl but even then, Owls can be formal in intimate relationships with outlanders (and tend towards dominating them when it happens).

- Owls do not do casual sex with outlanders or those outside the tribe (within the tribe is a different story, many Owls have sex for magical/ritual purposes only, but are not otherwise involved with the partner). If an Owl wants to have sex with you, they want a relationship with you, they see a future with you.

- If you get involved with an Owl, expect them to be protective of you, and probably protective of you mentioning anything about your relationship to the public beyond a few details. (They are a lot like demons in this respect.)

- Compliments are good, but there is a line where too many compliments will be seen as flattery and the Owl suspecting you want something from them. This doesn't go well. Even if you feel the need to tell your Owl friend how awesome they are all the time, try to tone it down a bit.

- Most important: do not, DO NOT wander in Owl territory without an escort, preferably one from within the Owl tribe. Their forest is heavily warded and patrolled and they perceive random wandering as an intrusion and potential attack.

As offerings Owls like what most Eshnahai like: hearty food, good drink, shiny things. They are particularly fond of things like poetry or stories you have written yourself or music you have composed yourself, or gifts of artistic objects made by you or specially chosen for them. Owls enjoy intelligent conversation and an exchange of wits (Owls are known for very dry wit, and also a love of bad puns); many of them smoke a pipe and will happily indulge in an evening of watching the moon and stars, smoking a pipe, and talking about life, the Universe, and everything.

THE RAM TRIBE

The Ram tribe are a tribe of elite warriors who serve as a military presence within Vanaheim. They are not just warriors with weapons, but are also specialists in crafting defensive charms, especially with regards to fiber magic and weaving protective magic in clothing, household coverings, and the like.

Tribal Structure

The Ram tribe is currently led by a female Ram named Elena, their chieftess, the widow of the former Ram chieftain (who was killed by the former Wolf chieftain during the second civil war), who has since married Raj the current Wolf chieftain, creating a strong alliance between Wolf and Ram tribes.

The Rams are a large group, scattered in several different groups that tend to be nomadic across Vanaheim, but the largest group of Rams has a consistent territory in the mountain range of northeastern Vanaheim. They tend to live in yurts and are primarily hunter-gatherers, usually with a herd of mundane (as in, non-elven-shapeshifter) rams and ewes to provide milk and wool.

Ram Culture

The Rams are extremely martial, teaching children the art of war as soon as they are able to walk, even if the children go on to be sorted into other tribes when they come of age. Rams specialize in hand-to-hand combat and their preferred weapon tends to be a sword or mace. All Rams are also trained in magical warfare, particularly the aforementioned crafting of defensive charms into weaving; it is not uncommon to see fierce warriors knitting beautiful things that are also meant as protective items.

The Rams are led by a chieftess, but are otherwise fairly egalitarian and the chieftess mainly makes decisions pertaining to whether or not to go to war. Rams are strongly clannish, and their customs differ from family group to family group, but they can usually be united under their chieftain or chieftess when a matter arises that concerns the tribe as a whole, such as going to war or other matters of defense.

Making Allies with Rams

It is strongly suggested that you not contact the Ram tribe unless you yourself are of a warrior temperament, and then be prepared to be challenged and tested until they find you suitable.

Rams appreciate good-quality fiber arts that you have made yourself, such as knit garments; they also appreciate goat and sheep milk and milk products such as yogurt and cheese. Rams can be entertained by song and poetry, especially tales of epic battles from Earth history. If building an altar to a Ram spirit, gifting them with a drinking horn will be appreciated, as well as fine weaponry, points if you forged said weapon yourself.

Rams are, of all the tribes, one of the easiest to offend so it is advised to be on your best behavior until you are very, very familiar with a Ram and very sure that letting down your guard and joking and being informal will not cause offense. Once a Ram lets down their guard and considers you a friend, they are fiercely loyal and lots of fun to be around.

Rams can be a lusty bunch, but like the rest of the Eshnahai will respect 'no' as a boundary if you are uninterested, or give a damn good time if you are. Unlike some other tribes, Rams can keep things casual, but if their heart is involved they may want to start a family, so that is important to keep in mind if you go there.

THE RAVEN TRIBE

The Raven's function amongst the tribes is one of the hardest to pin down. Ultimately, they are the transformers, initiators, alchemists of the soul. ...Linked with war and death, Ravens tap into the transformative power of these situations. Guardian of the grave, of the compost heap, Raven knows that in order to move forward, the past must be swallowed and digested in order to move on to the next leg of the journey. If Hare represents the process of creative transformation, Raven

has the opposite, catabolic function, clearing away the corpses so that new life can thrive.
-Catriona McDonald

The Ravens are all this and more, from what I have observed of their tribe. They are the most outgoing of the tribes, and the best people to go to for information about elven history and culture, yet paradoxically one of the most protective tribes of the realm, assisting the Wolves on patrol, and not being afraid to put nosy trespassers on "the Disney ride" or even drive those with bad intentions to illness or insanity to keep them away. The Ravens are fond of interacting with other cultures, learning about them, and having a cultural exchange, but also fiercely protective of elven culture, preserving its lore and traditions with iron talons. They are a paradox, a riddle, wrapped in a mystery, inside an enigma, but also the key to knowledge and the power that comes from knowledge applied with wisdom, in alliances formed in the Otherworld, and the study of the esoteric arts.

Tribal Structure

The Ravens were, until the spring equinox of 2014, led by a very, very old man who they call simply "Grandfather Raven". He was not the first Raven, but he is the oldest. Now, a woman named Serithia leads the Raven tribe. Jaerethsa'el (or Jarod to outlanders; one of this author's spirit companions) is the second-in-command of the tribe and also the head of the White Ravens (see below), a man who is typically addressed as "Lord Raven" within and outside of the tribe and may also be addressed as such by outlanders, a man who is the main historian of the realm, an archivist, and is possessed of a wicked wit.

He is a formidable warrior and battle-mage, but his real passion is the study of history and observance of cultures and psychology.

The Raven tribe also has a leading council of four, two women and two men, representing the four winds and four elements. They assist their tribal leaders in making important decisions in the tribe, and delegating various responsibilities within the tribe and where the Ravens are needed elsewhere in the realm and other worlds, including our own. They also assist Serithia and Lord Raven in priestly duties of the Raven tribe, such as observing the high days and lunar tides.

The Raven tribe "sponsors" a mystery school/cult called, simply, the White Ravens, a group of Ravens who dress in white and oversee dying and death rites in the realm, and also specialize in healing and rites of passage. Only a very small portion of the Raven tribe belongs to the White Ravens, and they are very secretive and have some rather strict taboos and binding oaths. Candidates for the White Ravens are observed for at least a year for being admitted into the fold.

Raven Culture

The Ravens are a fairly egalitarian tribe, and the leadership of Serithia, Lord Raven, and the Four is a loose one, with most Ravens being fairly autonomous to come and go and do as they please, so long as they remain within tribal law, and assist on group efforts where the presence of everyone is required (such as the Wild Hunt).

When a person is chosen to be with the Ravens, they are given an initiation ordeal in which the tribe shifts into bird form and tears their flesh off a piece at a time, stripping them down to the bone, and ingesting their body parts. The Ravens then shed their feathers and create a feather cloak which forms a "new skin" and puts the initiate back together. The body parts ingested by the tribe serves a purpose of "downloading" the initiate's thoughts and memories into the group mind, and the "new skin" formed from feathers allows the initiate to access the group mind. This does not work as a hive mind - each Raven remains an individual - but they have an awareness of the others, and an easier time with finding and communicating with other Ravens and can access information fed into the "collective" about people, places, and things.

The Ravens are, with the Wolves, considered one of the two "unseelie" tribes of the Eshnahai, due to their connection to death and destruction, and their tendency towards "extreme" measures of dealing with unwanted outlanders poking around in the realm.

Making Allies with Ravens

The Ravens believe in freedom of information, and are the best people to go to if you want to learn more about Vanic culture. However, the Ravens believe that everything has its price, and that nothing is truly free. The Raven tribe have a saying: "Knowledge is power. The other side of that equation is knowledge is liability." If they give anything to you, you will eventually be expected to pay it back or pay it forward in some way.

The Ravens are fairly flexible and can work with a human mentee by appointment or spontaneously; it will vary by individual Raven to Raven what their preference is, and they are usually adaptable to a "pet human"'s schedule.

The Raven tribe is particularly fond of creative people, and especially if you create something given as a gift for them, like a piece of jewelry or pottery set on a shrine to their tribe or a Raven guide. Some Ravens enjoy spending time in this realm with humans who can entertain them with poetry or song, and a bit of wine. The Ravens are, like most elves, highly sexual people and it is not unusual to be propositioned by one of them. They are not typically particular about gender, and tend towards kink, enjoying bondage and rough sex, especially drawing blood.

The Ravens are one of the harder tribes to offend, but it is generally a good idea to avoid mocking the dead in their presence, and they are not fond of censorship or ideologues. While there are things about human culture which Ravens appreciate and are fascinated by, there are other facets of human culture that they find illogical, undesirable, and downright ugly, and you should be prepared to answer questions about modern Western society and human behavior as influenced by modern Western society that may come off as intrusive and/or rude and condescending, but are mainly born from a desire to understand humanity better and try to find the good - the "shining" - in us, which they find increasingly rare in these times.

THE SALMON TRIBE

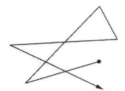

The pools in Salmon territory connect to the Well of Wyrd, and the Salmon tribe are first and foremost a tribe of diviners and seers. They are adept at scrying, most particularly. The Salmon tribe are best at seeing the patterns in the past and present and determining what would come to pass if these cycles continue; the Salmon tribe are often called upon to determine matters of Vanaheim as a whole, or the Vanir's relationship with other realms. They are keepers of history and lore and, with the Raven tribe, preservers of culture, particularly of bardic traditions.

Tribal Structure

Once a year the entire Salmon tribe gathers at the base of the World Tree, at the Well of Wyrd that feeds the roots, and have a tribal meeting and choose a new tribal king and queen by lots. Anyone in the Salmon tribe can become king and queen and it is indeed a position that most adults in the tribe have held at one point or another, sometimes more than once; the Salmon tribe is fairly egalitarian and non-hierarchical and the roles of Salmon King and Salmon Queen are more with regards to any decisions that need to be made on behalf of the tribe (listening to their tribesfolk first) and scrying/divining on behalf of the tribe.

The Salmon are fairly numerous and prone to having large families, but usually keep to their own tribal territory as to stick close to the pools and their source of power.

Salmon Culture

The Salmon folk are quiet, listening and observing much and speaking little. When they interact with others outside of the tribe it is rarely by accident, and deep connections can be forged rather quickly through non-verbal means.

The Salmon believe in constantly moving forward and not stagnating, and have been a big force in Vanaheim choosing to have more diplomatic relations with other realms and reaching out to humanity more actively again; the current prime minister of Vanaheim, Falaereth (or "Fal" to friends), is Salmon tribe, son of the most recent Salmon King.

The Salmon tribe tends to dress more formally and like most elves, are vain of their hair and some Salmon do particularly elaborate hairstyles, often strewn with shells and pearls, which is of some personal symbolic significance to them. The Salmon are known for being graceful and having beautiful voices and very kind and generous and hospitable to others.

Making Allies with Salmon

A Salmon ally can be helpful in learning divination and scrying, particularly scrying that involves water, and involves recognizing the patterns of the past and present and cycles repeating themselves and how to break destructive/toxic cycles.

Salmon are usually helpful if approached with good intent, and like most Vanir enjoy good food and drink, particularly seafood (though avoid feeding them salmon), ale and rum, and hazelnuts and hazelnut-flavored things. Salmon folk enjoy spending time at bodies of water, so it would be ideal to engage them at beaches, rivers, ponds, lakes, streams, or anyplace water is flowing. In a pinch, they can meet you in your shower, though this is not advised unless you're prepared for the relationship to be sexual.

Salmon are kind and nurturing, and regard working relationships with humans to be family. This may mean dealing with an overprotective spirit who gets on your case about past issues haunting you, and "rising above" and breaking painful cycles.

THE SEAL TRIBE

The Seals bring the manifestations of dreams and emotions into the physical world, they are givers of visions and inspiration. They interact with this realm as selkies, shedding their skin for a time to live and love with passionate, inspired, sensitive humans, but always the sea and their home will call them back.

Tribal Structure

The Seals are led by a chieftain and chieftess but the Seals are otherwise very non-hierarchical and spend their time mostly hunting and playing with family, sometimes finding beautiful humans in the waters and sending them visions and dreams and other forms of inspiration. The Seals are a fairly numerous tribe and are prone to large families, many of the children getting sorted out to other tribes when they come of age, though there is a phenomenon where Seals tend to have Seal grandchildren (not unlike the Frogs).

Seal Culture

Seals tend to dress in skins, leathers, and furs, and with simple jewelry of bone and shell. They have villages on the eastern shore of Vanaheim, just out of reach of high tide, with buildings made of driftwood and hides, decorated with seashells and seaweed. The Seals fish and hunt sea animals, and eat a lot of seaweed. The Full Moons are important to all the tribes but particularly the Seals, who will celebrate for three days non-stop with much singing, dancing, storytelling, swimming, and fire spinning.

The Seals are the tribe (other than Swans) most likely to get romantically involved with humans, with the aforementioned caveat that someday, they will return home.

Making Allies with Seals

The Seals are very friendly and approachable, and are easy to win over as allies. Like most Vanir they appreciate good food and good drink, with a strong preference for seafood and rum. It would be good to establish first contact at the ocean, or invite a Seal ally to spend time with you on a trip to the beach. Seals enjoy music and dancing and fun games and silliness, so if you can entertain them in addition to offering them, or just enjoy the beauty of the ocean together, that is a good way to begin establishing a bond.

Seals are very fond of sensitive artistic people, and are prone to falling in love with them and serving as a muse. It cannot be reiterated enough that getting involved with a Seal will likely not last beyond a decade or two, however the saying "tis better to have loved and lost" seems to apply here.

THE SERPENT TRIBE

The Serpents are equal parts priest, mage, bard, healer, scholar, and leader or counselor, fulfilling a similar role to elven society as the Druids did in ancient times. The Serpents are primarily known within the realm and to outsiders as master healers, but they are more than just healers of illness and injury. They are ultimately healers of the soul, and of wyrd itself.

Tribal Structure

The Serpents are led by a chieftain and chieftess, typically a consanguineous pair, and very often, fraternal twins. They claim a line of descent and initiation directly from the Serpent Twins, the first Serpents. Every pair of leaders of the Serpent tribe since have been hand-picked by the predecessors prior to their retirement or death; the position of chieftain and chieftess is usually held for life. The Serpents also have a priest and priestess, who are also supposed to be a consanguineous pair, fraternal twins. Sibling incest is not taboo in elven culture, and the twinbond is considered the most sacred of all marriages. The priest and priestess, as twins, are a polarity - yin and yang, day and night, sun and moon, and some balance of elements (such as fire and water, or air and earth). They perform rites for the tribe on the full moon and on the days of the wheel of the year which helps the Serpent tribe to do its job of wyrdworking.

The Serpents have a council of twelve, in addition to the chieftain and chieftess, and priest and priestess, who vote on important issues concerning the tribe.

The tribe is unique among other elven tribes in that most people who are born into the Serpent tribe, remain with that tribe, and candidates from other tribes are usually determined shortly after birth, with a representative of the tribe telling the parents their child is meant for the tribe. Occasionally, someone will wind up in the tribe after having been with another tribe for a time as an adult, and circumstances in their lives causing them to ansferred out" to the Serpents. There is at least one person from every tribe at all times within the Serpent tribe, which reinforces their connection to the wyrd of their land and their people.

Despite what the above might infer, the Serpents are also a fairly small tribe, one of the smallest tribes in the realm.

Serpent Culture

The Serpent tribe is extremely secretive about its inner workings; the author has not been permitted to speak of what he knows beyond what he has already given, and to say that the Serpent tribe "sponsors" a tribe-within-a-tribe, or a mystery school/cult, the Dragons. The Dragons consist of mated twin pairs. The work of the Dragons is seen as being of the utmost importance in the realm, and is also the most secret of Serpent business. All Dragons are considered Serpent-affiliated, even if they originate from elsewhere, but not all Serpents are Dragons.

Making Allies with Serpents

To work with a member of the Serpent tribe is to walk the knife's edge of pain - healing through venom, and the transformation process of shedding one's skin. The path of the Serpent is the path of ascension. It is difficult to slither out of the abyss and up the Tree, but it can be done.

Generally, if you are meant to work with a Serpent, they will find you and let you know. Their preferred method of contact is through dreams or approaching a person in an Otherworld journey. Otherwise, you are better off not going to them, unless you are told by another spirit to go find them and do business with them, in which case you have your work cut out for you.

THE SPIDER TRIBE

The Spiders' job is to weave wyrd. They are responsible for weaving things into place within Vanaheim, and with Vanaheim's connection to other realms. This is a very intricate, delicate, time-consuming job, like surgery. The Spiders can influence wyrd, but ultimately they are channeling the flows and currents of wyrd and manifesting it in their webs.

Tribal Structure

The Spider tribe is the smallest in number next to the Serpents. The tribe is almost exclusively female, with a few males who have the role of attending the women who weave so that they may do their job without interruption. The Spiders are led by a woman they consider their queen (though she is only the queen of the tribe, she is not the queen of all of Vanaheim), who gives birth to twenty-four daughters, one sired by a man chosen from each tribe, to "weave in" all of the energy of Vanaheim into the threads.

Spiders tend to be lesbians or mate with men who are Spiders themselves. They are one of the most insular tribes; children born within the Spiders tend to be Spiders themselves, but they produce children less often than other tribes because of how consumed they are with their work. The Spider Queen tests Spider women coming of age or who are advancing in the tribe; failure to pass these tests results in death. The Spider Queen assigns work to the Spider women, to weave different parts of the tapestry of wyrd.

Spider Culture

The Spiders are extremely secretive and protective of what specifically they do, beyond the general description of "they weave wyrd"; which generally means they bring people, places, and things into place, arranging things to happen. This does not mean they control everything - again, they do less influencing of wyrd, and more "tuning in" to what wyrd wants and being wyrd's instruments. I cannot get any more specific than this because this is the extent of what they want tribal outsiders to know.

The Spiders are, next to the Hares, the most xenophobic and the least likely to bring outlanders in and teach them things. Which is not to say it never happens, I know of at least one case where it has, but working with Spiders is not common and it is not desirable. The Spiders have to be carefully monitored because of how intense and time-consuming their work is, watching for insanity and illness due to energy drain. Spiders are usually assigned either one of the few male Spiders or a mate-helper from another tribe, to monitor and attend them as needed.

Vanir have a reputation for being kinky, and Spiders are kinky even for Vanir. Spiders are fond of complicated bondage, blood, and high levels of pain, inflicted on their partners. This is one reason why the men who are chosen to sire the Spider Queen's daughters are paid as well as they are. Spiders are extremely sadistic, and even more so among each other. The Spiders have had at least two coups within the tribe, with many Spiders being killed in a struggle for power and control of the tribe. As mentioned above, those Spiders who fail to pass tests given them are killed, and Spiders are routinely put through ordeal work as a way to correct any mental imbalances resulting from the intensity of their work, as a "reset button".

The Spiders, like the Serpents, live in a series of caves in a forest, but the Spiders live in a different series of caves than the Serpents do, in their own territory, which is directly adjacent to Serpent territory and the Tree that borders the worlds. Some Spiders choose to live outside of the Spider Caves in a series of cottages strewn across the Spiders' forest, but these are heavily warded and intruders (those without an invite or appointment) are trapped and killed.

The Spiders are the most insular tribe within Vanaheim and keep to themselves. They do have two representatives within Parliament as any tribe does, but beyond that they keep to their own territory and tend to not even show for the rituals that everybody else attends. Much of the reasoning behind this is how busy they are with the work of weaving wyrd, where they can be 'on shift' for days at a time.

Making Allies with Spiders

As mentioned above, you don't. You don't approach the Spiders looking for a working relationship with them unless you've either divined Spider and then checked with them or one of them has approached you.

If a Spider has approached you, it is either to teach you wyrdworking or have you assist with theirs - which is a training process that will take years, if not the rest of your life, and where you will constantly be pushed and challenged to do more, do better - or to have you serve them as an assistant, which requires learning about caregiving, energy work, and being there as an emotional support. Generally speaking Spiders normally do not trust outlanders with this job, but it might happen if you have a talent for energy work and care and feeding of spirits and have been shown through being under a period of observation for a long time that you are trustworthy.

As far as what Spiders like, that is highly contingent on your relationship with a Spider and what they ask of you.

THE SQUIRREL TRIBE

When the tribes were first blessed by Horn Father a long time ago, the Squirrels were among them. They were the only tribe to be completely obliterated during the first civil war in Vanaheim approximately 9000 years ago (the Serpents came close to total annihilation but escaped it with a dozen members); following the second civil war in 2012 and the reunification in 2013, the King and Queen made a charter by request of a handful of folks from different tribes who felt called to leave their tribes and form a new Squirrel tribe.

The Squirrel tribe serve Vanaheim as messengers as well as community organizers, coordinating important events and different jobs that need to be done, and helping to pool resources for large-scale efforts. They also keep track of comings and goings in the realm, including handling RSVPs from outlanders for events, which helps the border patrol (Ravens and Wolves) to do their job.

Tribal Structure

The Squirrels are one of the more informal, non-hierarchical tribes. The Squirrels have a leader they will refer to as their president, who is elected by the tribe to serve a twelve-year term, but their authority is not absolute, and they are required to hold meetings with the entire tribe and take counsel before making important decisions; the president otherwise checks up on and supervises various bits of business the Squirrels conduct.

The Squirrels are a fairly small tribe at present but are growing in number, though they will always necessarily be a smaller tribe due to their sphere of influence and line of duty.

Tribal Culture

The Squirrels are egalitarian to a fault, while the president represents them and will supervise things that go on, the president is held in check by the people, and everyone holds equal weight and importance in the tribe no matter how young or old.

The Squirrel territory is located in north-central Vanaheim, bordering Hare, Raven, and Boar territory. Their territory is heavily forested, and most Squirrels make their homes in tree houses that look like something out of a fairy tale, and are fairly cozy inside. It is typical for Squirrels to mate outside of the tribe (though occasionally there are relationships comprised of two or more Squirrels) and the mate from outside the tribe will live in the Squirrel's treehouse. It is also not unheard of for Squirrels who are romantically unattached to live together as friends, sharing a treehouse.

The Squirrels tend to dress rather plainly, in furs and leathers during the cold part of the year, and linens in warmer weather, typically of neutral colors. However they do favor elaborate jewelry, usually made themselves from found objects, and have an elaborate system of braiding in their hair (usually one or two thin braids on either side of the head, with the rest of the hair down) which signifies length of time in the tribe and their specific duty within the tribe (marked with a bead).

Like most of the tribes, the Squirrels have their own full moon rituals and seasonal rites in addition to attending the ones at the capital for everyone in the realm; the Squirrels bake a loaf of nut bread that they break together at the full moon to signify fellowship and cooperation.

Making Allies with Squirrels

The Squirrels are a pretty curious and friendly bunch, and enjoy meeting outlanders and getting to know them. Squirrels are often busy but can usually be persuaded to spend some time with an outlander if bribed with offerings and interesting conversation and activities.

Like most Eshnahai, Squirrels are usually fairly open to mating with an interested human, though whether it is just casual or involves feelings and expectations of something more serious really depends on the individual Squirrel.

Squirrels have a good sense of humor and are hard to offend, though they can bristle if they feel they are being taken advantage of and will get skittish if they feel they are being threatened in some way. It is always a good idea to politely invite a Squirrel to join you, and not summon them; it is also a good idea to not invade their territory (which tends to be booby-trapped) but make first contact in a more neutral location such as the capital (there are always Squirrels at the capital, and often in the marketplace), and wait on going to their territory until you are invited by them. To be invited into a Squirrel's home is an act of trust and respect on their part, and not something they do casually.

Squirrels are fond of nuts, nut bread, candied nuts, and things like almond-flavored or hazelnut coffee and liqueur. They will also eat stew, root vegetables, porridge, bread with honey, and really most things an outlander would offer of their hospitality. Squirrels enjoy music and poetry and play; being invited to do something like go on a jog or on a camping excursion pleases them greatly.

The Squirrels can be chatty, and can be quite silly and are overly fond of bad puns, so if you prefer your spirits to be more serious business, a Squirrel may not be a good fit for you as far as a guide/mentor. However, Squirrels love to be helpful and love to make people happy and feel at ease, so forging a friendship with a Squirrel will win an ally who brings you sunshine.

THE SWAN TRIBE

The Swan tribe are priests of the art of war and the art of love. They can transmute the rage of battle into sexual arousal, and vice versa, using passion to bring a warrior to battle-frenzy. They can divine the outcomes of battles, sing to give a warrior strength, or enchant weapons. They can turn aside arrows and strikes of swords. They have been known to protect people in this realm, and take human lovers who they champion. Understanding the link between love and war is the key to understanding the Swans and their magic.

Tribal Structure

The Swans are one of the smallest tribes in Vanaheim. They used to be much more numerous prior to the second civil war in 2012, and were drastically decimated. However, they have come back a bit in number. Every person in the Swan tribe bears arms and is trained in them. The Swans also cross-train with the Ravens. The Swans have a chieftain and chieftess who give each member of the tribe a weapon after having been a tribal member for three years; the chieftain and chieftess change hands when they are bested in battle, as anyone within the tribe may challenge them. The chieftain and chieftess are responsible for training new Swans.

Swan Culture

The Swans are extremely physically active and fit. However they enjoy luxury and fine things, and can be quite hedonistic in their enjoyment of good food, good drink, and good sex.

Unlike most of the Eshnahai who tend to be very polyamorous by default, a Swan will choose a single mate for life (or have a single male mate and a single female mate). After the bond has been established, there will be no other partner even in the case of infidelity or death.

Most Swans try to choose a mate from their own clan, but as mentioned above, some Swans choose mortal loves and have been known for them to go to Vanaheim upon death of the mortal form to be with them for life.

Making Allies with Swans

The Swans are very careful about choosing humans they work with, and will test humans before deciding to teach them, or give them further advancement in teaching. However, having a Swan as an ally can save one's life.

That said, Swans are extremely protective and possessive of people they consider theirs, which can sometimes/often make things complicated in this realm.

The Swans look for people with strength, people of a warrior temperament, not always physical - having fought many battles of life circumstances, fighting oppression, having causes one is passionate in and doing activism are all things the Swans value.

The Swans appreciate pretty things. They particularly are fond of jewelry, wreaths or cloaks or fans made of feathers, well-crafted wands, or handmade weapons (like if one does smithing, making a blade to put on a shrine for a Swan teacher/lover would be well-received). The Swans are also highly romantic and sentimental and will very much appreciate poetry or art done in their honor, or to convey the love and passion you feel about somebody or something.

Having sex with a Swan is not recommended unless you are fully aware of the implications that this means they are serious about you and they regard you as a mate, and you are OK with this. The Swans do favor rough sex when they have it, though there is grace and sensuality and palpable expression of love through the experience.

THE WOLF TRIBE

The Wolves were the first of the Eshnahai to reach out to humanity with the intent to teach humans how to fend for themselves. Their proper place in the structure of the Otherworld is that of protectors, guardians and guides. The Wolves are in charge of maintaining the Veil, or border, between Vanaheim and this world, for the protection of humanity as well as protecting the Eshnahai from unscrupulous or misguided humans. They are in charge of patrolling Vanaheim to deal with any conflicts that arise within, rather like police officers. They are also the main riders of the Wild Hunt, becoming a sort of military presence or "riot police" that deals with traffic from other worlds that might hurt elves or their human kin, as well as humans in Midgard who need to be "put down like rabid dogs" (this has in past years included violent criminals as well as political leaders).

The Wolves have always had a special relationship with the Hare tribe, they have a close bond with the Raven tribe by virtue of patrolling the realm and doing the Hunt together, and of course there are alliances formed during times of internal conflict in the realm. But by and large, the Wolves keep to themselves and only venture outside of their territory when needed or called upon.

Tribal Structure

The typical person to get sorted into the Wolf tribe will be a smart-mouthed, angsty kid who doesn't really fit in anywhere. Much like the military has whipped many into shape, teaching responsibility and respect for oneself and others, so do the Wolves.

Even with being sorted, it is not guaranteed one will "take" to the tribe, and so they have an initiation ordeal; a new person's first month in the Wolf tribe is very much like boot camp, and you either pass or fail. Most Wolves pass. The very few who have not are usually sent back to their tribe of origin (whatever their mother is) but this has only happened a couple of times in the entire history of the Wolf tribe.

The first initiation is that proverbial passing of boot camp. The new Wolf is given a task to perform, and then undergo a rite. This rite can be considered an energetic attunement, where one is granted a certain degree of immunity to iron, fire, and herbs that elves usually are susceptible to; one is also given a boost to the energy which speeds healing time from wounds and other injuries (but they are not invincible, just stronger than the average elf). A new Wolf should also be able to wolf-shift for the first time after receiving this attunement.

At this initiation, the Wolf's hair is also locked up, which is seen as a statement or marker that sets the Wolves apart, a source of pride, and contains energy stored up over time which eases wolf-shifting, the berserk, and the amount of power in attacks. Short hair on men is seen as largely unacceptable in the realm, so most elven men have long hair. From a practical standpoint, having locks means less time spent on hair, which is also good when you need to act quickly. In Wolf culture, the length of hair is also seen as a sign of virility - the longer one's locks, the more you're assumed to have prowess in battle and the bedroom, though anything beyond waist-length is not really practical from a battle standpoint.

There are three other ordeals which can be undertaken to advance in the tribe. The tribal structure consists of a chieftain, who can be male or female (but is usually male, since men sorted into the Wolf tribe outnumber women sorted into the tribe approximately 40 to 1), the chieftain's second-in-command who is chosen specifically by the chieftain, then a small group of people who have taken all three ordeals, and then finally the subordinates. Most people in the tribe only do the first two ordeals, and stop; to be considered eligible for the chieftaincy or becoming the second-in-command, a Wolf must do all three.

The chieftaincy itself is a long-term position; your average Wolf chieftain is the chieftain for about 2000-5000 years before retiring or dying. Retired Wolf chieftains can still remain in the tribe in an advisory position, or they may go to the Elders or another part of the realm. One of this author's spirit companions ("Clarence") was Wolf chieftain and was later on transferred to the Serpent tribe; the current Wolf chieftain goes by Raj (he was Clarence's second-in-command), and is very friendly, though a bit gruff.

The first ordeal after initiation, for advancement, consists of a fast followed by suspension in a tree and having the runes beaten into the Wolf. The second ordeal, the Wolf has their genitalia pierced. The third ordeal, the nipples are pierced. The reason for the piercings is multifold. First, people are often squeamish about their bits getting poked with needles, so it's a test of bravery. Secondly, elves are usually susceptible to iron, which includes steel which is made from iron. Having steel in their bodies is a sign of that immunity, and further modifies their energy. Finally, the Wolves have a reputation as being the best lovers, and the piercings make things more fun, for both them and their partner/s. (Worth noting is that the piercings don't tend to cause the steel "allergy" in a non-Wolf elven/fae partner who is handling them. This is part of what goes into the energy modification.)

If the second-in-command is to take the chieftain position, they must battle all the others who have taken all three ordeals, to prove themselves worthy of the position. There is a second part of the ritual, which involves extreme pain/fire endurance. This results in permanent scarring, which is notable as Wolves can usually heal without scarring, but the ordeal is designed to be painful and nasty, and the Wolf bears these scars as a thing of honor and pride.

Wolf Culture

The Wolf is a simple creature, of two loves: family, and work. A Wolf is happiest when helping others, and this is why subordinate Wolves are usually content being subordinate and not advancing past first or second degree - they are the "backbone" of the tribe as it were, they are valued for being that, and everything runs smoothly in the hierarchy. It is very, very rare for the second-in-command and/or the chieftain to run into problems from someone within the pack, but they have methods for dealing with their own if such an incident arises. That said, the second-in-command and chieftain are required to set a good example for the tribe - they cannot go around treating people like shit because they feel like it. There is confidence/dominance and then there is cockiness and arrogance, and the latter is to be despised. While the Wolves definitely are known for good-natured bantering within the tribe, which can get quite raunchy and raucous, they also believe that true strength is in building others up, not tearing them down.

The job of a Wolf is twofold - the duties described above, and then their own individual interests. In times past, individual Wolves tended to be bound to a specific tribe, or location, here in Midgard. The closest analog to what Wolves do that can be found in folklore, is the Irish faoladh or the Scottish wulver, and indeed some of them have done those particular jobs (one of this author's spirit companions was a Wolf who worked as a wulver for a long time). Wolves look after people. In eons gone by, when life was much nastier, brutish, and shorter, the Wolves trained human warriors. That said, while they can be benevolent towards humans, and can have "pet humans" that they look after and become fond of, they can still prey on humans, even if they only prey on unsavory humans (hence the reputation for being un-hostile - they're not hostile to most people), and they have filthy tempers and it is a bad idea to cross them.

All tribes have their way of making magic; the magic of the Wolves is blood, sweat, and tears, the power of the ordeal. They can give pain and blood, to spare it of someone else, or to heal. They can beat runes into people. The Wolf chieftain is an ordeal master and can be communicated with to arrange an ordeal in the Otherworld given by him, or by someone else who specializes in them (such as the Raven tribe).

Wolves are very, very strongly mate- and family-oriented. A majority of Wolves are monogamous, and those who aren't strictly monogamous usually have two spouses or only have occasional dalliances with a very close friend or two, otherwise are not really capable of having a full-on relationship outside of their mate. Since the ratio of Wolf-sorted women is much lower to that of men, male Wolves often have to take a mate outside the tribe, whereas female Wolves can be assured the pick of anyone they choose within the tribe who's not already taken, and female Wolves often have a harem. Wolves are expected to have children, and the family is seen as a source of pride. However, Wolves, like the rest of the Eshnahai, can control their fertility, and do not think people should have more children than they are capable of caring for.

Worth noting is that despite the tendency towards monogamy and emphasis on family, there is far less stigma towards children born outside of wedlock than there is in the rest of the realm. It is not uncommon for Wolves to marry a woman who has had a child outside of wedlock, or has had children from a previous marriage, and for the Wolf to adopt said children. Fosterage is a huge deal in the Wolf tribe, and seen as a sacred thing. Liminality is also sacred. They will take outcasts and give them refuge. They will father the fatherless, friend the friendless. They will give a place and a purpose to those who have none, even if that place is "beyond the hedge", in their wilds.

In the whole of Vanaheim, the Wolves are seen as being rather equivalent to (making an Earth analogy here) a biker gang who moves into a tough neighborhood and kicks out the drug dealers, gets crime under control... but are themselves noisy, boisterous, rough. Many of the elves fancy themselves to be refined and dignified, and Wolves have been sometimes seen as dirt, as riffraff, the people with the wild hair and wild personalities who refuse to be tamed, among a species that originated from the first taming of the wild. The Wolves are, in the Undying Lands, an unpleasant reminder that life feeds on life. The Ravens are their closest allies, and most closely aligned to them in work and temperament.

The Wolves are rough around the edges, and make no apologies for this. Wolves are loud, intense, wild, vibrant people, who are fond of hard drinking and lots of fucking. They like to party. They get an adrenaline rush out of the thrill of the hunt, and are sadistic enough to enjoy killing when it's called for, or otherwise meting out punishment to those deserving. While they may not be as refined and polite and "pretty" as the rest of the elves, they are fiercely loyal to those who have earned their loyalty, you could not ask for better friends, and they tend to have more consensus and cohesion within the tribe, a stronger, more tight-knit bond, than the other tribes which are prone to internal quarreling. Wolves are a brotherhood, with some sisters, and they love each other fiercely. It is because of this that they can pick on each other and say things to each other that nobody else can get away with (they are particularly fond of "your mom" jokes).

For all that Wolves may be death-dealers, bringers of pain and vengeance, a reminder that life feeds on life and sometimes it is necessary to cull so things can live... they are also arguably the most strongly alive of the Eshnahai, full of life and vigor and vitality and passion and zest. Every day is like dying in pain and reborn in joy, everything louder than everything else. They are the wild bunch. They are a living reminder not just of death, but that once upon a time elves and giants were the same people, and then things changed.

Making Allies with Wolves

Here are ways to get on Wolves' good side:

- They like alcohol. They like strong alcohol in particular (think vodka, but also whiskey, certain kinds of schnapps, etc).

- Entertain them. Can you sing? Make them laugh. Make them cry. Make them feel.

- Compliment their hair, and often.

- Be a good friend to your friends. Do good deeds. Be helpful. Carry yourself with pride, but also humility.

- Some Wolves will take sexual offers from outlanders, but this is not always a given, and has to go in tandem with having a good character, amusing them, etc.

In addition to this here are some cautions:

- Do not touch the hair without permission. (It is generally assumed to be OK to touch the hair if they are intimate with you.) Do not threaten to cut their hair, or they will cut you.

- Do not act overconfident and cocky, bragging constantly, and demanding respect that you have not earned. Wolves have a special hatred for self-identified 'alpha males', who think they're better than everyone else.

- Do not give unsolicited advice. They hate being told what to do, more than most people hate it.

- They loathe passive-aggressiveness. Be honest with how you feel. Say what you mean and mean what you say. Do not expect Wolves to play guessing games or be mind readers.

- In general, if you think "violence is never the answer", or you can't handle intensity, or loudness, or snark, or dark humor, you will not find yourself able to handle Wolves for very long.

Getting to Know the Eshnahai

There are multiple ways to get to know the Eshnahai (Vanic elves), and here are a few suggestions for establishing a formal working relationship with them.

Divination and first contact

If you are going into this "cold" – no prior history with them - your best bet is to do a divination regarding the tribes. You may feel a strong pull to the idea of one tribe or another, but it's important to do a divination first because what you think is a good fit for you, and what wyrd thinks is a good fit for you, are sometimes two different things.

I would recommend making a casting set with the tribal sigils found throughout the chapters on the tribes, which can be done with any material, though wood, stone (like small river rocks), bone, or leather would probably carry the best charge. During the new or waxing moon, set up a ritual space, light a candle, pour out an offering of milk and honey as a general good will gesture to the elves, and then divine, pulling one of the sigils from a basket or bag, and seeing which tribe comes up.

Once that sigil has been pulled, there are a couple of ways to go about finding a point of contact within that tribe.

The most reliable way to do this is to journey astrally to Vanaheim, specifically to the tribal territory. Different people journey differently. There is a wealth of information on altered states of consciousness available. It is assumed that if you are asked to go, you either have experience with altering your consciousness already or there is time for you to learn how. In some cases, a person will be shown how to get to Vanaheim by one of the Vanir Themselves (a deity or one of the tribal leaders). It is important to first ground and center, and then either use your spirit-taught form of journeying, or a breathing exercise where you feel your astral body project from your physical body, following your "threads of wyrd" out with the intent of reaching out to Vanaheim, seeing where it goes. This can be done as a regular meditation, though most need a little help.

Some people can journey from the high seat, used by such notables as Odin and Thorbjorg the Little Volva (and this seems to originate in Vanic traditions, as we will explore later on). There is something to be said about being up high shifting the body's sense of balance, which makes it easier for some to then shift their state of consciousness, and the symbolism of being "above" is helpful to prod the subconscious mind.

Others need some sort of physical anchor to Vanaheim, such as being in a numinous place with Vanic energies (one of the many reasons why finding sacred spots in the New World is so important). Even things like sitting on a rock, or being in water, can help with the transition between worlds. This author was personally gifted with a stone from Cannon Beach on the Oregon coast (a very liminal place where myself and others have felt the veil between worlds thin and even worlds overlap with this one, Vanaheim in particular) by Njord as an anchor to Vanaheim, and holding the stone does in fact help me to better access the realm when I journey.

I've found it easier to slip between the worlds if some part of me is submerged in water. The only issue with this is travel - you tend to emerge in one of two places: the shoreline or in the middle of The Lake. And most folks don't want to end up in The Lake (unless you're signed over to her [Nerthus] already). There are stangs on the shore cliffs, but they require a bit of a climb.

-Nicanthiel Hrafnhild

If you are worried about potentially getting lost or having something happen to you, there are two ways you can better ensure going where you're meant to:

-   you can journey while holding the sigil of the tribe you're visiting (or have the sigil drawn on you somewhere, in ink or oil, etc)

-   you can go to the capital city of Eshnahaliel, ask to see the Secretary of State (a Raven named Rumelia), and she or an assistant of hers will ask you some questions about your business there, and if they are satisfied with your answers they will give you a passkey (which is basically like a combination GPS device and ID badge to get through wards) or an escort to the tribal territory.

Eshnahaliel is dotted with a series of stangs that serve as transporter devices, and are watched, warded, and "fed" by grovekeepers. You may want to bring a little offering for the grovekeeper of wherever you're going, such as a gold coin (like a gold dollar piece), or something nice to eat or drink. It is a good idea to not ever be rude to a grovekeeper, and to be honest with whatever questions they ask you.

You may need to visit the tribal territory more than once before you find a point of contact. Most Eshnahai are friendly, though a bit wary of outlanders as they have had some bad experiences with people trying to fuck them over and appropriate their traditions, like using them to learn their magic and then trying to use it against them.

Unless they are of a tribe known to not visit their students/mentees often, I would recommend visiting with your contact person at least one to three times a week (ideally, every day, but I understand not everyone can do this), whether you journey Over There to meet them, or you find someplace to meet here (such as your place of residence, so long as hospitality is offered, or in a place in nature - for example, Ravens really like graveyards).

If you cannot journey, you could go the route of doing a ritual similar to invoking your Holy Guardian Angel, and with offerings (such as incense and drink, or milk and honey, or some combination thereof), invite someone from the tribe into your life, to work with you and teach you. You may have to do this more than once - the ritual will probably get someone's attention, but they may want to observe you for awhile. Once you establish contact with the spirit, you can arrange to start meeting together, spending time together.

A lot of your working relationship may just be spending time together in each other's company, getting a feel for each other's energy, and exchanging perspectives on things. This too can be seen a lesson.

Depending on your sexual preference and comfort level, you may find that the elf you are working with wants to be sexual with you. Elves are as a rule respectful of boundaries, so if you are asexual or otherwise uninterested, they won't push it, but I highly recommend elf sex if they and you want to go there, it is a beautiful, sacred experience, and a lesson in magic and energy work in and of itself. Contrary to what some believe, elf sex will not kill you. It may make your life more interesting and complicated, but it otherwise is good. While Eshnahai are as a rule pansexual and polyamorous and kinky, there are exceptions to this, and attitudes towards sex may vary from tribal culture to tribal culture, which has been noted in the chapters on the individual tribes.

It would be good, after a time, if the spirit you are working with wants that, to do moon rituals together, and celebrate the Wheel of the Year together, which will be explored later in this book.

For people who are "headblind" and cannot sense spirits at all, it is perfectly acceptable to pay regular respects to elven spirits with offerings, to pray to them for guidance or help, and express gratitude for the blessings of this world, and the blessings that particular tribes give (such as Cranes and eloquence, Bulls and prosperity, etc.).

If you have prior history with the Eshnahai

If you are elven-souled, or you have some other connection with them (for example, a friend of mine was married to one in a previous incarnation, while not Eshnahai himself), my advice is trust your gut. If you have a feeling you were associated with a particular tribe, it's worth exploring that, and re-establish contact with them. If you remember having a mate or other family members from back then, they will usually welcome you seeking them out, if they are still living.

All of what is said above still applies, except without doing the divination (unless you really feel it's necessary). It would be a good idea to journey there or call upon the elves you had a connection to, to come and meet you if they are still around.

The chances are very good if you had a life in Vanaheim, and a tribal connection, that you had some sort of job, and you may be expected to resume that job when you visit Over There (or you may not, depending on what it was), and there will be more expectation on you to uphold your tribal values and be a good representative of your people in this world, than someone who is just human. This is not always the case - I know of at least one person who was Eshnahai and had a specific tribal affiliation but left the realm, and has a point of contact in that tribe now but no obligation or expectation to do anything with the tribe or pick up where they left off. But this is the exception, more than the rule.

It is of course perfectly acceptable to leave the past in the past, but I've found from my own very painful experience that trying to deny who and what you are to "be human now" doesn't work so well, and there are advantages to re-establishing old bonds.

Faux pas tend to vary from tribe to tribe, for example it is considered highly inappropriate to touch a Wolf's locks without permission and usually they only want other Wolves or their family touching the hair; Hares consider you rude if you want them to visit you and aren't offering food and drink of some sort, while other tribes may be less particular. It really depends on who you're working with, because the Eshnahai are not a monolith and culture can and will vary from tribe to tribe. Some tribal-specific faux pas have been addressed earlier in this book.

However, here are some general pointers on etiquette that could be applied with just about anyone over there:

- Don't bring up the wars unless someone specifically talks to you about them. This is considered an *extremely* sore and sensitive subject, a number of war vets there have trauma and don't want to talk about it. Period.

- Mind your manners, say "please" and "thank you".

- At least initially, gifts are a good idea. Most Eshnahai are fond of alcohol (especially mead or good scotch), bread with honey on it, porridge or stew, or sweets like cake, pie. Eshnahai are also fond of things like music being shared with them, art done of themselves, poetry, or spending time together (like taking a walk with you), so if you can't give food/drink offerings for whatever reason, giving them something novel from this realm is usually a good way to get their attention. Once you have an established relationship you can relax a bit with this.

- Do not give your word unless you intend to keep it. Eshnahai will attack someone for oath-breaking.

- Don't have iron around unless you're dealing with a Wolf, Raven, or Serpent. The Eshnahai consider this offensive.

- The Eshnahai are not fond of the Aesir and if you are very obviously affiliated with the Aesir you may get a less than friendly reception. There are and have been exceptions to this - Eshnahai don't tend to hold people's parentage against them, usually - but things are not as tight with the Vanir and Aesir as a lot of people think they are. Not at all.

- If you are visiting Vanaheim astrally, it is a good idea to either have an escort within the realm (such as a tribal contact) or get a visitor's pass from the Secretary of State at the capital. Stick to the roads and paths, use the stangs (big decorated poles that serve as transporter devices) to get around, don't go in any buildings or out of the way places without an escort. You may not enter any temples with weapons on (there are only three temples within Vanaheim). If you do not have an escort or a visitor's pass you are a lot more likely to be stopped by a Wolf patrol and asked questions about your business and possibly sent back if they think you don't belong there, or they may just keep you from entering the realm altogether (this is especially true if you "smell like" the Aesir).

- If the Eshnahai offer you food and drink in their realm it is seen as extremely rude to refuse. A number of "experts" will caution "don't take food/drink from elves in the Otherworld because they'll enslave you" but that does not apply to Eshnahai. Other elven/fae groups the bets are off, but Eshnahai are anti-slavery as a rule and there are laws about doing non-consensual things to people. It is also against the law in Vanaheim to poison people. Moreover, Eshnahai food is some of the best ever, and has some wonderful energetic effects. If the Eshnahai are giving you alcohol and there is a toast, it is considered polite and good to toast your host and/or hostess with 'may your fields be fertile and your trees evergreen' (regardless of whether or not they're farmers, it's a common Eshnahai toast and is symbolic).

- If you are a guest in someone's home, it is considered polite to offer help with things like dishes or other work that needs to be done, though they may tell you they don't need it, in which case that's OK.

- The Eshnahai value hospitality and generosity and loyalty and that could be said to be one thing the Eshnahai have in common across the board, they try to demonstrate that with others and they honor that when they see it in other people.

- Keep in mind that not all Eshnahai have the same cultural references that modern humans do. However sometimes Eshnahai may surprise you - most of them know who Elvis and Madonna are, for example.

- Do obey any instructions or rules that are given to you by the tribe or individual escort you are dealing with. This doesn't mean let anyone boss you around, but it does mean that any rules that are given to you are expected to be observed and you may be in violation of a law by breaking them.

- Do not take any "souvenirs" unless one of the Eshnahai gives it to you.

- Some spirits are particular about their privacy, some are not so much. It is a good idea to check in with People before you talk openly about any experiences you have Over There, especially if you are planning on being public with your experiences (such as on a blog).

If you stick to the above you should be fine.

Don't be surprised if building relationships with the tribes takes more than one visit. Often, the first time you meet a particular group, you will be put to work to see how serious you are. There are valuable insights to be gained from the labor itself--much like the Zen Buddhist saying, "Before enlightenment, chop wood, carry water; after enlightenment, chop wood, carry water."

Corollary to this, the lessons from the tribes will overflow into your waking life as well. Pay attention to how a particular tribe influences different aspects of your life. Often times, you will be asked what you've learned between visits, as well as what you've absorbed in Vanaheim itself. The Vanir are nothing if not practical—if you can't transfer an experience from one world to the other, you should seriously question its verracity.

-Catriona McDonald

For those of us who are asked to journey, we have quite a task ahead of us. We are dealing with an entire pantheon that most regard only as an afterthought, yet have disregarded to our own peril. The knowledge that we uncover is very often not for ourselves alone, but is also meant to be shared with others to find as they are led and need dictates. Even in our enthusiasm to share and pay homage to these great Powers as well as help our fellow travelers, we must still observe protocol in what we share. Many of us will find ourselves being told by the entities we encounter not to share certain things, whether because it is only relevant to our own relationship with them, or there is a mystery that must be preserved among a few of like mind. It can be very difficult, especially when wanting to corroborate this gnosis for reality checks, to have much that cannot be told. Yet that is part of the package, as well.

So, here is to safe travels, and safe returns, knowing what to share of the journey, and what to preserve in one's heart, and making use of it all, that Vanaheim may continue to open itself to travelers without fear of its sanctity being violated in thoughtlessness, and the power of Vanaheim may touch Midgard once more, and bless us, even as we bless them.

The Differences between Aesir and Vanir

It has been asserted by some modern heathens that the Aesir and Vanir are not tribally distinct, and so this list was made to show both critics and those who might be leaning in favor of the Vanir and Vanic ways that the Aesir and Vanir are not "all the same"; there are differences in how the gods present themselves as well as key elements of their worship.

CHARACTERISTICS OF THE VANIC CULT

- The Vanir are known for consanguineous marriage, such as the unions noted in the primary sources between Njord and his sister (most likely Nerthus), and Freya and her brother, and via SPG of the King and Queen as well as citizens of Vanaheim unnamed by lore.

- The wain seems to be the most important symbol of the Vanic cultus. Frey and Nerthus are both noted as having a wain that goes on a yearly procession, and Freya also has a wain pulled by cats. The only Aesic god noted to have a wain is Thor[10], who is married to Sif, a probable Vanir goddess, and as such carries her influence (and as explored earlier in this book may be of Vanic origin).

---

[10] While it is common belief that Frigga has a wain, this is not mentioned in primary sources and can be considered "fakelore" or purely personal gnosis.

- Another important symbol is the ship, which only Frey and Njord have connections to out of the Norse gods. Even when the Northlands mostly cremated their dead, many cremations involved burning ships. Many burials were in ship-shaped stone formations known as "stone ships".

- The Vanir are more immediately associated with animals than the Aesir. Frey and Freya ride a boar and a sow respectively, and cats are sacred to Freya and synonymous with her witch-cult. Frey is also connected with the stag through the antler, and stallions were kept in his honor by Hrafnkell Freysgoði as well as his people at Thrandheim, Norway. Sea birds are sacred to Njord, and livestock, especially the cow, is connected with Nerthus. There are also the tribal divisions within Vanaheim.

- During the Ertebolle/Funnelbeaker era and through Proto-Germanic culture, beaker shaped vessels were found in graves as well as homesteads. The beaker may have been of significant purpose in Vanic rituals.

- Bodies were found in lakes and bogs throughout Northern Europe in Neolithic times. Nerthus' victims were sacrificed in a lake, and the sacral kings of Yngling blood were usually also drowned.

- Frey and Njord are the two deities mentioned in oaths taken on the oath ring in *Landnamabok*. Ullr is mentioned elsewhere as having an oath ring. The Vanir probably initiated the custom of oathing on a circle shape in their time (symbolic of the circle and cycles of life), which carried over into blended Aesic and Vanic religion.

- There was no cremation during the time of the Ertebolle and Funnelbeaker cultures, and the practice of inhumation in a mound was common long after the Aesir-Vanir war and blended religion, among Frey's historical devotees (re: Thorgrim in *Gisla's Saga*). The practice of utiseta most often involved sitting on a burial mound, and the elves were also noted to dwell in mounds throughout the land.

- In Ynglinga Saga, Freya was said to practice *seiðr*, and that it was commonly practiced among the Vanir. Following the Aesir-Vanir war, Freya taught *seiðr* to Odin, who was most interested in using it. There seems to be two forms of *seiðr*, oracular and magical.

  o Oracular *seiðr* required a ceremonial costume, and an elevated seat to perform, as well as chanting songs to help alter the state of consciousness. This was explicitly mentioned in the account of Thorbjorg, and we know Odin has a high seat called Hlidskjalf (or High-Shelf), which he likely built after Freya taught him, and it is mentioned that Frey used Odin's high seat and saw Gerda when sitting there.

o   There was magical *seiðr*, which will be explored later in this book.

- Male practitioners of *seiðr* were often called *ergi*, which has connotations of cross-dressing and homosexual behavior. When *seiðr* was seen as more of an evil thing through the lens of Christian superstition, to call someone *ergi* was as good as calling someone a *seiðr*-worker, and both the magical and homosexual components were an insult seen as worthy of serious criminal charges in medieval Iceland. The priests of Frey at Gamla Uppsala horrified the Odinsman Starkadr with effeminate dress and mannerisms, and Tacitus mentions a few accounts of cross-dressing priests, particularly in the rites of twin gods (a common trait of the Vanir). While in the modern day many who claim to be *seiðr* practitioners are oathed to Odin, *seiðr* originated as a Vanic practice and followers of the Vanir have every right to claim it as our own.

- The "magic number" of the Vanir cult seems to be four rather than nine: four for the ruling Vanir of "the heathen era" (Njord, Nerthus, Frey, Freya), the four dwarves Freya slept with to acquire Brisingamen, and the four oxen Gefion (likely one and the same as Freya) used to plow the Danish island of Zealand. Four is also representative of the four seasons and four directions (especially as presented in the four angles of the diamond that is the Ing rune), and the four elements of Wiccan practice (earth, air, fire, and water).

- The Vanir cult itself seems to have started during the late hunter-gatherer period of Europe, in the beginnings of horticulture, and began to be blended with the Aesir cult when "civilization" was coming from elsewhere. The four most prominent deities of the Vanir – Frey, Freya, Njord, and Nerthus - are brother/sister pairs who are noted as mating with one another, most likely in rituals to preserve fertility of the land. Njord and Nerthus have connections with the ocean and lakes/rivers respectively, and Frey and Freya have connections with the land, Frey of grain crops and Freya of fruit and flowers (also Frey with the harvest and Freya with spring). Njord, Frey, and Freya also all seem to be invested in the quality of human life and influence prosperity and love as well as familial relationships. Nerthus seems to have investment in the Earth itself, and keeping humanity mindful of the holiness and awe of the Divine.

- The Vanir cult seems dependent on priesthood, which carried into blended Vanic and Aesic religion. Frey and Nerthus are noted as having a priestess and a priest respectively, who is in intense communion with the god and performs their yearly procession to bless the Land and its people. Frey and Njord are mentioned in *Ynglinga Saga* as being the priests of the gods following the Aesir-Vanir war. The question is, what were they sacrificing, and who were they sacrificing to? I believe at least part of this is collecting the offerings given from man to gods, and in return blessing men. But from a Vanic perspective, they are also giving of their inherent sacral/hallowing nature to the Aesir, in frith.

CHARACTERISTICS OF THE AESIC CULT

- The Aesir are known for exogamous marriage: Odin and Frigga are not brother and sister, Baldur and Nanna are not brother and sister. In *Ynglinga Saga*, Odin made the brother-sister relations of the Vanir illegal at least in Asgard, and Loki remarked upon Frey and Freya being caught having sexual relations in Lokasenna, which would have been considered extremely scandalous with the ban on sibling marriage.

- The Aesir are typified by their tools. The Vanir also have tools/weapons - notably Freya's Brisingamen, Njord's axe and Frey's sword/antler - but they are not known immediately by these tools as the Aesir are known by theirs:

  o Thor's hammer, which functions by dispersing lightning rather like a policeman's taser. (The hammer was later worn by heathens during the conversion era to differentiate themselves from Christians who wore crosses, and the hammer can be seen as a symbol of the Aesic cult par excellence.)
  o Odin's ring Draupnir, which makes nine more like itself every ninth night, and as such would put him as a "ring-giver", as many ancient Germanic kings were called.

Odin also has a spear called Gungnir, which would be an easy weapon for a layman to craft and use, effective for quick and painful killing of foes, and creating horrific injuries for ordeal purposes. A spear was also more efficient to throw over the head of the opposing army - a practice of the Vikings as a way of Odin claiming foes and war-dead - than a sword, axe, or something else.

- Frigga's distaff. While Holda and Frigga are both spinners, Holda is a solitary and does it for the comfort of her own cottage, whereas Frigga has a great hall and clothes many and probably makes tapestries as well.

- Heimdall's horn. The argument as to whether or not Heimdall is a Van or Ase is mentioned earlier in the book, but he uses his horn as an alert and an alarm.

- While the Vanir guard the fertility of the Earth, the Aesir seem to be in charge of its progress. Thor is, again, something of a divine policeman. Frigga is a hostess and a politician in her own right. Heimdall is a warder or "security guard" if you will. Bragi is a god of poetry and song. Odin is a god of higher learning and "knowledge as power" through ruling society, and of warfare. Loki, though of Jotun blood, is often counted among the Aesir and can be seen as a figure of chaos which sometimes helps the natural order, sometimes does not.

- Sacrifices made to Odin were usually hanged (often criminals; see also "the nine nines" mentioned by Adam of Bremen), or slain opponents in battle (the blood-eagle was common). Odin Himself hung on a tree during his Yggdrasil ordeal, literally dying and reborn to gain power. We have no evidence of runes prior to 200 CE in the Northlands, we can assume this was done after the Aesir-Vanir war, and when Aesic and Vanic religion were blended in the Northlands.

- The practice of cremation began in the Northlands during the Corded Ware/Battle Axe culture, the time when we see people coming from elsewhere and most likely bringing the Aesir gods with them. In fact, it is an explicitly Aesic practice, noted in *Ynglinga Saga*:

  o Thus he (Odin) established by law that all dead men should be burned, and their belongings laid with them upon the pile, and the ashes be cast into the sea or buried in the earth. Thus, said he, every one will come to Valhalla with the riches he had with him upon the pile; and he would also enjoy whatever he himself had buried in the earth. For men of consequence a mound should be raised to their memory, and for all other warriors who had been distinguished for manhood a standing stone; which custom remained long after Odin's time.

- Rune magic was a practice known to Odin as well as to Rig-Heimdall who gave the runes to humanity. While Odin gave the runes to all tribes to use, it originated with the Aesir and is much more theirs.

- In addition, rune magic was often accompanied by something called galdr. Unlike what you will read in most Neo-Pagan texts about runes, galdr most likely did not involve singing the names of runes themselves, but rather a verse of poetry that served as a charm. Odin and Bragi are both noted as gods of poetry and inspiration, and it seems that weaving words together effectively was seen as magical. There are some Vanir tribes that also work with the magic of poetry and song (most notably the Cranes) but this is not as immediately associated with them.

- The number of the sacred Aesir mysteries is nine: Odin hanging on Yggdrasil for nine days, and having a ring that produces nine more of itself every ninth night. It is noted that while nine nights is the time Frey waited to marry Gerda, and the time Njord and Skadhi stayed in each other's homes, this was not until after Frey and Njord came to live among the Aesir.

- There are a few characters in the primary sources called Thorsgoði, but not any called Odinsgoði apart from the mentions of sacrifice made at temples, and the worshipers of Odin who were kings, and no Tyrsgoðar or of any other Aesir gods. Can we assume that Odin and the Aesir lacked an organized priesthood the way that the Vanir and Thor did? (Again, Thor is married to a goddess who is most likely Vanir, and would be influenced by her.) Who knows? However, it does seem the Aesir cult is notable for lack of priestly figures, who are consorts of the gods or at least carry their presence and luck with them to bless the people directly.

Vanic Traditions for Today

As mentioned in the previous chapter, there were distinct elements of the Vanir cultus that were not shared by the Aesir cultus, and vice versa. It is important to know these things to understand our gods better. Some modern Vanic pagans may also look at these things as traditions that are rightfully ours, and go about the process of re-claiming them for a Vanic-centered spirituality. The problem is with any older traditions, they are based in the context of the needs of the people and their lifestyles at the time. We have changed enough that it is impossible to do things exactly as they were once done. With that said, we can still look at these things and think about how to modify them to work in today's world, or even the original spirit of what was done and how that would manifest itself today.

Here are some thoughts on traditions that can be updated for modern Vanic religion; most of these can be integrated into one's ritual format of choice.

THE WAIN

Both Frey and Nerthus were said to have wain processions in antiquity. A wain could be built for a yearly ritual to carry the gods to their people. One might consider having a public wain procession for Frey at Midsummer or Lammas, or a public wain procession for

Nerthus at Imbolc or Ostara[11]. One could even consider doing both, if one feels close to those two deities among the Vanir. If not ready or able to do a public ritual, the wain could also be pulled on the land to bless the area where you live, or one's household could have a private celebration with the wain.

One thing that was noted in the account of Nerthus' wain procession, and of the king who consulted Frey (as Lytir) as an oracle in his wain, was the presence of the deity making the wain feel "heavy". A private ritual could be had before the procession to invoke and perceive the presence of the deity within the wain, and commune with the deity and bless the wain prior to the rite.

GROVES AND STONES

While there is nothing wrong with having a Hof - indeed, the accounts of Frey's priestess and several of his priests report his temple; Nerthus had a temple on an island - there is some merit to worshipping the Vanir outside, in nature (and indeed, one could do both).

Those who wish to carry on the tradition of a sacred grove should find some site in their bio-region that, first of all, is legal to use (i.e. not someone's private property without permission), and where it feels right to worship the Vanir. It would help if this site were on or near a body of water (see below). The grove should be dedicated, and worship regularly performed there. A relationship should also be built and maintained with the nature spirits of the area, and one should endeavor to

---

[11] Depending on when the end of winter and first signs of spring are in your area; in some places one may need to wait until even April/May for this

regularly "check in" and keep the area clean and safe. With a time, a pile of stones (re Freya's favorite Ottar) and/or a small stone circle (re the megaliths of Europe built during "the Vanic era") can be raised to further sanctify the area.

Within the grove, or at home, a mound or small hill could be chosen as a place to offer to the wights, and maybe even plant flowers for their enjoyment. When needing guidance from spirits, one could sit on the mound overnight to commune with the spirits and receive visions from them.

OFFERINGS

While many Germanic pagans prefer to utilize a drinking horn and there is nothing wrong with this, some may consider switching to a ceramic beaker-shaped vessel. These were found all over northern Europe ca. 4000/3000 BCE. The symbolism of the vessel is itself very Vanic – it is made from clay of the earth, put into a fire, and holds liquid (when full) and air (when empty). When one is celebrating with the Vanir, they may wish to have a metheglin (herbed mead) or a tea made of mildly ethenogenic herbs (e.g. mugwort) to relax their state of consciousness enough to be in the proper frame of mind before the Powers.

(Note: pregnant women should not ingest mugwort.)

The victims of Nerthus (per Tacitus as well as Germanic folklore) were sacrificed in a lake, and the sacral kings of Yngling blood were known to be drowned. The bog bodies found during "the Vanic era" confirm this is the Vanic way of making a sacrifice. Ergo, modern offerings in Vanic rituals could be done by making an offering into a body of water such as a creek, river, pond, or lake. Great care must be taken that the offering does not disturb the ecosystem, so biodegradable offerings would be best. One thing that could be done in place of flesh sacrifice is to make an effigy of dough - a human figure - and yourself or your household or group pass around the dough effigy and give it "life" with very strong feelings, such as gratitude and awe (usually), or fear (if one needs to appease Nerthus for the safety of the land). The doughman could then be placed in water with the proper ritual, and break down naturally.

OATHING

Frey and Njord are connected with the oath ring, as is Ullr, and it seems that oathing upon a ring was a Vanic custom brought to Asgard. An oath ring could be specially made and dedicated to Frey and Njord, so if one needs to oath, they can take it upon the ring in the name of these gods, and see the cycle - the process begun by the oath - to completion.

DANCING

The priests of Frey mentioned in the account of Starkadr were said to make "effeminate gestures". Some scholars believe this refers to dancing, because bells and clapping were also mentioned. Many modern-day devotees of Frey and Freya feel strongly drawn to dance, and so there might be some time in a Vanic ritual dedicated to song and dance, to express our joy towards the gods and entertain them. This could be augumented by wearing bells, which are mentioned in some folklore to scare away evil spirits, and attract the fae folk (who are Frey's charges).

SEXUAL SYMBOLISM

Frey is often depicted with an erect penis, and archaic images of Freya sometimes show nudity. The few surviving myths of Freya are largely based in something sexual (the giants wanting her for a bride; her relationship with her favorite Ottar; sleeping with the dwarves for Brisingamen; teaching Odin magic and being listed as a concubine; as Gefion sleeping with a king to win land). The "Venus figures" found all over Europe during "the Vanic era" depict exaggerated breasts, and could probably represent Nerthus/Earth Mother. Those modern-day Vanic devotees who feel comfortable doing so could honor the Vanir skyclad, or create or utilize images of the gods, and ritual tools (e.g. the wand) which have sexual symbolism. For those who are Wiccan, the Great Rite could be done in honor of Frey and Freya. Sex magic (whether with partner or solitary) could be helpful as a regular practice in the life of a Vanic pagan.

SEIÐR

For those who feel they are on a spirit-work path, *seiðr* is a practice that is ours. One does not become *seið-folk* overnight, and will take years of figuring things out, and practicing them, but it is a worthy endeavor for contributing to the Vanic tradition. Some theories on *seiðr* are further into this book.

PRIESTHOOD

As mentioned in The Differences Between chapter, Frey and Nerthus were said to have priests, and Freya's favorite performed priestly activities; in addition, the Thorsberg Chape finding (ca 200 CE) have runes that translate as "The servant of Ullr, well-renowned". The only Aesir god definitively mentioned to have a goði is Thor, who is (possibly) half-Vanic. It is apparent that priesthood was important to the Vanic cult and not so much to the Aesir cult (which might also account for modern American Asatru attitudes that "we don't need clergy"). Those who feel called to service could look at either promoting the cultus of their individual patron, and being a "public resource" for those who want to know them better; or modern-day clergy skills such as counseling, the legality behind various practices, etc.

RITES

Besides the wain processions, some distinctly Vanic rites that could be performed are:

- The Maypole ritual, symbolic of weaving wyrd around the World Tree, with the May Queen and King representing Frey and Freya, or the Fair Bright Queen and Lord of Plenty

- A modified Aecerbot for Nerthus at Imbolc or Ostara - whenever winter is thawing and spring is in the air.

- Making an offering to Njord at the sea for safe travel of self/others (or, metaphorically, a safe transition and inner peace during a difficult time in one's life); gold coins or alcohol would work.

- A ritual surrounding hunting, dedicated to Ullr, Frey, or Horn Father.

- invoking Frey at a wedding

- The Alfablot in fall/early winter where the elves are offered to in order to protect the land and one's household

- leaving out offerings for the elves during Yule, and feasting with ham in Frey's honor

This is far from being a complete list of everything that can be done to revive the Vanir cultus, but it is a start, and hopefully will be of inspiration.

Vanatru: Frequently Asked Questions

What is Vanatru?

The word Vanatru is a neologism that means "true to the Vanir", and this author is unsure of who coined it, but is aware it came into usage in the 1990s. The term Vanatru is used to describe the religious practice of those heathens or pagans who

- have one of the Vanir as a patron – Frey, Freya, Nerthus, and/or Njord – or one of the deities speculated to be Vanir (e.g. Ullr, Herne, Holda)
  or

- work more with gods considered Vanir, than Aesir, whether or not they have a formal patron
  or

- work with the Eshnahai (citizens of Vanaheim unnamed by lore), with or without worship of the Vanir named as gods

Some who identify as Vanatru worship only the Vanir (for various reasons), and some who identify as Vanatru worship the Vanir primarily and the Aesir secondarily.
It should be noted that one does not have to be exclusively focused on the Vanir or exclusively Germanic/Norse pagan to be Vanatru. There are some Vanatruar who practice one or more other pagan traditions in addition to Vanatru (including this author).

N.B.: Some modern Anglo-Saxon pagans use the neologism Wenan to refer to the gods known as Vanir to the Norse, and refer to their religion as Wen-Troth.

Why not just call yourselves Asatru? Asatru means "true to the Gods", and the Vanir are the Aesir.

For starters, only some of the Vanir have joined the Aesir: Frey, Freya, and Njord. The world of Vanaheim did not cease to exist following the Aesir-Vanir war. Besides Frey, Freya, and Njord, in the opinion of this author, there are other deities that are Vanir, which has been discussed earlier in this book. There is also the aforementioned corroborated gnosis regarding the Eshnahai, the citizens of Vanaheim, who have their own separate culture and customs from the Aesir.

Moreover, Frey, Freya, and Njord going to live among the Aesir and allying with them does not change who they are and where they come from.

While this author is aware the term Asatru originally meant "true to the gods" and was inclusive of both the Vanir and the Aesir, over the last two decades (00/10s) the term has been used increasingly to mean "true to the Aesir", specifically.

Didn't it say in Voluspa that following the war, the gods decided who would be given tribute?

Yes, it does say that in Voluspa. This passage from the Voluspa is often cited as the basis for the argument that the truce made between the Aesir and Vanir means the Vanir should not be regarded separately and there is no need for Vanatru as a separate focus in Germanic paganism.

To a certain extent, one can see why this argument would be made. While Vanaheim continued to be its own world and was not absorbed into Asgard, many feel the overwhelming majority of the Vanir who live in Vanaheim have names lost to us with time, and are largely unconcerned with interacting with humanity at this time and receiving worship. There are a few speculated reasons for this, and the most common speculations are that the Vanir withdrew their favor when the Aesir religion became dominant, or that the Aesir manipulated the Vanir following the truce (the latter is a shared gnosis by several individuals).

However, from 2007 on there have been accounts of Vanatruar given access to Vanaheim and the host of unnamed Vanir, and the information of these experiences is beginning to be shared with the public, and bridges rebuilt between Vanaheim and Midgard.

With that said, citing the passage in the Voluspa as reason why "Vanatru is not a real religion" is a flawed argument.

For starters, the Eddas were written down 200 years after the conversion. They were from a Christian perspective and not meant to be used as liturgy. We don't know how literally to take the account, but we know this much: history is always written from the perspective of the conqueror/s (as one example, the Bible demonized the polytheistic Semitic tribes). It seems that the worship of the Vanir was indigenous to northern Europe (see below) and suppressed by invaders bringing the Aesir religion with them, and while some beliefs and practices were kept, much was lost. The account of "deciding to who would go the tribute" may be factually true, or it may be history written from the perspective of the conquering Aesic religion. We don't know how the Vanir actually felt about it, or even how extensive this proclamation was. It may have been true of Asgard only, as one example.

This much we know: religion in the Northlands was not "pan-Germanic"; practices varied widely from tribe to tribe, household to household. There was no ancient "Asapope" giving proclamations as far as what all Teutons should do. Curiously, there was no Aesir/Vanir dichotomy on the continent of Europe, what you saw rather was a focus on one deity or a pair of deities who were revered as ancestors and/or guardians of a tribe. Through the accounts of Tacitus and other historians, it seems that the worship of Vanic gods like Nerthus and Ing, and Vanic traditions such as the wain procession, were carried on all over the continent of Europe. Thus it seems these tribes were, in a sense, "Vanatru".

Finally, regardless of what the Eddas said 800 years ago, we live in the here and now. Much has changed since the lore was recorded. One of the things that has changed is we now have the technology to destroy ourselves and our planet – Nerthus herself – is in a state of crisis like never seen before. It makes sense that at such a time as this, the Vanir would be calling forth a movement focused on relationships with them, to help bring things to balance, and because they are gods, they will do this whether other humans approve or not.

How do Vanatruar feel about the Aesir?

Some Vanatruar (but not all) view the Aesir as separate but equal gods, and give Odin and his kin their due on the holytides and as it is appropriate to do so. Some Vanatruar do not worship the Aesir at all, for various reasons, whether due to lack of personal connection with the Aesir, or a bad experience with one or more of the Aesir gods, being asked not to by the Vanir, etc. Whether one does or does not worship the Aesir, we are polytheists and if we recognize the gods as individuals we will realize different people deal with the gods differently, and thus the Aesir are not bad or wrong – just different.

For those of us who do not feel kinship with the Aesir, and may even wish to keep them at a wide berth, most of us still do not wish to bash or defame them as it's bad manners to disrespect gods.

How many people practice Vanatru? Where can I find Vanatru lore?

It is unknown how many people practice Vanatru, however this much is certain – at present, Germanic polytheism is a minority within paganism, and we are a minority of a minority (although it does seem we are growing in number). Part of what complicates the matter of establishing a statistic is that (to this author) the bare minimum criteria for someone to call themselves Vanatru is a focus on the Vanir. Beyond that, worship of the Vanir can be done in an Asatru format, a tribalist format, or even a Neowiccan or Druidic format, or something outside of extant religious traditions altogether.

Since many Germanic polytheists focus heavily on the Aesir or see the Aesir and Vanir as a blended pantheon, the idea of Vanatru is considered highly controversial and most of us who publicly identify as Vanatru are independent free-thinkers enough that we are, when found, at best de-centralized and don't agree on everything. For example, some of us consider Vanatru to be its own separate religion that re-claims and explores the history and mysteries of the Vanir; some do not and are more or less 'generic heathen' with one of the Vanir as their patron.

With regards to 'Vanatru lore', the short answer is there is no such thing. We have a few surviving myths featuring the Vanir gods, which were heavily colored by Snorri's Christian bias. We have a few surviving stories of historic people who were devoted to one of the Vanir (usually Frey). However, we have no Vanic equivalent of the Sagas and Eddas. We have archaeology that points to a progression of pantheons in the Northlands, and recorded folk customs which seem like a survival of Vanic practice, but short of building a time machine we will never know for sure. With that said, for many who identify as Vanatru, the most relevant thing is the direct experience of the Vanir in the here and the now. The only thing we have close to 'Vanatru lore' is the corroborated gnosis of some who work with the Vanir and perceive their influence in the world to be a certain way. While that might not be good enough for people who want heavy documentation and citation, our religion is not a fossil, it is alive and well.

What makes Vanatru so different?

It is often said that the Aesir are the gods of civilization and the Vanir the gods of nature, and while this is basically true, it is also a gross oversimplification of the Powers and their working in the worlds (as the Aesir also have connections to nature, and the Vanir to the preservation of tribal structures and cultures). However, many Vanatruar see Frey's family as being inherently different from Odin and his kin, and seek to explore that and celebrate with rites other than the standard Heathen rites of blót and sumble (or in addition to), including (but not limited to) magical workings, sacred sexuality, and attuning with the elements.

Many Germanic polytheists have a tendency to treat the gods all the same, with the same offerings and ritual format given to all. With many who identify as Vanatru, there is an effort to approach the Vanir on their own terms, with their own rites, exploring their own mysteries and culti.

Finally, Vanatruar seem less likely to be reconstructionists, as the essence of our religious experience is based on place and presence – being here in the world we live in, and taking things as they come, not by our assumptions of how they 'should be'. This does not mean that one is 'doing it wrong' if they are reconstructionist and Vanatru, or that there is anything wrong with reconstructionism in and of itself, but the Vanatruar known to this author have seemed less concerned with past history and more concerned with making a living tradition.

Wheel of the Year and Lunar Tides

The Eshnahai (Vanic elves) don't really have a religion in the way that humans understand the concept. What they have is connectedness, to each other and the land in both worlds, and humans they see as their kin, and what they have is magic, working to bless each other, the land, and our people. Elves live and breathe magic, and it is common for an elf to do something magical every day. But the solar and lunar cycles are seen as times of special power and potency.

There are two types of holiday festivals in Vanaheim, lunar and solar. The lunar festivals are monthly, on the full moon. The full moon festivals last for three days. During the three days each Vanic tribe will have its own full moon celebration, and the King and Queen will mate at the capital to bless the land and people with the energy of their lovemaking, which people are encouraged to observe and then go home and mate with each other - men with women, men with men, women with women, men with men and women, women with women and men, and so on and so on - to continue to add to the energy.

The solar rituals are the solstices, equinoxes, and cross-quarter days. While the eightfold Wheel of the Year is a modern pagan invention, the eight holidays are in fact celebrated in Vanaheim, albeit the theme of said holidays is somewhat different from how they are presented in mainstream paganism.

ESHNAIA AGRETA – SPRING EQUINOX

The Vanic New Year is the spring equinox in March, called Eshnaia Agreta (esh-NIGH-ya ah-GREY-tah), or Green Awakening.

The night before the spring equinox, each tribe holds their own ritual of cleansing, building a large bonfire wherein a symbolic token (such as words or an item representing the thing) of anything that transpired within the last year that they want closure with, such as traumatic or unpleasant experiences, is thrown in the fire. Those who need to grieve or be angry are given space to do so around the fire, and typically songs are sung to aid the grieving process. When the atmosphere feels cleaner, someone from the tribe is chosen to light torches or staffs from the fire, and fire dance, symbolic of beauty born from pain.

The day of the spring equinox, the Hare tribe dances through each territory, leaping to bring the world into bloom, flowers springing up where they land. This is also the day that Nerthus's procession goes out; for the next six weeks her wain will travel through Vanaheim and Midgard, for peace and prosperity of land and people.

Some suggestions for observing Eshnaia Agreta here:

- The night before the spring equinox, one can burn persistent negative thoughts or experiences of the past year, such as by writing it down and throwing it into the bonfire, taking some time to reflect and grieve as necessary (particularly with song as an aid); dancing would be a good way to end the rite but is not necessary if you are not comfortable.

- If one can journey to Vanaheim, going to the capital and watching the Hares begin their dance (watching them go out and return, with a feast while the gathered folk wait for the Hare dancers to return) would be fine.

- One can dance this side of the fence on the day of the equinox, or plant flowers (or dance after planting flowers). One can light candles and/or make offerings such as libations to bless the Hare tribe for their gift to the land.

- One can honor Nerthus as her procession goes forth; her procession could also be enacted here.

Eshnahai greeting/blessing for the holiday: *Blessed Green Awakening! May the road rise up to meet you, may your paths be green and gold, in this coming year.*

Nerthus Procession

The most explicit mention of Nerthus and her cult is the account of Tacitus in 98 CE, stating that Nerthus was worshiped by several Germanic tribes and her yearly festival was held among them. We unfortunately do not have mention of the time of this festival, however, I am inclined to believe it would be sometime in the spring for ease of travel, as well as the lakes not being too frozen to receive sacrifices, and symbolizing the return of life to the land, getting her blessing on the growing things.

Furthermore SPG amongst Vanic practitioners states that her procession goes out into Vanaheim and Midgard and back in the spring.

So, while there is nothing in the primary sources to indicate that Nerthus' feast is on the spring equinox, I do think the spring equinox is as good a time as any to observe her wain procession.

This is a rite I composed in 2008 for the Kindred I had at the time, to honor Nerthus' procession.

Preparation:

- There will need to be a wain. As an oxen-drawn wain transporting attendants is not going to be practical, an acceptable substitute is a small handcart, perhaps a modified wheelbarrow. It should have four wheels and high sides, it should be decorated somewhat elaborately so it doesn't look like "just an ordinary wheelbarrow", and should have a pole to draw it. The wagon in the Oseburg ship burial is an example of this. The wain should be able to fit into a car as well as be able to be drawn along a sidewalk or into a field. If you are a Vanic hearth who will be doing the Frey ritual at Lammas, it is possible to use the same wain for both deities provided it is decorated with appropriate Vanic symbolism.

- There will need to be an image of Nerthus, particularly as it will be cleansed afterwards by her attendants. I personally connect Venus of Willendorf with Nerthus, whether or not the image was actually representing her in those times, it is very her between the body shape and the lack of having facial features (as Nerthus is veiled or wearing a mask, so most people do not have to be killed for looking upon her).

- While many heathen rituals are led by a Goði or Gyðja who may not have a strong personal connection to the deity involved, for this ritual I feel the rite must be overseen by an oathed dedicant of Nerthus or someone who is a priest of another Vanic deity with oaths to serve all the Vanir by extension. In keeping with Vanic mysteries of having the Nerthus-priest pull the wain in her procession, and the Freysgyðja in his, it is preferable for the priest in this rite to be male-identified, but not mandatory, and it should be a male who is willing to wear a skirt, bells, etc.

- There are some Godfolk who may be able to bring the wain to every Kindred or other pagan groups in their area, both with regards to being welcomed by the groups as well as being able to set aside a week or so to travel around. In a place where compatible heathens and pagans are few and far between, it may be more practical to invite one's Kindred and/or some chosen and respectful friends to a select area to meet the wain as it arrives. This would be preferable, and in any case the rite must be held by an inland body of water such as a lake, creek, river, or pond.

- The wain will be prepared by the priest with a secret rite. Because the procession was done at the will of Nerthus who informed her priest it was time, the Nerthus image should be carried by the priest somewhere on their person for three days prior to the rite, even if it means bringing the statue or framed print to work with them and sitting it on the desk, or putting it in their purse or briefcase. The priest should also take Nerthus to bed with them, placing the image on the bedtable or under the bed if the statue/print cannot be slept with. This serves to heighten the connection with Nerthus sufficiently that the image will be charged enough to fill the wain with her power.

-   The priest should inform those attending to bring food for a potluck, the priest can also bring some things like mead, a drinking horn or beaker, and some food such as bread or salads.

-   The priest will need to select four people willing to help cleanse Nerthus after the rite. The priest should make up a bag with a vial of salt water, a vial of essential oil, a candle in a safe holder, and an herbal recaning stick for the cleansing of Nerthus after the rite. The priest will also need to make or procure a strawman, and have a bag of diabetic stickers, alcohol pads, and latex gloves because a blooded strawman will be sacrificed to Nerthus in lieu of human sacrifice being illegal.

Ritual Outline

1. The priest will have spent three days charging Nerthus' image, and hallows the wain by placing

Nerthus' image inside whilst chanting her name. The priest should be sensitive to the move of her presence filling the wain with her power.

2. The priest loads the wain with food items brought to share among the folk, as well as the drink and drinking horn. The priest will pray over the food and drink to bless people with Nerthus' might.

3. The priest goes to the ritual site, singing to Nerthus on the way there. Presumably the priest will get there by car, at which point the car should be parked enough of a ways off that the priest can pull the wain a bit to the site, singing and chanting while the wain is pulled.

4. The wain arrives at the ritual site and the priest proclaims this place a holy frithstead in Nerthus' name. Weapons must be laid down (including cell phones).

5. The priest invokes Nerthus into the stead, and loads the horn with drink to share in her blessings. As the horn is passed around the circle, each participant should speak words of praise to Nerthus and her kin. The remainder of the drink will be poured into a blessing bowl.

6. There is a sacred feast, with a blessing on the food beforehand, thanks given to Nerthus. Some food should be selected beforehand to give specifically to Nerthus, preferably left at the base of a tree or buried. The priest also pours out some mead from the blessing bowl, with thanks to Nerthus. Some of the drink is deliberately left in the bowl.

7. After the feast the priest will go around the circle with the blessing bowl and an asperger. Each person will ask Nerthus for a boon, and the priest

will sprinkle the person head-heart-shoulder-shoulder, speaking Nerthus' blessing upon them. The priest should be open to the move of Nerthus for prophecy or a specific blessing.

8. At this time the priest gives a final benediction and all but the four attendants should depart from the ritual site.

9. The four attendants accompany the priest in removing Nerthus from the wain and setting her on a rock to be cleansed. This is a time when there must absolutely be privacy, for it is a holy occasion. The attendants should be filled with reverence and awe in directly feeling Nerthus' presence among them. One attendant will be given the salt water to rub onto the image. The next will hallow the image by passing the lit candle around it in a circle nine times. The next will anoint the image with essential oil. The last will hallow with smoke from the recaning stick.

10. The priest will then take out the strawman and speak of it being a sacrifice, put the strawman down on the rock, and don latex gloves. Each attendant will present their hands. The priest will prick the middle finger of both hands of each attendant, for them to drip blood onto the strawman. The strawman is then dropped into the body of water, as Nerthus is hailed by the priest and attendants. The priest will then address the attendants that a holy thing was done, and as the Earth is in her fullness of glory, so Nerthus' glory was witnessed, and beauty and terror are inextricably entwined. The priest and attendants should spend the next few days being mindful of

their relationship with nature and the Earth, and those who live upon it.

Solitary Adaptation

If the solitary is able to procure a wagon and make it into a "Vanic Wain", they may want to do this and draw Nerthus' image around their neighborhood or backyard, to bless the land. The solitary will then feast and share with Nerthus. The blooded strawman can be omitted, what could be an acceptable substitute is the solitary blooding some herbal tea of a calmative or mildly ethenogenic nature (such as mugwort), giving half to Nerthus, and using the other half to perform utiseta (sitting outdoors, preferably overnight) in private communion with her.

LIMNAIA ASTHREANAD – APRIL 30ᵀᴴ/MAY 1ˢᵀ

At the end of April/beginning of May is Limnaia Asthreanad (lim-NIGH-ya ahs-THRAY-ah-nahd), or the Dance of Lovers. This dance commemorates the growing season in Vanaheim, blessing the greening and blooming of the land.

A giant pole is erected at the capital of Vanaheim, and citizens come from around the realm to dance and weave ribbons around the pole, their choice of ribbon a color that represents their hopes and wishes for the year, anything they would like to bring to fruition (red for love, green for prosperity, blue for healing, etc).

After the dance at the pole, there is a feast, a giant banquet (both catered and potluck, so there is plenty of food for everyone) as a band plays, and after the food and music, the little ones are taken home by their caregivers and the ritual begins.

In the weeks prior to the holiday, there are three baskets in which participants will put their names in the hopes of being chosen to serve as Lovers and bless the land. At the ritual, the King and Queen choose two names from each basket: one female/female pair, one male/male pair, and one male/female pair; the King and Queen themselves represent a couple outside the gender binary (the Queen being a femme/androgynous trans man), so there are four couples to represent different kinds of love, eight individuals to honor the sacred number of eight, the number of infinity.

Each couple positions themselves in a different location around the stone circle: the male/female couple in the North, the King and Queen in the East, the male/male couple in the South, and the female/female couple in the West. The couples mate, each of them giving their own special energy of love and ecstasy to the land and people; around them in the capital's green there is a giant orgy, with everyone who wishes to do so mating with whomever they please so long as the parties will it.

There are some who will not participate in the sexual festivities for whatever reason and their own participation is sacred, with drumming or dancing for the rite, or doing creative things, which adds to the energy of joy and passion to feed the realm. The Dance of Lovers can thus be said to include lovers of life, not just those who offer their sexuality for this rite. Thus the growing season is blessed, as the hearts and works of the people are as well.

Some suggestions for observing Limnaia Asthreanad here:

- If one can journey, the ritual (both the dancing around the pole and attending the orgy) is open to tourists so long as visitors can observe ritual etiquette (which includes getting consent of anyone they wish to mate with for the orgy).

- If one can't journey, one can "anchor" the ritual bio-side by crafting a pole and weaving a ribbon or handful of ribbons around the pole (by yourself or with others) in colors representing your wishes for the year (and maybe even some runes on the ribbon representing said wishes or spelling out the words of things you want to manifest), and then either having sex (solo or with partner/s corporeal or non) and giving the energy as an offering to land, gods, or using it for magic (to help "power" the manifestation of what you want to manifest in the growing season), or if you are asexual or not able/wanting to participate sexually for whatever reason, you can do something that brings you joy (such as music and dancing as one example) and offer that energy.

RASTHUAS RIHANANSAI – SUMMER SOLSTICE

The summer solstice in June is Rasthuas Rihanansai (RAHS-thoo-ahs ree-HAHN-ahn-sigh), or Lights of the Phoenix, which is observed over three days.

On the night before the solstice the Lord of Plenty and Lord of the Black "battle", with the Lord of the Black "winning" to herald the end of summer and the beginning of the harvest season and the dark time of the year.

On the day of the solstice the Lord of the Black and the Fair Bright Queen mate publicly to further reinforce the ending of summer and the beginning of the harvest and dying season. The Lord of Black ties the Fair Bright Queen down and cuts him with a ritual knife before mating roughly with him; the knife will then be given to the Fair Bright Queen to use at the next turn of the wheel to sacrifice his own twin.

On the day after the solstice many weddings are performed, which is a favorite day for weddings in the realm (though not the only day that Eshnahai can marry); as the daylight often lasts past midnight in Vanaheim, it gives newlyweds all night to make love and celebrate their union. On this day the King and Queen celebrate their unions with their respective outlander consorts, to strengthen those bonds as well as send energy from Vanaheim to other worlds and strengthen Vanaheim's presence and the Vanir's influence in the web of wyrd.

Some suggestions to observe Rasthuas Rihanansai here:

- If one can journey, one can go to Vanaheim to observe the solstice festival, the mating of the Fair Bright Queen and Lord of the Black.

- One can have sex (solo or with partner/s) through the night of the summer solstice, giving the sexual energy and ecstasy as an offering, "invincible summer" that will sustain you through the coming winter.

- One can keep vigil the night of the summer solstice doing something non-sexual, such as activities that are pleasurable and fun where the energy can be used to "keep the fire burning" later, perhaps by charging a candle to light during the dark half of the year.

RUNEKTA MARUSANAT – AUGUST 1ST/2ND

At the beginning of August is Runekta Marusanat (ROO-nek-tah mah-ROO-sah-naht), or Feast of the Fallen. This day marks the beginning of the harvest season and the Lord of Plenty is sacrificed by his twin the Fair Bright Queen, using the same knife that blooded the Queen on the summer solstice. The King is cut down to feed the land as payment for its yield, and lies dead for several hours on the ground, with the Queen keeping vigil as the Lord of the Black walks the King through the lands of the dead.

While the King lies dead, blood is collected from every adult in Vanaheim, into bowls carried by attendants from the Serpent and Boar tribes.

When the Lord of the Black decrees that the debt has been paid, the Queen brings the King back to life, breathing life into him until the King awakens, and then the Queen penetrates the King (usually the Queen is penetrated in rites involving them both) to help anchor his soul into his body. When the King spends his release it is collected into a bowl. His seed is then mixed with the blood that was taken from his people and baked in a hole in the ground into loaves with the first sheaves of wheat from the first harvest. As the bread bakes there is music and dancing to celebrate the return of the King, and then the bread is finished, the first loaf of bread is taken by the Lord of the Bull tribe to give to the Bull lands, the largest producers of agriculture in Vanaheim, and the remainder of the bread is shared among the people, to build solidarity.

Some suggestions to observe Rasthuas Rihanansai here:

- If one can journey, one can go to Vanaheim to observe the sacrifice and return of the King.

- One can keep vigil for the King by lighting a candle and celebrating his return with merriment and feasting.

- One can offer blood to the Vanir and to the land.

- One can bake bread or (if not able to bake, or eat grain like wheat, or if you just don't like bread) prepare some other sort of food, preferably something in season in your area.

- This is also the time when Frey's procession goes forth within Vanaheim, and Frey can be honored during this time as well.

Freysblot

We know from the account of Tacitus that Nerthus was brought about in a wain once a year, and feasts were held in her honor as well as the tribe ceasing conflict and keeping peace. From archaeological evidence we know wains were a major part of what can be considered "the Vanic era", found in bogs as well as burials. There is some evidence Frey himself is connected with the wain:

Ing was first seen by men among the East-Danes,
till, followed by his chariot,
he departed eastwards over the waves.
So the Heardingas named the hero.
Anglo-Saxon Rune Poem

Frey might also have been one and the same as Lytir, noted in *Hauks tattr habrokar* in the *Flateyjarbok*, where a Swedish king consults the god Lytir, whose ceremonial wagon was taken to a sacred place wherein the god entered it and then rode back to the King's hall, answering questions there. Lytir is etymologically related to the Old Norse word *hlutr*, meaning "lot" and "foretell". There are a few Swedish place names that may contain elements of his name, including Lytisberg and Lytislunda. We know from the account of Frey's folk at Thrandheim that he spoke to them and foretold the future, and it would not be unheard of for a Vanic Power to be skilled in prophesy. I am inclined to believe Lytir is one of Frey's by-names and further evidence of his connection with wains. Finally, we have this explicit mention of his procession in Gunnar Helming's Saga:

"...I think it is better you stay here this winter and accompany us when Freyr makes his annual journey. But I must tell you that he is still angry with you."

Gunnar thanked her well. . . Now the festival time came, and the procession started. Freyr and his wife were placed in the carriage, whereas their servants and Gunnar had to walk beside. When driving through the mountains, they were surprised by a tempest and all the servants fled. Gunnar remained. At last he got tired of walking, went into the carriage and let the draught cattle go as they liked. Freyr's wife said: "You had better try and walk again, for otherwise Freyr will arise against you." Gunnar did so, but when he got too tired, he said: "Anyhow, let him come, I will stand against him."

Now Freyr arises, and they wrestle till Gunnar notices that he is getting weaker. Then he thinks by himself that if he overcomes this load Foe he will return to the right faith and be reconciled with King Olaf. And immediately after Freyr begins to give way, and afterwards to sink. Now this Foe leaps out of the idol, and it lay there empty.

Gunnar broke it into pieces and gave Freyr's wife two alternatives: that he would leave, or that she might declare him publicly to be the god Freyr. She said that she would willingly declare what he liked. Now Gunnar dressed in Freyr's clothes, the weather improved and they went to the festival. People were very much impressed by the power of Freyr, because he was able to visit the country in such a tempest, allthough all the servants had fled. They wondered how he went about among them and talked like other men. Thus Freyr and his wife spent the winter going to festivals. Freyr was not more eloquent towards people than his wife, and he would not receive living victims, as before, and no offerings except gold, silk, and good clothings.

Gunnar Helming's Saga, Flateyjarbok II.

In the account of Frey's procession in Gunnar Helming's Saga, it is said to take place in the wintertime. The winter by our modern calendar would have Sweden too snowy for a chariot and walking servants. Likely, the winter procession was what we know as fall (which was indeed counted as winter by Old Norse reckoning), when the temperatures began to drop significantly but it was not too snowy and icy to move about.

However, Frey's cult was not just known to Sweden but seems to also have been known in England, hence the rune named for him in the Anglo-Saxon Futhorc. In England, the festival of the first wheat harvest of the year, Loaf-Mass - known to us as Lammas – was celebrated at the beginning of August. It was customary to bring a loaf from the new crop to church, and tenants were bound to present freshly harvested wheat on their landlords at that time. The Anglo-Saxon Chronicle refers to it as "the feast of first fruits". The celebrations on this day usually include singing hymns, praying, and decorating churches with baskets of fruit and food in the festival, and is known in modern Britain as Harvest Home.

Barley would also be harvested at this time. "John Barleycorn" is an English folksong about the character of John Barleycorn who suffers attacks, death, and various indignities which correspond to the different stages of barley cultivation, such as reaping and malting. John Barleycorn is a representation of the spirit of barley. It is widely thought by scholars that John Barleycorn also represents a practice known to the English pagans, representing the ideology of the cycle of harvest. It is notable that every other European pantheon has a dying and-reborn god connected to crops and the only deity explicitly known to die and reborn in the Northern pantheon is Baldur who has no connection to agriculture, but is more of a societal Power. It is a commonly held gnosis that Frey (and later on, the Lord of Plenty, continuing a custom Frey started) takes the figure of the sacrificed crop god of the Northern pantheon, going through the John Barleycorn ordeal each year at Lammas to appease the Green World and Death and ensure food for another year.

Some scholars have speculated the historical figure Sceaf Scylding (Sheaf Debt-ing) is another by-name for Frey:

... Sceaf; who, as some affirm, was driven on a certain island in Germany, called Scandza, (of which Jordanes, the historian of the Goths, speaks), a little boy in a skiff, without any attendant, asleep, with a handful of corn at his head, whence he was called Sceaf; and, on account of his singular appearance, being well received by the men of that country, and carefully educated, in his riper age he reigned in a town which was called Slaswic, but at present Haithebi; which country, called old Anglia, whence the Angles came into Britain, is situated between the Saxons and the Goths.
-Gesta Regum Anglorum

This would definitely relate to the verse in the Anglo-Saxon Rune Poem. As I've often said, "short of building a time machine we'll never know", but research and gnosis inform me that Loaf-Mass is Frey's feast, commemorating his role as sacral and sacrificed King, presiding over the harvest.

In corroborated personal gnosis, Frey's procession comes after the Land is appeased with sacrifice, and his vitality flows through the realm; there is celebration after mourning, joy after sorrow. This is a rite I made in 2008 for my Kindred at the time and friends of the Kindred, for Lammas Day itself, to celebrate Frey's procession to bless the land and its people with Life.

Preparation:

- There will need to be a wain. As mentioned in the Nerthus rite, it should be small enough to be transported in a car but substantial enough to carry a statue and some goods. A heavily decorated wheelbarrow will suffice. In the case of a Vanic hearth which has also done the Nerthus rite for the equinox, Frey and Nerthus can share the same wain for their different festivals.

- There needs to be an image of Frey in the cart, preferably a statue. The wain will be consecrated by Frey's image being placed in it (see below).
- While many heathen rituals are led by a Goði or Gyðja who may not have a strong personal connection to the deity involved, I feel this particular rite must be overseen by an oathed dedicant of Frey, and preferably a Freysgyðja. If a Freysgoði is to perform, he should wear a skirt, and definitely as many bells as he can stand. The priest will attend the wain, conduct the rituals, and oversee the gifting.

- There are some Godfolk who may be able to bring the wain to every Kindred or other pagan group in their area, both with regards to being welcomed by the Kindreds as well as being able to set aside a week or so to travel around. In a place where compatible heathens and pagans are few and far between, it may be more practical to invite one's Kindred and/or some chosen and respectful friends to a select area to meet the wain as it arrives.

- The wain will be prepared by the priest with a secret rite, that is, by the statue of Frey being "charged" by either anointing the statue with one's sexual fluids or blood (such as with a diabetic sticker). For hygiene's sake there should only be a small amount of personal fluids and the Frey statue should not be handled by others, particularly as it will be the priest's own statue and representative of their personal connection to Frey.

- The wain will be loaded with gifts of food and drink, both to gift Frey as well as those who have come to honor him. Loaves of homemade bread, especially that baked by the Goði or Gyðja, is most appropriate, as are baskets of fresh organic fruit and vegetables, and perhaps some bottles of mead or ale whether home-brewed or bought from a decent brewery. Beyond that, gifts can be at the priest's discretion, whether it be a bag of gold dollar coins with some attendants taking one a piece, or amber beads; I also find having an antler, a sword, and figurines of horses and boars is nice, as well as candles consecrated by the priest for people to take and enjoy Frey's light.

- Those who are planning on attending the rite should be informed beforehand to come to the rite with a gift for Frey. The rite is based on the principle of 'a gift for a gift'. Everyone takes something from the wain representative of Frey's blessings, and in return gives something which will be given by the priest to Frey, whether it is food and drink items or something more tangible for the priest to keep on Frey's altar and use only for him.

- The priest should procure a pleasant-smelling essential oil for the purpose of blessing the gathered folk.

Ritual Outline

1. The priest privately consecrates the cart with sexual fluids or blood on Frey's statue, and a galdor chanting the names of Frey (Frey, Ingvi, Lytir, Sceaf) as the statue is added to the cart. The priest should be sensitive enough to feel Frey's presence filling and hallowing the wain.
2. The priest loads the cart with gifts from the folk to Frey, praying over each one that they may bless the people in his name.
3. The priest goes to the ritual site, singing to Frey on the way there. Presumably the priest will get there by car, at which point the car should be parked enough of a ways off that the priest can pull the wain a bit to the site, singing and chanting while the wain is pulled.
4. The wain arrives at the ritual site and the priest and wain should be welcomed with a toast, with words spoke in praise of Ingui and his kin.
5. The gathered folk may help themselves to any of the wain's goods.
6. When all have gone through the wain, they give back bounty of their own, items of worth for Frey's enjoyment.
7. The priest will bless the gathered folk, anointing each attendant with an Ing rune on their forehead, in blessed essential oil. The priest can go around the circle and say something such as, "The blessings

of Ingui upon you, so your body and spirit may be well fed." This is also the time when the priest should be open to Frey's move, if there is a prophecy to be made or a special boon to be given. If the priest is very sensitive to Frey's presence among the folk, the priest can blow at each individual's forehead, visualizing light going into the forehead, and "charging" the person's etheric field.

8. The priest calls one final blessing of Frey upon the gathered folk, and then formally closes the rite.

9. The gathered folk can share food together, eating and making merry. The priest also joins in the celebration.

10. The priest returns home, and gives the gifts to Frey, including their own private gifts (such as food, drink, and other items). Food and drink should be burned, buried, or placed at the base of a tree. Tangible items should be placed on Frey's altar for his use or enjoyment. It may be that the following year Frey asks for something to be "re-gifted" to a person, having been charged with his energy the whole year.

11. After the priest gifts Frey at their personal altar, the priest will purify the cart with the smoke from an herb such as sage or mugwort, and then take a purification bath. For some time after Lammas, the priest should reflect on what things are most deeply fulfilling in their life, and work at preserving that and perhaps moving to the next level. In any case, Lammas should be a time of appreciation and gratitude for the little things that are in fact big things, the stuff of life itself.

Solitary Adaptation

If the solitary is able to procure a wagon and make it into a "Vanic Wain", they may want to do this and draw Frey's image around their neighborhood or backyard or local park, to bless the land. The solitary will then feast and share with Frey. Some time can be spent communing with Frey and drawing his renewed vitality into oneself, for personal healing whether of an emotional or physical nature, preferably a bit of both.

SELENESTRA MADONATAL – FALL EQUINOX

At the fall equinox in September is Selenstra Madonatal (seh-len-ES-trah mah-DOUGH-nah-tahl), or the Festival of Gratitude. This is essentially the Vanic version of Thanksgiving, where people feast with their families and count their blessings of the year. It is common for people to light lanterns or candles for each of their blessings and float lanterns down the rivers.

This is also a time of reconciliation and restitution. People will ask to be addressed with any grievances others might have against them, and apologize for wronging others intentionally or not intentionally; people will often settle their differences by breaking bread in fellowship.

This holiday is fairly low-key compared to the other holidays, with most people observing at home or making a trek to the rivers to set their blessing-lanterns afloat. However the King and Queen do make an appearance at the capital, where they hang blessing-lanterns from the folk who wish to give them on a "giving tree", the lanterns staying lit for a fortnight, and they bless a loaf of bread that is broken among the gathered folk in solidarity.

Suggestions for those who wish to observe this holiday:

- If you work closely with an Eshnahai guide, they may be willing to allow you to celebrate with their family (though you should let them invite you, don't ask to be included in their family celebration), or you and just they may light candles or lanterns together and break bread in solidarity.

- You can light candles or lanterns at home as you give thanks for your blessings over the past year, and let people in your life know that if you've wronged them you're sorry; this is a great time of year for reconciliations and clearing the air. That said, if you don't want to deal with the issue of grievances and apologies for whatever reason, nobody will fault you for it, it is not mandatory.

- You can break bread or give a drink libation to be shared with yourself and your gods and/or spirits, thanking them for the gifts they have given you, and as a gesture of fellowship.

RASTHUAS MAHAREYAN – OCTOBER 31ST/ NOVEMBER 1ST

At the end of October is Rasthuas Mahareyan (RAHS-thoo-ahs mah-hah-RAY-ahn), or Lights of Remembrance.

On this day, individual households will remember loved ones (whether blood or chosen family or people who were well-respected) who passed on over the past year and light candles in their memory, as well as candles for loved ones who passed on in years prior. Their memories will be honored, and a meal and sweets left out for any spirits who choose to visit.

There is a large Rasthuas Mahareyan ritual put on by the Raven tribe, more specifically the White Raven cult, where a list of all the Eshnahai who have passed on in the last twelve months is read by the Lord of the Black, name by name, with a moment of silence and a candle lit, and those who knew/loved the deceased can approach the ritual space and lay down a candle for them also. One by one, candles are lit until the ritual space has hundreds of candles, and then the lists are burned, and the Ravens dance - some of them fire-dance, with the fire that burned the list of names, and as they carry the fire they psychopomp the souls of the names on that list into the afterlife, to wait re-entry on the wheel of incarnation and join our people once more.

There are a couple of different ways one can observe Rasthuas Mahareyan here.

- For those who can journey, the ritual at the capital is open to the public, though it is recommended you only do this if you know any Eshnahai who have passed on in the last year. You can light candles on this side, to commemorate those who passed on. White candles are best, though any color will do. It is appropriate to observe the ritual, come up to the ritual space when the person/s you are commemorating have been named, light the candle then, and then continue to observe, watching as the ritual concludes and the Ravens dance and ferry the souls to the other side.

- If you cannot journey, or simply choose not to, a second option is just to name your own dead, whether blood or chosen family or spiritual ancestors, human or non-human, and light candles as you take a moment to remember them, and leave out some sort of food or drink offering for any hungry spirits who might visit. (You can forego the latter if you live in a place where this is problematic or not practical to do, or you could make a libation outdoors.)

Eshnahai greeting/blessing for the holiday: *Blessed Lights of Remembrance. May your beloved dead never thirst.*

RASTHUAS ESSONSARAS – WINTER SOLSTICE

The winter solstice is Rasthuas Essonsaras (RAHS-thoo-ahs es-son-SAH-rahs), or Lights of the Serpent, where the "fire within the earth" is given to begin awakening the land.

On the night before the winter solstice, the Lord of Plenty and the Lord of the Black "battle" again, with the Lord of Plenty "winning" to gain control of the land again. As the men "battle", women mate to enact the union of Star Mother with her reflection in the Void, exploding the Multiverse into being through orgasm.

On the day of the winter solstice, the Lord of Plenty in his fierce guise (similar to Krampus) and the Fair Bright

Queen mate to bring back the light. The remainder of the nights are gift-giving and feasting, particularly to provide a nice meal for the elves who are riding on the Wild Hunt, which is a strenuous job.

There are a few different ways one can observe Rasthuas Essonsaras here.

The night prior to the solstice

- For those who can journey, there is the option for women to go to the temple at the capital and join with an elven partner in an all-female orgy (please note this means anyone who identifies as female), enacting the mystery of Star Mother seeing her reflection in the Void, falling in love with her reflection, and mating with said reflection, the orgasm exploding the Multiverse into being. There is the option for men (anyone who identifies as male) to go to the World Tree and watch the Lord of Plenty and Lord of the Black "battle" at the Tree, giving seed to the ground as the Lords "fight".

- For those who cannot journey but are OK with sexual ritual, one can have queer sex with a spirit or a bio-partner and offer up the energy to Star Mother or the Lords, thanking them for the gift of light and life.

- For those who do not do sexual ritual for whatever reason, a candle may be lit for Star Mother and praises sung, or a white candle for the Lord of Plenty and black candle for the Lord of the Black, with offerings made.

The night of the solstice

- For those who can journey, the ritual at the capital is open to the public. There is a "Krampus and Perchta" procession (with the Lord of Plenty dressed in his fierce Krampus visage, reflecting his role as a child of Horn Father, and the Fair Bright Queen dressed as Perchta) will happen around the ritual site, with Krampus flogging people who have been "naughty", and then Eshnahaliel's Prime Minister (his name is Falaereth, he is Salmon tribe) is dressed as Yulefather and giving small gifts to the gathered attendants, before a buffet.

- Following the buffet, those who brought children take their children home, and then the Lord of Plenty and the Fair Bright Queen will mate on the stone table in the center of the stone circle, to bring back the light. It is not mandatory to attend this part, one can come for the first part of the event and go home before the elf sex, but it is OK to stay for the elf sex if one wants to. One may then take the energy and mate with partner/s (whether corporeal or non-corporeal) if they want to, helping to "push the wheel".

- For those who cannot journey, but are OK with sexual ritual, one may perform with their partner/s (in any number and gender combination, corporeal or non-corporeal), giving the ecstasy of their love and pleasure as energy to help aid the return of the light.

- For those who cannot journey and do not do sexual ritual, candles may be lit and offerings made to the Lord of Plenty and Fair Bright Queen, and the Vanir as a whole. It is also good if one can, to keep a vigil until the dawn, and praise the rising sun.

The remainder of the holiday

For each of the twelve nights (the night of the winter solstice, into the new year) one can offer to the heads of each tribe, doing two tribes a night for twelve nights, so all twenty-four tribes (Serpent, Raven, Wolf, Cat, Hare, Bear, Bee, Bull, Deer, Fox, Ram, Salmon, Spider, Swan, Wolf, Horse, Eagle, Owl, Seal, Frog, Goose, Crane, Otter, and Boar) are covered; one may also offer to twelve Vanic deities. These do not have to be big elaborate rituals but can be simple offerings, and indeed simple is good if you are inviting them into your home, as a family thing, making them feel welcome.

Eshnahai greeting/blessing for the holiday: *Blessed Lights of the Serpent. May the sun rise and shine upon you and yours.*

RASTHUAS JA'ENLADATA – FEBRUARY 1ST

The last holiday of the Vanic year is Rasthuas Ja'enladata (RAHS-thoo-ahs JIGH-en-lah-dah-tah), in early February, or Lights of the Winter Storm, where lights are burned through the worst winter storms of the year as a reminder that soon the spring will come. This is the holiday of the Fair Bright Queen, whose power begins to rise again in anticipation of the spring, his season.

• • •

The Fair Bright Queen arrives at the ritual site at the capital, wearing a crown with unlit candles. A representative from each of the twenty-four tribes wields a wand and draws down light from the stars to light each candle. When all the candles are lit in his crown, the Queen lights a candle for each of the tribes to bless them, as the King dances around the Queen, spinning fire, a token of offering his power so that the Queen's power may rise. When all of the tribal candles are lit, the Queen removes his crown and places it on the snow, and the King and Queen mate ritually on the stone table in the sacred circle; the Queen's seed is shot into the melting snow within the circle of his crown, and the first sign of green growth appears, which will survive the rest of the cold season. The mating of the King and Queen empowers the candles with light and life and the gift of joy. When the mating is done, the tribal representatives take their candles and each tribal candle is used to light a candle for every individual within that tribe, so the Queen's light is given to all of Vanaheim and the land can begin to thaw from the winter and people's spirits can be lifted in hope.

Some suggestions to observe this holiday:

- One can travel to the capital to watch the ceremony, which is open to the public.

- If one does not journey or does not care to watch ritual sex for whatever reason, it is acceptable to light a candle for the Queen and/or candles for each of the tribes, and then from the Queen's candle light candles for yourself and your loved ones, for "thawing" in your own lives, the promise of the new year and new things and prosperity coming to you. One can also dance as the candles burn, offering the energy of happiness and freedom to flow through you into the Otherworld and from the Otherworld into you.

FULL MOON RITES

The full moon is especially important to the Eshnahai. Each tribe of the Eshnahai has their own full moon ritual, usually with a communal meal, drinking, music and dancing, sometimes stories, and sometimes sex. There is also a ritual held at the capitol, in the stone circle on the town green, where the King and Queen mate - an echo of the union of the Serpent Twins, our progenitors, and to affirm the sacredness of love in all of its forms - and in their passion and ecstasy, raise energy to nourish and protect the land, and bless those who have gathered to watch.

So, in building connections with the Eshnahai, celebrating the full moon would be an important part of that practice, but there are many ways to go about it. Here are some suggestions.

- Making an offering to the King and Queen, such as wine, or blood, or milk and honey, and either journeying to the capital to watch their ritual mating and receive the blessing of the energy raised, or have your own sexual celebration. This can be done solo, or with a partner or multiple partners (whether corporeal or spirits, such as other elves), and in any combination of genders, reinforcing the energy raised with your own, feeding the land and people. Love in all its forms lends energy to theirs, and connects our people, and it is good.

- In lieu of sexual activity, one can also sing or dance, or play a musical instrument such as a drum, raising energy with that, or doing another creative activity, such as writing, art, etc.

- Under the light of the full moon, offerings can be poured out to the elves of the Otherworld and the land spirits, asking that they be blessed, and blessings shared between you. You can then drink in the light of the moon and its power, and carry the light within you, pushing it into the things you do.

- You can journey to visit with the tribe you are affiliated with, and participate in (or observe) their full moon ritual.

- You can do all or none of the above, and do an act of magic, or use the energy of sex or creativity or the joy of celebration with elves to empower a working.

Whatever you do, remember that this is a time of merriment. There is reverence to be had, for sure, in the beauty of the mating dance, the beauty of the worlds bathed in moonlight, the beauty of fellowship and connection, but there is also mirth to go with it. Do not worry so much about "doing it wrong", the important thing is doing, and receiving joy, light in the darkness, to sustain you for the weeks ahead.

The Purpose of Clergy

(from a Vanic perspective)

Heathenry, as a whole, is still having debates 40+ years into its revival as to whether or not clergy is needed, or is an outmoded concept. The main arguments I have heard against the concept of heathen clergy are

- that the hereditary position of Goði as a semi-spiritual leader/semichieftain/semi-lawyer is outmoded and not applicable to today, when most people are not born and raised in heathenry and thus cannot generate a hereditary priesthood

- that it is a hangover of conditioning by Abrahamic religions

- that "Tru Heathens" do not need an intermediary between self and the gods

- that the modern priesthood now serves as an "elite class" to debate theological matters not previously debated in elder heathen times because life was too busy for such speculation, and is thus extraneous and cluttersome

- that there is no need for lore interpreters, because most heathens are home scholars

Without turning this entire chapter into a rebuttal, I would say first and foremost that while it is the ideal for Norse pagans to be well-versed in the lore, many have not more than a basic understanding of the Eddas and some of the Sagas; most have not read Saxo, Bede, Tacitus, and the extensive folklore from medieval and Renaissance-era Scandinavia, Germany, and England. We need to debate theological matters now because heathenry has been effectively dead or at least dormant/underground for over a thousand years and most of our knowledge of what was done was lost, and what we do know of is largely not applicable to today and must be updated in some way.

And while I think all people should strive for deeper connection with the gods and be their own priests, the fact of the matter is most people don't have a "godphone" – if we were all mystics, the world would stop functioning. Many people are in fact capable of being devoutly religious without having intense god-contact, and yet because of their devotion they deserve to at least periodically be able to be touched by the gods - which is where I feel the true purpose of mystics and spirit-workers comes to play.

If one is planning on becoming clergy within a Norse pagan context, the first and foremost reason should be to serve gods by serving the community. Obviously the ideal setting for a heathen clergyperson will be one who has a local religious community of some sort. There are now some folks who are solitary or mostly-solitary and have clients from far and wide, by the modern virtues of increased mobility, uprootings as a result of that (such as for work, military service, etc), decreased compatibility with those in one's immediate locale by way of increased mobility, and social networking via the Internet. I believe there is validity in this practice as times have changed and will continue to change as society advances. But ideally, one will be working with a reasonably-sized local group if they aspire to be clergy.

The wrong motivations for becoming clergy are to be elite or have some kind of renown, or lord it over others and spend time arguing with them about why their way of doing things is wrong, and how "real" religion is done, beating people over the head with piety and ridiculous (and often ableist and classist) standards. It should be seen as a way to contribute to the greater good, not as a way to be right and prove to the world that you're better than other people.

A further requirement at least based in my own past (negative) experience is one who will put themselves out there as clergy needs to have their own shit together before they try to help anyone else. This is not to say the clergyperson cannot have issues, as that would be most of us, and there's something to be said about previously going through hardship to help those who are currently experiencing it. However, if continual personal chaos is going to interfere with the ability to be there for others depending on you, and make good judgments when people come to you for advice, the role of priest is not one you should assume until things are more stable, or if you are a priest you may consider taking a break until life settles.

It goes without saying that a clergyperson should also be above reproach. If one has a serious criminal background or is otherwise notably flawed ethically, there is going to be doubts about your sincerity and capability. If you have a reputation as being an aggressive shit-stirrer, it might also be a good idea to wait a few years and build up a good reputation rather than promoting oneself as clergy and finding it hard to gain "a following".

Again, it comes down to the greater good. If a person is not going to be able to serve a community (whether local, online, or some combination of the two) – if you don't like people for whatever reason (and there's nothing wrong with that!), if you're not capable of putting in the work of dealing with people who come to you for guidance or assistance, clergy is not the right choice, and selfishly insisting upon it and thrusting one's incompetency on others looking to you for guidance is quite frankly contributing to decay. There are other ways to be a part of something meaningful, without being in that sort of leadership position.

Indeed, one thing the greater pagan community seems to have a problem with is "too many cooks in the soup", too many wannabe priests and priestesses, and not enough laypeople, and an attitude (particularly among some Big Name Polytheists) that the ones who matter most in the community are the spirit-workers, the priests, the "elders", and a pooh-poohing of laypeople (and then saying things like "laypeople are important and there's nothing wrong with them" when they're called on it, meanwhile contradicting themselves at every point), to where a lot of people feel like they have to be in a priestly role in order to contribute or be "good enough" for the gods, and nothing could be further from the truth. Just looking at ancient polytheisms, the priests were few and far between. The religion was held up by individuals and households, the common people. We need this now as well.

For those who would aspire to be on this path, skills for a Norse pagan clergyperson start with extensive knowledge of primary and secondary sources, being able to express their thoughts on its relevance, in a coherent and meaningful way, to apply it to the here-and-now rather than intellectual masturbation over semantics.

I also think having at least some sort of a "godphone" is important. You don't have to be a spirit-worker or mystic, you don't have to be "spooky" and hear from the Powers constantly. But doing ritual because "it's what our ancestors did" is not enough. A group ritual inevitably has to be led by someone, and the person leading the ritual should not speak words and go through the motions with a blank head and an empty heart. A person leading a ritual should think of themselves as a "conductor", both in the sense of electricity and orchestras. A ritual done properly will be satisfying for the people involved as well as pleasing to the gods, and there should be enough know-how of meaning behind what is said and done, and how to feel and flow the energy raised, to be able to understand what is good and what is mediocre and what is not acceptable at all.

While again all of us should strive to be our own priests, the person with the "godphone" should offer it to their group, as a master who leads, a servant who serves, and an equal who apart from the godphone is no better or worse than their kinsmen. If the aspiring clergyperson can work *spae* or some other art where they can communicate with the gods and pass the messages to their people who seek such knowledge, so much the better.

And perhaps most importantly, a Norse pagan clergyperson should have a good understanding of ethics and be able to give proper counsel to those in need. We live in very troubled times, now more so than any other time, even if life is longer and has more luxuries. People need encouragement and support. This is not the same thing as being allowed to drain from the clergyperson, and indeed clergy should have good boundaries with their clients as not to be taken advantage of. But oftentimes talking to a priest is helpful as it treats the spirit – the root of many wounds - and so one who feels called by the gods to become clergy should keep this in mind. It is the easiest part of the job to abuse, the most challenging if done properly but also most rewarding. In fact, this is why I am most opposed to the sentiment that heathens don't need mediators. It takes full-time dedication to be there for other people who need counsel and rede, and to study and meditate enough in order to continually improve one's service.

Even if the system of hereditary clergy is not applicable to today, the fact of the matter is, the elder heathens did in fact have clergy, and probably for all these reasons mentioned (except the primary sources then would have been stories passed down). It's just common sense. We need doctors and police and clothiers and farmers and smiths; we also need those who can give support when it is needed so these folks can keep doing their jobs, so their place in this world – in their families, amongst their loved ones – is not void.

I have heard at least one person say that in the issue of heathen clergy, one should honor all of the gods equally. If we're looking at the lore, we see far too many examples of people called Freysgoði or Thorsgoði, including a woman named Steinunn Refsdottir who owned a temple to Thor and composed a flyting in his honor against Jesus.

These were people dedicated in service to specific gods. They most often had temples dedicated to these gods. While it was common that an entire village would be dedicated to a god and under their rule with certain customs, it was also common for people to travel to different temples to pay the gods respect, a popular site being Gamla Uppsala. We can see the clergy dedicated to a specific god had general priestly functions but I also believe carried the energy and luck of that deity within them to bless the people, and certain qualities that would make them specialists. We know Frey was sacrificed to for marriage, and Odin for war. It makes more sense for a Frey-priest to bless a marriage, and an Odin-priest to bless an army. Among other things.

From a Vanic perspective, we see in the primary sources that priesthood was a common Vanic practice, not so much with the Aesir gods. Nerthus had an attending priest who lived in isolation on an island in communion with her and came out only for her yearly procession, and Frey had an attendant priestess who kept a temple as well as did his yearly procession and was oath-wed to him. In *Hyndluliod*, the human male Ottar is called Freya's "favorite", and Freya herself speaks:

> An offer stead to me he raised,
> with stones constructed;
> now is that stone
> as glass become.
> With the blood of oxen
> he newly sprinkled it.
> Ottar ever trusted
> in the Asyniur.

It is likely that Ottar was a priest-consort of Freya.

This is not to say that the Vanir never had priests who were the same gender as their deity - we come again to the mention of men called Freysgoði. It is likely (though not guaranteed) that the "servant of Ullr" mentioned on the

Thorsberg chape was also male. Nor am I trying to dissuade those who feel called to the priesthood and Vanic Powers and happen to be the same gender as the one they serve. There are few enough people truly serving the gods and community, for starters, and I won't presume to play Vanaheim's bouncer. However, it is notable that the priests of Frey at Uppsala who so horrified Starkadr were said to be "effeminate", and Tacitus mentions the worship of twin gods whose priests cross-dressed. It would seem in a Vanic context that the ideal is either for the priest of a deity to be of the opposite gender, or to cross-dress or break other gender roles when performing the deity's services. I am not saying this is mandatory, and as heathenry in the United States has become very gender-normative - with one (in 2008 at the original writing of this book) well-known heathen blogger who encouraged women to be "traditional" and has gone as far as to scorn followers of Frigga who are childfree - this will likely raise some eyebrows if not attract backlash. But as far as the cult of the Vanir, it does seem that at least with some deities, they prefer this of their priesthood, while it is not mandatory, and it seems that Vanaheim as a whole challenges our conception of gender roles and gender norms, being a more egalitarian society.

In some cases, the priest or priestess of a Vanic deity was also their consort. The human priest is a representative of humanity, a "door" between Midgard and the Otherworlds. In the full knowledge of one's human body, thoughts, emotions, and limitations, and still experiencing the Vanir god's love for that, both personal and yet impersonal... transformative and transcendent... draws Vanaheim's health and fertility into our world, the power and vitality of the Vanir into ourselves. It is a great honor to please and love the gods, building up energy in that union, and then using the energy to bless the community. While the Vanir gods can be served without all of the overtly sexual woo-woo, there is a charge from the love and lust between the Power and priest-consort, that is like nothing else in the Multiverse and is the stuff of fertility creating life itself, truly "a gift for a gift".

It is also common that getting intensely involved with the Vanir (whether the gods or the Eshnahai, or both) will result in one's life being transformed, often in a painful way, akin to a death-and-rebirth process. Serving the Vanir as priest, then, not only involves standard clergy skills, but a deeper understanding of the nature of sacrifice and what it is to be a sacrifice oneself, for to be touched by the Vanir - especially intimately - means one will never be the same. It is giving the bounty of the fertility gods to the people, to teach the people to appreciate their embodiment. Priests of Aesic deities usually have more of a responsibility to educate as well as be a ward for their tribe, and priests of the Vanir can do this also, but the gift of the Vanic priesthood to their own tribes is celebration, which is all too infrequent and half-hearted with the struggles of the world. Celebration to some extent encompasses mourning and grieving, which is another thing our modern society has forgotten in the need to stifle feelings for the convenience of other people, or work, or "life as usual". A Vanic priest can help others grieve and mourn in a healthy, cleansing way, and indeed teach others to do this, as they work through burying their own deaths and losses in the soil of Vanaheim. But it also encompasses the goodness of the world, and a Vanic priest may find themselves giving relationship counseling to their clients, or counseling on work/life balance, or anything that has to do with embodiment and living more fully and completely.

As the wains of the Vanir gods go on processions through the roads of the world, so it is the duty of a Vanic priest to go the extra mile to bring the gods to the people, for celebration and renewal, for abundance and vitality.

Seiðr: The Wyrding Way

A number of Germanic polytheists do not approve of the word witch as a self-identifier, saying one should use the word *seiðkona, spaekona, haegtessa,* or something of the like. Part of the reasoning seems to be based in Wiccaphobia, part of it seems to be based in the Old Norse Terms Are More Authentic mindset, but at least some of it seems to be based in the confusion over witchcraft and *seiðr* being the same thing. There are similarities, but they are emphatically not the same thing.

For starters, we get into etymology and word usage. While the word is related to the Old English séoðan ('to seethe or boil' but also means 'to prepare or purify the mind'), words cognate that were in a specifically magical context are *siðen* and *siðsa*, and in a way that suggests it was only practiced by elves (*ælfe* or *ylfe*); these seem likely to have meant something similar to *seiðr*, and would lend credence to the myth of *seiðr* being a Vanic practice.

However, as is noted, it was only practiced by elves, and I can safely say that if there was in fact *seiðr* in Anglo-Saxon England, chances are good someone would have made note of such a thing, so we can assume *seiðr* is not an Anglo-Saxon practice.

Seiðr is often translated as "witchcraft" in Modern English manuscripts, but it should be noted that as far as the Anglo-Saxon language, witches were not referred to as *seiðr* practitioners, they were called *wicca* (m.) or *wicce* (f.), or another specialized label such as *scinnlaeca* (which translates "sorceror" but is a compound of *scinn*– "skin/phantom" and *læca* – "leech/healer", lit. "phantom-healer").

We do have two distinct forms of witchcraft seen in history: sorcery and folk magic.

The Church issued edicts against basic folk practices during the Conversion Era, such as women adding their menstrual blood to food to seduce a man, or using their man's blood or semen to help cure an illness (as two examples), or doing things in a certain place of power (wells, old trees, springs, groves). Folk magic relies more on symbolic associations and thus sympathetic magic. Practices in later centuries, such as the witch's bottle and putting shoes inside the walls of an old house, seem to be remnants from this time. Folk magic was practiced by the common people, and not generally distrusted until after the conversion, as this witchcraft generally ran the gamut of protecting and enhancing the home life, the sex life, fertility of body, crops, and animals, and healing: positive magic, for the most part.

Sorcery was more 'high magic', and involved more complex spell craft (particularly for healing purposes), divination, and things like 'faring forth' and shapeshifting. The sorcerers - *scinnlaeca* - of old became the cunning-men/women of later history, who were sought by the community for help. While potent, this is still different from the discipline and the magical act of *seiðr*.

Seiðr is something completely different. To begin with, it is said in the primary sources to originate with Freya and the Vanir:

Njord's daughter Freya was priestess of the sacrifices, and first taught the Asaland people the magic art, as it was in use and fashion among the Vanaland people.
    -Ynglinga Saga

Freya was said later to teach the art to Odin. The kind of magic that Odin worked, which was also noted in stories of "wicked women" in the Sagas, consisted of:

- shapeshifting
- calming fire and storm
- changing the weather
- raising the dead to speak with them/gain information
- bringing sickness and even death to people if he saw fit
- robbing the health, intelligence, or other strength/s of one and giving to another

Since we know Odin was taught *seiðr* by Freya, we can assume these were part of the *seiðr* as practiced by the Vanir in Vanaheim.

Groa (of the eponymous *Groagaldr*) is another noted *seið*-worker, who speaks nine spells over her son Svipdag when he raises her from the dead (this in and of itself a *seiðr* practice). The charms were as follows:

- to cast away the irksome by strength of will
- that Wyrd herself would protect and guide him
- rivers that would drown him flow to Hel and be diminished
- stopping foes and turning their minds to peace
- power to break bonds and fetters
- power to still storms at sea, and navigate tranquil waters
- to stop frost and cold from having ill effect
- that the spirits of the dead do no harm

- that giants may not attack but give wisdom and abundance when met

Seiðr is most noted for being baleful magic, with multiple examples in the Sagas of *seiðr* being used to harm others. In Friðjof's Saga:

> Then they sent two women skilled in magic, Heiðr and Hamglama, and paid them to send such a storm upon Friðþjóf and his men that they might all be lost at sea. So they practiced their magic; they fared to the seiðhjallr with charms and sorcery.
> . . . Then Friðþjóf and his men found that the ship made great speed, but they knew not whither they had come, for that so great a darkness fell on them that the stem was not seen from the center, what with driving spray and storm, frost and snowdrift and bitter cold. Then Friðþjóf climbed up in the mast; and when he was mounted up he said to his fellows, 'I see a marvelous sight. A great whale circles the ship, and I suspect that we must be near some land, and he would not let us near the land. Methinks that King Helgi does not deal with us in friendly wise: it is no loving message that he sends us. I see two women on the whale's back, and they must wield this hostile storm with their worst spells and magic. Friðþjóf and his crew managed to smite the women, and they disappeared, the whale submerged, and the storm dissipated. But back ashore it was seen that "while the two sisters were at their incantations they tumbled down from the seiðhjallr, and both their backs were broken.

From Ynglinga Saga again:

> Then Drífa sent for Huld, a seið-kona, and sent Vísbur, her son by Vanlandi, to Sweden. Drífa prevailed upon Huld by gifts that she should conjure Vanlandi back to Finland or else kill him. At the time when she exercised her seiðr, Vanlandi was at Uppsala. Then he became eager to go to Finland; but his friends

and counselors prevented him from doing so, saying that most likely it was the witchcraft of the Finns which caused his longing. Then a drowsiness came over him and he lay down to sleep. But he had hardly gone to sleep when he called out, saying that a mara rode him. His men went to him and wanted to help him. But when they took hold of his head the mara trod on his legs so they nearly broke; and when they seized his feet it pressed down on his head so that he died.
    -Ynglinga Saga, ch. 13

    Seiðr practitioners in Iceland were distrusted by the common people even before the conversion era. The word *ergi* was used as a pejorative for men who practiced *seiðr*, comparing receptiveness to the spirits to being a "bottom". (This does not mean that *seiðr* required a man to be gay, however; sexual orientation has nothing to do with whether or not one can seethe.) At least one account of *seiðr* has a *seiðkona* meeting an untimely end with a sealskin bag (although contrary to popular modern heathen belief, it was not 'the community' neutralizing a threat, but another *seiðkona* murdering out of jealousy). The reason why *seiðr* was distrusted seemed to have a lot to do with fearing the power of the practitioners - after all, a person who has the knowledge of how to heal someone also has the knowledge of how to hurt them; if you call on a professional to hex your neighbour, the person also has the power to eventually turn that curse on you if it suits them.

    However, the lore was written by Christians, and there are other pieces of lore that were strongly colored by Snorri's perspective. From a logical standpoint, it seems *seiðr* was demonized, just as accounts of tribal shamans largely have focused on harm done to others even if that was only a small part of what they actually did. If we look at the broader picture, we also know that the Vanir are deities of nature, and by extension the fertility and abundance that comes with it. The "endgame" of the Aesir initiating the war with the Vanir was likely to bring the three major players into Asgard, and their powers with them. The Aesir, being power-hungry, war-like gods, lacked the force of fertility and health in their world. Before the truce, the Vanir were winning the war against the Aesir with their battle magic - which *seiðr* definitely looks like. But I also believe *seiðr* was their ability to heal and revitalize, as well as harm.

So we know a bit about what *seiðr* was used for, but most of us don't know how it was done. In the accounts of *seiðr* in the lore, we mostly have records of the results, not the actual process. Indeed, the majority of those trying to reconstruct the practice of *seiðr* call it 'oracular *seiðr*' and do seership work by trancing on a high seat. A few of these believe that deity or spirit possession can also be called *seiðr*, even though we have no instances of these practices in the primary sources (which isn't to say it never happened, just that there was no record of it). But all of this is guesswork. And this is not really a surprise. The lore of the Vanir cultus was all but stamped out. We have a few surviving myths, but not enough to call it a body of 'Vanic lore'. *Seiðr* as a practice with Vanic origins would also be something deliberately muted when it was brought up.

However, from a Vanatru perspective, it is still worth exploring, as a form of magic that is truly our own. So we go on what very few clues we do have, and fill in the blanks through Divine inspiration. We know the end results of *seiðr*, here are some clues as far as what *seiðr* was and was not, and how it was done.

Seiðr seems more akin to shamanism than to folk magic or sorcery. Just like traditional tribal shamans have worn costumes, Thorbjorg the Little-Volva wore a costume, and we can assume that the *seið*-folk had a special costume they wore both as items of personal power as well as to set them apart from the common folk and denote their status and commitment. Moreover, the *seið*-folk were *seið*-folk all the time, not just when they were accessing altered states and casting spells. To do the magic associated with *seiðr*, it could not be done without a tremendous amount of self-discipline and power. And as mentioned above, the *seið*-folk were often feared and mistrusted, as indeed many shamans were in their tribes.

More so than the current groups and individuals claiming to reconstruct and revive the practice of *seiðr*, I posit the theory that the closest analog we have to what *seiðr* actually looked like was the (fictional) Bene Gesserit of Dune. The Bene Gesserit had an intense personal discipline of mind and body - most notably a martial art called "The Weirding Way" - and formal rites of passage to gain power, including a ritual where a drug (the spice melange) was ingested to meet with and access the memories of the female ancestors. The connotations of this for Germanic polytheists should be obvious. The Bene Gesserit, like the *seið*-folk of old, were feared, and known for influencing and manipulating others, but for all that they were hard with others, they were hardest on their own. Their power was hard-won - it was not merely a practice, but an entire way of life.

Seiðr is etymologically akin to "seething", and if we use the definition of *seiðr* as seething, I would explain it as follows:

The act of magic by *seiðr* would likely involve an emotional and/or kinesthetic experience. Since many accounts of working *seiðr* involved a high seat, we can assume this was for a reason. It seems that being up high does aid the body into shifting consciousness, and on a deeper level can be seen as symbolic as sitting upon the World Tree, particularly if the high seat was specially prepared with the sole intent of working *seiðr* upon it. I personally think "seething" to create specific acts of magic - like the tribal shamans doing their work - was achieved by sitting upon a high seat and shaking or rocking and breathing differently while letting the mind go. Doing this lets the one who seethes literally slither into that veil between worlds, and work from there.

To do magic by *seiðr* involves making the Web of Wyrd seethe with you. By seething, you bring what is within, outside. In seething, you access primordial fire and ice, internally. You access the fire that melted ice and made water, the waters in the Well, the threads that are the waves and currents leading to Wyrd's Well – the threads that interconnect all life on Earth, the nerves and blood vessels under our skin, shoots rising up through soil. Seething puts you in a state where you can move wyrd around, to line up this world with your own inner worlds, or the Otherworlds. By twisting and manipulating the threads and currents of wyrd, you can cause paths to intersect or break apart, you can heal or harm a body or mind, you can influence how things play out on the land.

When you come back, you feel intense burning cold, the shock of being fully in this world again, but the threads have been changed, by your own internal changes. When you are in that space of extreme cold fire, it is easy to freeze or burn wyrd and speed it up or slow it down. It is a rare person who can truly hit that "Dagaz moment" and use it to effect change, and most people who can access that state are generally aware of the workings of wyrd and serving as a catalyst of wyrd, and its potential consequences.

Seiðr is being able to seethe deep enough to be in both worlds, access the primordial currents of wyrd and/or the collective unconscious. It is literally making yourself a microcosm of the macrocosm.

Because it is an intense working, it takes its toll on you physically when you come back, more so if you do not know how to ground, do not practice psychic hygiene, and do not know how to take care of yourself. People who regularly practice a magical discipline cannot eat, rest, and do as everyone else does, but must be particularly mindful of how their lifestyle affects their mental and physical well-being.

It goes without saying that magic is not a mandatory part of the Vanic tradition. Yet, for those of us who have abilities and aptitude, and who honor the Vanir, exploring and re-claiming the lost art of *seiðr* might help us to further the interests of our Powers, ourselves, the Land, and the ones we love.

Vanic Virtues 2.0

By Nicanthiel Hrafnhild

If there is one thing pagans enjoy doing, it's making lists – lists of correspondences, of offerings, of in- and out-group – and the subject of ethics (though in almost all other ways ignored) is no exception. Even heathenry, which prides itself on supposed independent thought and individuality, has *two* lists of acceptable behaviors, depending on how tribalist one is.

So here's another. The purpose of the following list is not to dictate right and wrong action; in fact, it should never be used for that, nor should any mere list – those actions should be derived from living rightly, which is something such lists are merely a tool to guide into. Neither are the virtues below the sum total of every possible good thing someone who follows the Vanir should strive for, just some of the most important to Vanic culture, and most lacking in many discussions of paganism.

Vanic Virtues:

- *Beauty* – Above all else, strive for what is beautiful, because that which is beautiful in form, in function, in purpose, in relationship, is what is good in the working of the cosmos. Now, this is not strictly physical beauty, the definitions and parameters of which are fickle and subject to social change, but beauty of character, of intellect, of well-made and well-loved items and people. Everything is beautiful, in its own way, and learning to see and embrace that beauty is key to understanding how the Vanir work.

- *Passion* – Accompanying beauty is passion for life, for love, for enjoyment and doing the work of right living. Those without passion are adrift on the waves, and outside of the confines of mental illness (which is often an antithesis to passion but is not to be considered a personal fault), those who choose not to embrace passion are indeed lifeless, hopeless, and could easily be mistaken for automata.

- *Naturalism* – The Vanir are, among other things, the powers of Nature and all it encompasses. To then claim to worship them, and deny the agency, importance, and power of their domain and subjects is gross blasphemy. Those who honor the powers of nature should be first to embrace their non-human kin on an equal level, as all part of the great design. This may take many forms, as all of us have different strengths and spheres of influence, but the trifecta of reduce, reuse, recycle should be at the core of any practical and truly-honoring Vanic practice.

- *Serenity* – this is the counterbalance to passion, which unchecked can lead to carelessness and recklessness. Pursuit of stillness, of harmony and balance serves as the bank to control the flow of passion to beautiful and natural ends. Someone in the embrace of tranquility cannot be moved by mere appeals to emotion or manipulation, but seeks to move in ways that are aligned to the pattern.

- *Openness* – The guiding principle of nature is More and Different is Better, and left to its own devices without significant outside intervention, it will tend to wild leaps of evolutionary diversity – witness the examples in our own world of isolated islands featuring hundreds of animal and plant species found nowhere else on the planet. With this understanding, we too should seek to honor and respect our diversity, and also that the key to communication and interconnectedness is to remain open to possibility and wonder.

- *Wildness* – We are animals, just as the other creatures of the world, but we are the only animals that have the ability to consciously and willfully deny our positions in the pattern, the only ones (as far as we know!) who consider themselves above "all that". We train our children, those most connected to the truth, to deny their animal selves, to be "proper" and "civilized", when all the world is calling us, begging us, to remember that we too used to dance in the mud, call out in the night, swing through the trees singing the songs of the birds, that we knew for a certainty that elves and dragons and unicorns lived in the forests and mountains (they still do, you just need eyes to see them!). Shake off the shackles of civilization and dance wild like a maenad or a troop of baboons. Sing to the moon and the sun without care for who is listening.

- *Love* – The most powerful force in existence, it keeps the planets and stars in their dance, connects us to the surface of our world, and draws hearts together. It should never be scorned or mocked as weak, and when love is returned, all the spirits weep for joy. We are all family on this earth.

Living Vanatru: What It's All About

Everyone has to start from somewhere, and this chapter was written in mind for those who are new to the idea of Vanic paganism and feel it is right for them.

Most people will tell you if you are new to a religious system, to read the source material. If you are working with historical deities, it does make sense to look at what was written of their mythology and how they were worshiped. However, there is not much in the lore pertaining to the Vanir.

There are mentions of the Vanir in the Ynglinga Saga (Aesir-Vanir war and truce), Viga-Glum's Saga ("the wrath of Frey!"), the Saga of Heithrek and Hervor (King Heithrek was a devotee of Frey), the Sorla Þattur (the story of Freya's Brisingamen), Hyndluljod (Freya taking Ottar to Hyndla), Skirnirsmal (Frey's lovesickness for Gerda), and the portions of the Prose Edda dealing with Njord's marriage to Skadhi, and the other account of Frey winning Gerda which also discusses (briefly) his slaying of Beli.

There are examples of worship of Frey in the Sagas, such as Gisla Saga (mentions Thorgrim, a priest of Frey), the Saga of Hrafnkell Freysgoði (a priest who kills someone for riding a horse dedicated to Frey), and Gunnar Helming's Saga (Frey-in-a-wain v. Gunnar Helming), but these are few and far between, and the Sagas are hardly the best example of human behavior.

Finally, there are occasional mentions from historians such as Tacitus, who mention the procession of Nerthus in a wain.

Reading these historical texts can be somewhat important to get a background reference, but what is mentioned of the Vanir is scanty compared to Aesic deities like Odin and Thor, and seems to be written from a heavily Aesic bias. And ultimately religion cannot be experienced through a book – it has to be lived.

This means actually making an effort to connect with the Powers involved. Offering food and drink is a show of hospitality; you can share a meal and some quiet contemplative time in your home, and make your home welcoming to them in some way. However, as the Vanir are the Powers of Nature, the best place to commune with them is in their element. It is good to go to places where their influence can be felt. You can worship Njord at the ocean, or on a fishing trip at a lake or pond; Nerthus likes marshy places as well as forested areas. Freya enjoys places with lots of flowers (and flowering trees), and gardening (especially where growing food is concerned) is just as much a devotional act to Frey as prayer.

In general, going outside is important to understanding the nature of the Vanir and living in a Vanic way. Get involved with something that means going outside on a regular basis, if you're not already doing so. Breathe some fresh air, get some sun – or better yet, some rain - and watch nature all around you. Get familiar with the climate and terrain of your area, the little subtle differences in flora and fauna as the seasons change.

As the Powers of the Land, the phrase "think globally, act locally" really does apply here. Be an example to others. Be the change you wish to see in the world. Make sure your neighborhood is clean in both greenery and deeds. Recycling and picking up litter are things we can do mindfully to pay respect to the Vanir and the land-wights. Participate in your hometown. Vote (even if only with your pocketbook). It is your deeds that matter, not just your devotion. Devotion can be expressed through deeds. Look out for your family and friends, and for your local community, the Land and its people.   Don't contribute to urban decay and the ills of modern society.

Finally, it is important to work on personal stability, to have a healthy connection to this world – enjoyable activities, good relationships - and know it is not somehow "not spiritual" or "less spiritual" to enjoy what creature comforts and material things you can. Fertility, to me, includes health of body and mind as well as creativity, it is not just limited to reproduction. Prosperity is not just material, but is about the abundance of life and getting as much out of it as you can, whether rich or poor. Vanic pagans should be aware of their role in the co-creation of their own destiny, and always be mindful to seek their maximum benefit as well as the greater good.

But at the same time, Vanic pagans should be able to stop and smell the roses, to take time out and be grateful for where they are at. Express gratitude as often as you can. When you feel the need to complain about something – and there is much to complain about in today's world – also try to think about what is good, in your life - the little things as well as the big things, all important, contributing to making life worth living. Life is a gift, and to affirm this and know even the small things are sacred, is the core of living with the Vanir.

Visions of Vanaheim: The Road Home
(A personal story)

I have been pagan since the 1990s, and in 2004 I took Frey as my *fulltrui*, and married him, and for the next seven years served him as priest. From 2007-2010 I was one of the figureheads of the Vanatru movement, under the name Svartesol, and being one of the only public resources on the Vanic cultus at the time, I got fairly popular on the Internet. I wound up burning out because a lot of people thought priest = on-call counselor and I didn't have the boundaries then that I have in place now, and I also attracted a lot of haters within reconstructionist heathenry who thought I was "doing it wrong" – I have been threatened, cyberstalked, and harassed.

Because I burned out, in September 2010 Frey let me go. I did not break my oaths to him. I did not ask for release from my oaths to him. He released me. Prior to this I had been trying to do everything I could to work on my relationship with him, and when he released me I was very, very hurt, even though I understand in hindsight that he was doing what was best for my mental health – I needed a break from everything. After Frey released me and we divorced, I wound up unpublishing the original version of this book because it was a painful reminder of the breakup in and of itself and also people thought I was still with Frey and were continuing to ask me to godphone for Frey on their behalf, which was also a painful reminder.

I tried to walk completely away from Vanatru for awhile, burned out and reeling from what I perceived as rejection from the entity that had been the most important thing in my life for seven years. For a brief time that worked, but I had a Vanaheim-shaped hole in my heart, and things like exploring Celtic polytheism were a bad fit for me.

Since I was a little kid, I knew I was not human. I believed I was an elf. Not only did I believe I was an elf, but I had vivid memories of Back Home, including having a twin brother who I believed would come for me and take me home again. If you called me human, when I was little, it was the worst insult and I would throw a huge temper tantrum. Because I was "special", and thus treated accordingly (read: special ed., school shrink visits, etc), I learned fairly quickly to start Presenting as Sane; I eventually stopped talking about being an elf. But "the elf thing" never went away – my favorite cartoons as a kid were David the Gnome and The Littl' Bits because it was the closest thing I had to elves on TV, I was an animist long before I was pagan and liked to spend time outside communing with nature spirits, I had imaginary friends who were elves, and I got into Tolkien at age 12-13. But I learned to stop talking about it. I even to some extent rationalized it away.

I still rationalized it away even when my spirit companion (who I refer to as "Clarence", a close analog to his actual name) arrived in 1996, even though he fit all of the profile for that person from Back Home who was coming for me, including the eyes that haunted my dreams. Oh, the eyes. The warm brown eyes full of love.

When I was 19, the dragon dreams started. At this point, I was confused. I didn't think I could be an elf *and* a dragon, and the dragon stuff was tied into some magic and energy work I was doing, me starting down the path of a Guardian. So as that was more immediately relevant, I started to take on the identity of "dragonkin" except this was back in the 20th century before I had regular Internet access; I didn't know there were other people like me, so for years I had no one to talk to about it, and that was my dirty little secret. That, and my spirit companion.

When I found the otherkin community many years later, I identified as a dragon originally. But "the elf thing" wouldn't go away, and because I was dealing with the Vanir, it became more relevant, and it was frustrating because I didn't know what was going on. I did, however, learn to shut up about elves again, because the spirit-worker crowd I was associating with by and large didn't like elves and my UPG about them would get criticized and shot down. In hindsight I wish I had said "fuck you" and broke off to do my own thing years ago, but instead, I lay down and took it until I couldn't anymore, and by the time that happened, enough damage had been done that it took me about two years to unpack everything and figure out where the indoctrination ended and my own legitimate spirituality began.

Which was when the non-human thing was yet again thrust in my face.

To further compound the issue, my spirit companion was having "pointy ear attacks" and it became pretty obvious he was an elf. At first we were like "la la la go away" about it because we didn't want to be "special" (we already were "special" enough just by him existing and needing to have a more active place in my life rather than swept under the rug like I had for years) but it got more and more frequent and more and more obvious. And then finally, I had a dream:

Dream last night: I was with Clarence, who had pointy elf ears, and was wearing a grey cloak and "typical elf clothing" underneath (although he still had on stompy boots, lol). He helped me to escape a crowd, and we got on a small boat and sailed around. The scenery was amazingly beautiful, with forested islands, and a very clear sky and sea. When we came to land, he took care of me (I had been wounded) and I told him how beautiful he was, and I once again went into feeling unworthy due to my own body image issues (e.g. scarring). He told me that I am beautiful to him because he loves me, and he spoke endearments to me in a language that sounded like Quenya (?) and we were intimate and he did some healing work on me. I woke up with him holding me, and felt very safe and loved.

-from my personal journal, June 13, 2011

After this dream it became apparent that this wasn't going away and we had to deal with it. On the summer solstice of 2011, my spirit companion and I did a working to "unfetter" ourselves and begin the process of figuring stuff out once and for all. We had more elf dreams, and a couple of weeks later, Clarence suggested we journey to Vanaheim, where I had not been since the Breakup. We went there, and I asked point-blank, "What the fuck is he?" of Clarence, and the Person whom I asked replied, "He's one of us," in this tone of voice like you are explaining something to a very slow, silly child.

And then the Person said, "And you are, too."

From what I found out, the elf life and the dragon life were the same – my elven self could shapeshift into a dragon form, and back, the dragon being the protector and caretaker of a place where some of my blood ancestors hail from. I had an untimely death, and after several incarnations wound up in this body, the life where I was meant to remember and return. My elven mother had been chieftess of the Cat tribe at one time, and Loki was my sire – they had an exchange of learning magic from each other, and business quickly became pleasure. My spirit companion was my twin and mate from back then (yes you read that correctly, that is A Thing with the Vanir, I do not condone human/human incest, this is different) and made a deal with wyrd to help me, which involved having his memories wiped, on the condition that they would be returned when I figured things out (they had to be wiped to not complicate things more than they were, and yes, honestly if we had that information any sooner, it wouldn't have helped and probably would have made things worse because we were not ready before).

Now understand, after the breakup with Frey, I didn't want to deal with the Vanir. I was hurt, understandably so. I was very reluctant to get re-involved with them again. When I got the bomb dropped on me that I had been Eshnahai (Vanic elf) in a previous incarnation – my first incarnation, my soul is elven – I was *not happy* about it, you could hear me grumbling all the way in Niflheim.

Once we got the big memory "download", we were told to report home for duty, which made me even less happy. But I eventually got over it (being re-united with "Jarod", the man we were in a triad with, helped immensely) and after awhile realized that this is where I belong. I'd felt that Vanaheim-shaped hole in my heart because this is my home, my People. And so I accept it, and even embrace it now, and we walk between worlds, doing various jobs together to influence both worlds, weaving bridges between Vanaheim and Midgard, picking up where we left off. I may be in a human body for awhile, but my Work isn't done, and indeed there are some things that need to be done while I'm here in Midgard. For the record, I don't think I'm all that because

I'm elven-souled; that and three-fifty will buy me a cup of coffee. I am very aware of the limitations of my human form, and I'm just this dork who isn't anybody particularly important bio-side – being who/what I am in Vanaheim does shit for me here. But, trying to ignore that part of myself and "just be human now" doesn't work for me. I'd been running from this my whole life, but this is wyrd.

I identify as Vanatru now, as I did in 2004-2010 when I was serving Frey (and then stopped for a couple years for what should be obvious reasons), but my approach to Vanatru is different than it was then. I don't deal with the Big Name Deities much. This isn't to say I don't deal with them at all – I am on friendly terms with Frey and visit Njord every time I go to the Oregon coast, for example – but I would not identify myself as a worshiper of the Vanir (honor yes, worship not so much). I do spirit-work (rituals, magic, divination, channeling, as well as our astral family life) with Clarence and Jarod, and I interact with various Eshnahai when I journey to the realm (though this has been less what it once was). I am a member of the Serpent tribe (and the Dragon mystery cult), which has been... interesting (let's go with "interesting").

But even though everything about my life is wrapped up in the Vanir and my service to my People, it's taken me awhile to feel comfortable using the label again because of the change in my religious practices, and it's taken me an even longer while to feel comfortable with the fact that wyrd seems to have tasked me as being a public resource about the Vanir, Vanaheim, and Vanatru. The last time I did this, I burned out. I understand why now, and take steps to avoid this (I have better boundaries now, cleaner motivations, etc) and so far I am doing a pretty good job.

That said, it's a tough job. One of the things that I have been tasked to do is re-release *Visions of Vanaheim* (which you are reading right now). I spent the first half of 2014 working on a new edition of the book. Some of the old material from the first edition is here, but some of the old material has been cut out for various reasons (whether extraneous or because there are some points of view I no longer agree with or things I said that I find problematic in hindsight), and there is a lot of new material – for example, bits on the tribes, and the Wheel of the Year as it is celebrated in Vanaheim. Doing the new version of the book was difficult. It wasn't just difficult in and of itself with the new material, but it's been difficult because of the issues attached to the book, namely having to revisit my past (including and especially my relationship with Frey and the breakup, as well as a long-term bio-relationship with a contributor that went pretty badly pear-shaped) as well as some difficult issues within the months I was working on the book (such as having relationship difficulties with Clarence which have been smoothed over). Also, I've had to do a lot of spirit-work to get the book done (such as journeying, or getting information from my spirit companions, which is exhausting).

So it's been work, it's been work that is very painful at times. But I do it because I love my People, and I want there to be accurate information out there so people in this world can better connect with my People, which benefits both worlds.

And I do it because there might be others out there like me, needing to find the road home, and it would be nice if they didn't have to get lost in the forest getting eaten by bears for years, like I was. This isn't to say that everyone should have this journey handed to them on a platter – my struggle makes my belonging sweeter, and deeper, and fiercer – but just the same, I spent years in loneliness and pain trying to figure shit out and piece it together, and if I can spare somebody even a tenth of the bullshit I went through, it's worth it.

Glossary of Terms

DISCLAIMER: The writings in this book operate under the assumption that you at least have a beginner's knowledge of the Northern religion. However, it is best not to assume this, or that the way I define a technical term is the way you relate to that term.

So, I have provided this glossary for the benefit of my readers. Rather than giving a very long and detailed list, I have narrowed the glossary list down to those words that are most likely to cause confusion and debate without people realizing what I mean by these terms. What I state here in my glossary is definitions of words as I apply these words in my own writings: I do not assume that my definitions of these words are the same for any and all people in or out of the Northern religion.

AESIR

The dominant tribe of the Northern gods, which seems to have the domain of civilization and society, including functions such as education, war, police, and entertainment (poetry, song, hosting). Examples of the Aesir include (but are not limited to) Odin, Frigga, Thor, and Bragi.

ALFAR/ELVES

Generally used in the context of "light-elves" but can also include "dark-elves", beings that live in Ljossalfheim and Svartalfheim and also have a presence in Midgard (as exemplified by something like 75% of the Icelandic population believing in elves, and a government expert having to certify a space is "elf-free" before anything can be built[12]). Some modern heathens refer to their male

---

[12]http://www.vanityfair.com/politics/features/2009/04/iceland200904? printable=true&currentPage=all

ancestors as "Alfar", however references to the Alfar in the primary sources are always to elves, which can be thought of as powerful nature spirits, possibly demi-gods, closely related to the Vanir. Frey is noted as being the lord of Ljossalfheim, given to him as a tooth-gift.

ASATRU

Literally, "true to the Aesir". Whilst many Asatruar see the Vanir deities as included in the Aesir, there is still a focus on Aesic deities such as Odin, Frigga, and Thor. Asatruar typically hold to the Nine Noble Virtues, and organize themselves in groups called Kindreds. Asatru is a modernized Scandinavian-Norse flavor of heathenry and is the most common form of heathenry in the United States. Asatru is a heathen denomination, but in the opinion of this author, the words Asatru and heathenry are not interchangeable.

BLÓT

A term, cognate with "blood", to denote the main sort of ritual in heathen practice. Originally, in Blot a livestock is given and the attendants are sprinkled with its blood. Since most modern heathens do not have the land, livestock, or knowhow to give an animal rightly, many heathens use the word blot to describe a ritual where the gathered attendants are sprinkled with mead and do rounds on the mead horn.

ECLECTIC

The author uses the word "eclectic" to describe a practice of paganism where gods come from many different pantheons and elements of different cultures are mixed and matched, often combined with modern practices.

"ELDER HEATHEN"

Term used by this author to describe the heathens who lived before the conversion of the Northlands to Christianity.

FAINING

From the Old High German word "fagende" (fah-YEN-da), meaning "to celebrate". This usually involves an offering, whether it's food and/or drink, poetry or song given, or something else, that the deity being honored can appreciate. This word is cognate with the Old Norse word *forn*.

FAKELORE

Something that is widely thought by Heathens and/or pagans to be in primary sources, but upon extensive study is not in there anymore and in fact is either personal gnosis or a scholar's speculation passed off as fact. A few notable examples of this include the belief that Ullr rescued Frey and Freya from the giants (Rydbergism); that Frigga rides a chariot drawn by rams (UPG); or that Heimdall is Vanir (speculation).

FULLTRUI

Literally, "full-true" or "fully-trusted". This word is still used in Modern Icelandic legal terminology to denote "legal representative". In *Viga-Glum's Saga*, the word "fulltrui" was used where the word "protector" stands in modern English translation, when Thorkel made a sacrifice to Frey. While having a *fulltrui* was not necessarily a common practice in elder heathen times, it was not unheard of and was not just limited to kings or very important people. The practice of taking a *fulltrui* is much more common in modern heathenry, albeit it should be approached with care, and nobody is obligated to take a patron, unless of course, that is the deity's decision to make. This author sees the *fulltrui* relationship as being reciprocal - the deity represents your best interests before the other gods, and you are likewise a representative of that deity's interests on Earth. While nobody can or should become a clone of their deity, they do tend to influence their devotees to a large extent.

GODFOLK/GOÐI/GYÐJA

The word "Goði" translates literally as "godman", and "Gyðja" as "godwoman". In elder heathen times, the Goði presided over the town blot at holytides, including the marriage and burial/cremation of the town's residents, and gave individual counsel, including decisions of law. In today's heathenry, the Goði is usually over an individual local/regional Kindred, and only has jurisdiction within that one Kindred — though they may be respected, or not, by heathens in other groups, they are not the leader for more than one group. Today's Godfolk are, besides leading a Kindred, performing clergy duties such as marriage, funerals, and the like, and often (but not always) trained in some kind of pastoral counseling methods. While many Godfolk are trained by clergy ordination programs of established heathen organizations, having an ordination does not mean necessarily having a group to serve as Goði, and there are a few who are recognized by their group and/or other individuals as Godfolk without having an ordination in place.

"GODPHONE"

A colloquial term used by this author to describe those who can talk with the gods (not hallucinating or deluding oneself), are said to have "a godphone".

GOD-TOUCHED

The author does not use the terms god-touched and god-owned interchangeably. God-touched is someone who may have specific deities communicating with them, and intervening/interfering in their lives. When this is to the dismay of the person involved, the word "god-bothered" is sometimes used. "God-touched" as used by the author denotes a more positive camaraderie with the deities.

HEATHEN

Old English word literally meaning "of the heath". Contrast with Latin *paganus*, meaning "of the countryside". Very broad umbrella term that can and will include Asatru, Anglo-Saxon Heathenry, Forn Sed, Fyrnsidu, Theodisc Geleafa (Theodish Belief), and Irminenschaft. There is no central authority for "all heathens", whereas there may be people taken as authority figures in some of the heathen denominations listed above, to say what is and is not acceptable for that denomination. As the word "Heathen" means "of the heath" it can be thought to be inclusive of all gods and wights of the Northlands. Anyone who worships the Northern Gods may call themselves heathen based on the broadness of the word. (However, due to some using the words "heathen" and "Asatru" interchangeably, not everyone wants to.)

JOTUN/JOTNAR

The Jotnar are a tribe of gods in Northern cosmology who represent the forces of chaos, e.g. the primordial elements such as fire, frost, storms, the sea, etc. Examples of Jotnar include (but are not limited to) etin-brides such as Gerda and Skadhi, friends of the Aesir such as Aegir and Rán, and the Norns, who are said to be frost-thurses.

KINDRED

The author uses the word Kindred in the heathen sense to mean a group of people who have formed a religious community, similar in function to a church or coven while not being the same thing. The main function of a Kindred is for like-minded people to honor the gods together, as well as perhaps have lore and/or rune studies, and have fellowship together, rather like a surrogate family. While the majority of Kindreds are led by a Goði or Gyðja (priest or priestess), some Kindreds rotate leadership according to what holytide it is/Who is being honored. Some Kindreds require oaths for membership, some do not.

LORE

The primary sources, such as the Eddas and Icelandic Sagas, as well as historical accounts of Saxo Grammaticus, Bede, Tacitus, Jordanes, Adam of Bremen, and folkloric sources such as the Grimm Brothers.

MAGIC

Magic is the art of affecting change, whether temporarily or permanently, with people, places, plants and animals, objects, and events. Magic is both ceremonial (High) and common (Low). Examples of High Magic in the Northern Tradition would be runes and *seiðr*. Examples of Low

Magic would be kitchen witchery, home remedies, folk charms, and the like.

OTHERWORLD/S

The author uses the term "Otherworld/s" to denote worlds that are not Midgard (this plane), such as Ljossalfheim, Jotunheim, and Asgard. The author also considers worlds outside the Northern Tradition, e.g. the sacred Otherworld/s of the Celts, Hellenes, and Egyptians among others, to be accessible through Yggdrasil. Traveling to a world outside Midgard in a trance state is referred to by the author as Otherworld journeying.

PAGAN

From the Latin *paganus*, literally meaning "of the countryside". While the word heathen means pretty much the same thing, most heathens prefer not to call themselves Pagan due to its connotation with Wicca and other forms of pre-Christian or post-Christian belief not founded in Germanic culture.

RECONSTRUCTIONIST

The author uses the term "reconstructionist" to denote attempts at trying to resurrect the pre-Christian belief systems of European cultures, from one of two standpoints: 1. as if Christianity never happened at all, and things naturally progressed to the point they are now, 2. the way life was prior to the conversion, which would include "tribes" or the idea of intentional communities. The author has also seen most "reconstructionist" heathens to say that if it wasn't in historical documents, it didn't happen, and things such as UPG are highly frowned upon.

RECONSTRUCTIONIST-DERIVED

The author uses the term "reconstructionist-derived" to denote groups that work with European pre-Christian belief systems, and may respect what has been recorded in historical documents, but use that as a springboard to find a deeper understanding of the gods — the lore is a means to an end, rather than an end in itself.

RUNES

The alphabet of the Northlands. The best-known rune row is the Common Germanic (also called Elder Futhark) of 24 runes; there is also the Younger Futhark and Anglo-Frisian or Northumbrian Futhorc (with 29 and 33 runes, respectively). The word *run* means "mystery" and the runes are said to be discovered by Odin after a nine-day ordeal of hanging from Yggdrasil, and shared with the different races of beings in the Nine Worlds accordingly.

SEIÐR

Seiðr can involve cursing/hexing, weather-working, or healing. Freya is said in *Ynglinga Saga* to be adept at *seiðr*, which was commonly practiced by the Vanir, and to have taught it to the Aesir.

SPAE

Literally, "to speak". A form of prophecy in the Northern Tradition, most commonly seen in the accounts of "*spae-wives*" who traveled through the land and would predict events for households, whether good or ill.

SUMBLE

A less common ritual than blot, but more serious. The standard sumble format is toasts-oaths-boasts, three rounds over a horn. Some participants of sumble will have three as a minimum and have the sumble go all night. Traditionally the drink for sumble is mead, although a very good ale or something special — something that you wouldn't commonly have — can be substituted. Because of the luck-changing nature of the ritual, that is, making oaths before the gods and witnesses, and honoring past deeds, sumble is typically only done with one's kinsmen (Kindred and/or family), and not done very often (usually once a year at Yuletide, or not more than 2-3 times a year).

UPG
Abbreviation for Unverifiable Personal Gnosis, that is, gnosis (information) about a deity or something of a spiritual nature that cannot be proven in the primary sources. For example, a common UPG that cannot be found in the primary sources is that Freya enjoys strawberries and chocolates for an offering. If a number of people share a UPG it becomes Supported Personal Gnosis, or SPG (sometimes also called Peer-Corroborated Personal Gnosis, or PCPG, but the author dislikes this term for various reasons).

VANATRU
A form of the Northern religion that puts primary emphasis on the Vanir (not necessarily exclusive).

VANIR
The Vanir are the tribe of gods in Northern cosmology whose primary domains seem to be cultivating the land and the sea (agriculture and fishing, sometimes hunter-gatherer), and by extension they are connected with prosperity, fertility/sexuality, and the quality of life.

Examples of Vanir include (but are not limited to) Frey, Freya, and Njord.

WEREGILD
Literally, "man-gold". A word used to denote appropriate compensation for a wrong done to self or kin. The key word here is "appropriate", as in proportion to the deed. The *weregild* for slander would be different than *weregild* for theft would be different than *weregild* for murder.

WIGHTS
An Old English term meaning "living thing", cognate with the Old Norse term *vaettir*. This author uses "wights" in the context of "spirits of place", whether land spirits, plant spirits, sea or rock spirits, or house-wights (known as *tomten* or *nisse* to the Scandinavians).

WITCHCRAFT
The author uses the term "witchcraft" to describe what is essentially known as "Low Magic", that is, non-ceremonial (and often non-ritual) practices utilizing common objects and simple steps to work magic, to effect positive or negative change with people, places, things, and situations. Witchcraft can be a part of a religious practice — it makes a nice compliment to various forms of paganism — or it can be wholly separate.

WOO
A colloquial term used to describe communication with supernatural entities, whether verbal or visual, that gives information, instructions, or other sorts of connection with the spirits, or things like astral experiences. The word "woo" appears to be pejorative in origin, and yet used

rather humorously if not self-deprecatingly by spirit-workers and related pagans. The author will sometimes use the word "woo" tongue-in-cheek when describing mystical experiences. It is not by any means a scientific term or one that should be used seriously.

WORKING WITH (A DEITY)
While it has been argued that a relationship between deity and person is not "co-", as in working with a co-worker, the author prefers to use the term "working with" in the context of a magical or ritual working to affect change, whether large or mundane, and/or to do the deity's Work in Midgard, especially if that deity is one's patron. The gods and spirits sometimes rely on humans to promote an agenda, or awareness, or help other humans they care about.

WORLDVIEW
Literally, the way one views the world. This is usually comprised of the way one was raised and the experiences of formative years + experiences later on in adulthood. This author is fond of saying that it is virtually impossible to "reconstruct" the worldview of the elder heathen as we no longer live in a heathen society nor a heathen majority, and most of our worldview in the Western world will be colored by Abrahamic religion + secular Western culture whether we want it to be or not.

WYRD
Wyrd is seen by the Norse as layers in the well, and by Anglo-Saxons as threads. I think these views are compatible rather than contradictory, as both pertain to the Norns. Wyrd is seen to be an accumulation of one's deeds

— the past affects the present, the present affects the future. It is possible to alter the course of one's wyrd just by making a decision, even a small one, but it could be argued that there are multiple directions a person's life could take and all are probable, and all courses overlap at certain points, getting one ultimately to where one is supposed to be. The word "wyrd" is cognate with our modern word "weird".

YGGDRASIL

Literally, "Ygg's steed", a name for the World Tree upon which Ygg (Odin) hung Himself for nine days and nights to gain knowledge of the runes. The World Tree of Northern cosmology is home to the Nine Worlds, as well as being such as Ratatosk the gossiping squirrel, and Nidhogg who gnaws the roots of the World Tree (when he's not eating the souls of the wicked). While the Eddas give an account of Odin as having made Yggdrasil with his brothers out of the body of Ymir, this can be thought of as a "late" creation myth as Odin-like figures did not appear in the Northlands until around the Bronze Age, and the domesticated cow (Audhumbla) was also much later. Whatever creation myths there were prior to this, have been lost and may or may not be able to be reclaimed through personal gnosis and speculative research.

Nornoriel Lokason is a thirty-something mage and spirit-worker living in the greater Portland, OR, area with his  spirit companions (a demon and two Vanic elves) and a cat. He has been an occultist since 1991 and a pagan since 1995, and his spirituality could best be described as dual-trad Vanatru and Abrahamic pagan. He is an artist and poet in addition to being an author, and enjoys thrifting, metal, and communing with nature. He keeps a blog at http://serpentslabyrinth.wordpress.com